More Praise for *The Confident Leader*

"To date no book has comprehensively dealt with the underlying problem of how to get outside of your comfort zone to think and succeed big in business. Many wonderful books have been written addressing these issues from many different angles, but ultimately we know we must push ourselves beyond what's comfortable to get better results, and Larina Kase shows you exactly how."
—Michael Port, bestselling author of *Beyond Booked Solid*

"*The Confident Leader* is going to be a great hit with those who want to be wildly successful. What a fresh new idea and powerful solution for turning procrastinating into achieving!"
—Rita Emmett, author of *The Procrastinator's Handbook*

"Larina's book shows us how to confidently and successfully move out of our comfort zones and help our employees do the same thing. Do what she suggests and you'll build teams filled with committed, engaged people who'll help you and your organization succeed."
—Sharon Jordan-Evans, coauthor of *Love 'Em or Lose 'Em: Getting Good People to Stay*

"In my over 25 years of leading and coaching various sales teams, I have read many leadership books. *The Confident Leader* is different in that it covers the unfamiliar territory of what makes someone even more successful as a leader. It really opened my eyes to my possible potential and caused me to look at being a leader in a different and unique way. I would recommend this book to anyone who desires to grow themselves as a prelude to growing others."
—Al DiLeonardo, CEO of Cutco Cutlery

"Effective leaders are lifelong learners and students of human behavior. But even the best leaders sometimes get stuck in the dreaded 'comfort zone.' Larina's new book reminds us that that is a dangerous place to be. Fortunately, *The Confident Leader* provides a wealth of research- and practice-based advice that is a valuable resource to novice and experienced leaders alike."
—Harrison Monarth, *New York Times* bestselling coauthor of *The Confident Speaker*

"'Dare to dream' is fine . . . but what about 'dare to do'? What could you do with your business, your work relationships—your whole life—if your doubts and fears became igniting fuel to make it all happen? Read this book to find out how."
—Dr. Max Vogt, founder, Monster Productivity Institute

"What separates effective leaders from exceptional ones is their ability to motivate themselves and others, even in the face of great difficulty. Dr. Kase provides a clear step-by-step plan for addressing both day-to-day difficulties and big-picture challenges. Inspiring and practical, this book is what ambitious leaders need to become even more successful."
—Mark S. Schweiker, president and CEO, Greater Philadelphia Chamber of Commerce, 44th governor, Commonwealth of Pennsylvania

"A must-read for people who are ready and willing to take their lives and careers to the next level! Larina provides the reader with practical steps to achieve one's vision and be an exceptional leader."
—Carol Gallagher, Ph.D., managing partner, Alliance for Excellence; author, *Going to the Top*

"The #1 obstacle that keeps coaches from helping clients change is simple: Change is hard, and staying the same is easy. This book provides the ultimate solution, helping people make any change they desire (no matter how scary or seemingly impossible), and helping coaches achieve unbelievable results with their clients."
—Milana Leshinsky, bestselling author, *Coaching Millions*

"*The Confident Leader* is support, strategy, and an implementation plan all wrapped into one book. Larina focuses on what I know to be one of the most important aspects of running a profitable business: our ability to become exceptional leaders. *The Confident Leader* will teach you how to lead your customers to solutions, lead your employees or contractors to passionate work, and lead your industries to excellence."
—Sheri McConnell, president and founder of the Association of Web Entrepreneurs and the National Association of Women Writers

"Confidence is an outcome. It is also the dividend you'll earn by reading this impressive book. *The Confident Leader* provides a step-by-step road map for helping you face fear, embrace discomfort, and pursue demanding challenges. If your aim is to enlarge your leadership influence, actualize your professional potential, and yield astonishing results—without getting an ulcer!—this book is for you."
—Bill Treasurer, CEO, Giant Leap Consulting; author, *Courage Goes to Work*

"True leadership entails the ability to motivate yourself and others toward a common goal. As a leader it takes strength, wisdom, and a vision to forge new territory and keep moving forward. Dr. Kase's book is a powerful guide to help you stay the course and ensure that each day moves you toward your vision."
—Nicholas DeBenedictis, CEO, Aqua America, Inc.

"I've seen plenty of people both fail and succeed. The difference between the two is leadership ability. This book is a must-read for anyone desiring success in any area of life, business or otherwise."
—Frank Rumbauskas, *New York Times* bestselling author, www.NeverColdCall.com

The Confident Leader

The Confident Leader

How the Most Successful People Go from
Effective to Exceptional

Larina Kase
Psy.D., MBA

Mc Graw Hill

New York   Chicago   San Francisco   Lisbon   London
Madrid   Mexico City   Milan   New Delhi   San Juan
Seoul   Singapore   Sydney   Toronto

1 2 3 4 5 6 7 8 9 0   FGR/FGR   0 1 4 3 2 1 0 9

ISBN 978-0-07-183172-7

MHID   0–07–154988–9

McGraw-Hill books are available at special quantity discounts to use as premiums and sales promotions, or for use in corporate training programs. To contact a representative please visit the Contact Us pages at www.mhprofessional.com.

Library of Congress Cataloging-in-Publication Data
Kase, Larina.
   The confident leader : how the most successful people go from effective to exceptional / by Larina Kase.
        p. cm.
   Includes bibliographical references and index.
   ISBN 0–07–154988–9 (alk. paper)
1. Leadership.   I. Title.
   HD57.7.K374 2009
   658.4'092—dc22
                                                                      2008010261

To my husband, John.
I look forward to life's journeys,
even the most challenging ones,
when I'm with you.

Contents

Part II: How Confident Leaders Turn Problems into Dynamic Opportunities

Chapter 15: Handle Conflict and Difficult Situations with Ease 219

"I Want to Improve My Skills in Managing Conflict and Dealing with Difficult People"

Chapter 16: Master the Challenge of Championing Change 233

"I Want to Innovate, Create Powerful Change, and Make a Real Difference"

Acknowledgments

This book was in the making for several years, and along the way many wonderful people generously gave of themselves because they believed in me and in these ideas. They walked with me through this journey and improved not only the book, but me as a writer, thinker, coach, and person.

I would like to thank my family, including my parents, and John, Nicole, and Jamie, for bouncing ideas around and helping me to navigate outside of my comfort zone when greater patience and persistence than I naturally possess were needed. I thank them also for being wonderful role models of proactively pursuing ambitions and living life to its fullest. To Moraima and John, from whom I have learned so much, and to Roger and Arnelle for being Confident Leaders in their fields and lives. To Donna, Chuck, Jen, June, Cesare, and Earl, who are always supportive.

One of the first people I told about my idea for this book was Sam Rosen. His enthusiasm has been consistent over the past five years, and his guidance has been invaluable. More recently, input from Christiana Briddell and my other WeHabitat partners has been much appreciated.

This book would never have become a reality were it not for the tireless support of brilliant marketing strategist and innovative, creative thinker Mark Levy. His clear and decisive perspectives truly made the tough things easy, and have kept me motivated and focused on what's most important. Words cannot express my amazement at how his mind works and the depth of my gratitude.

I want to thank my literary agent, Rita Rosenkranz, who has represented me for some time, with *The Confident Speaker* and now with this book. She helped shaped this project through many iterations and went well beyond the call of duty for a literary agent. Rita's influence on this project has been substantial, and her belief in me as a writer has been incredibly inspiring.

I am grateful for my editor, Donya Dickerson, who has a remarkable ability to conceptualize and edit for both detail and the big picture to address the reader's needs, and who has been enthusiastic about the book from the beginning. I also want to thank Janice Race and her freelance team, who have excellent eyes for detail, as well as the rest of the group at McGraw-Hill for their contributions to this book.

I am fortunate to have many talented colleagues with whom I enjoy collaborating: Max Vogt, Marilee Adams, Deb Ledley, Indira Pahria, Miles Lawrence, Cindy Greenway, Rhonda Embry, Angela Nielsen, Tom Beal, Milana Leshinsky, Terri Levine, Kevin Hogan, Robert Isaacson, Cathleen Fillmore, the coaches and faculty at Penn State's Smeal EMBA program, and the women in the Internet marketing group. They are too many to list here, and I am fortunate to have learned from so many bright people.

I want to acknowledge my clients, whom I'm privileged to serve, and who have showed me just how much we are capable of changing and achieving. The concepts in Part 2 are based on issues that my clients struggled with, had the courage to confront, and ultimately mastered to become even more successful.

Finally, I would like to thank the thought leaders who generously contributed their ideas to this book (in the expert interviews) and who serve as exemplary models of Confident Leaders: Michael Port, James Kouzes, Joe Vitale, David Allen, Tim Sanders, Mark Levy, Annie McKee, Seth Godin, Rick Brinkman, and Jen Groover. They have all influenced me greatly, and I am honored to share their insights with the readers of this book.

PART I

THE SIX GROWTH STEPS USED BY CONFIDENT LEADERS

1

Step 1: Get Your Exceptional Vision

What Change Do You Want to Make and
Why Is It Important to You?

JOE SAT ACROSS from me at his oversized mahogany desk in his enviable corner office. Joe's friend who had referred him to me had told me that Joe had always been a superstar. In college, he was a star football player, president of his fraternity, and active in several local charities. At 6 feet, 2 inches with tousled deep espresso-colored hair, olive skin, and penetrating hazel eyes, Joe never had a hard time getting dates in college.

Joe was an extremely good-natured guy from a close Italian family with a great sense of humor and a high level of loyalty. His friends all loved him but couldn't help being slightly jealous of him. He'd always seemed to have it so easy. Joe was the guy you hated because he had it so good, but then you felt bad about hating him because he was just so darn nice.

Now, at only 39 years old, it appeared that things hadn't changed much—he still had it all. He sat before me in his twenty-first-floor executive office suite. His feet were clad in Italian leather shoes and rested on an exquisite rug. In a glass frame on his desk sat a photo of his gorgeous

3

wife and their two kids outside their new $2 million beach house. Essentially, Joe was living any businessperson's dream.

But Joe's eyes told me a different story. They darted around the room, falling first on me, then on the dark chocolate-colored leather armchair I sat in, then on his family photos, then on his computer screen. His eyes conveyed an insecurity that was odd because he came across as very confident, too confident even. Joe smiled when he spoke to me. His smile, while dazzlingly white, didn't quite put me at ease. It gave me the feeling that he had something to hide. I knew that Joe harbored a secret. Perhaps he hadn't even admitted it to himself.

He seemed tightly wound up, like a spring that could uncoil any minute. As we spoke, I heard the beeps of new e-mail alerts coming in, and Joe appeared to subtly cringe each time because he couldn't check his messages when we were in a meeting, as that would be rude. And Joe tried very hard not to be rude.

Joe, despite having the job of most people's dreams, was caught in an internal struggle. He reminded me of someone following the adage, "Never let 'em see you sweat," but his palm was sweaty when he shook my hand that day. I thought about how eager Joe was to begin coaching, and I was curious. Why was Joe so successful, yet so in need of assistance?

"Joe," I said, "you've achieved an incredible amount, especially for someone as young as you. Yet ..." I continued, "I get the sense that you aren't fully enjoying it. Let me ask you, what are you successful in spite of?"

"Hmmm?" Joe was confused.

"By all appearances, things have come easy for you, but I can tell that it hasn't all been as easy as it seems. What has held you back from being even more successful or more at ease with it all?"

"That's a great question, and I wish I had an answer," Joe replied. "I definitely want to find out. I want to accomplish even more and enjoy it all much more!"

"Think about it this way: What torments you every day? What causes you to have sleepless nights? What makes your blood pressure rise as you're riding the elevator up to work? What makes you think, 'I hope this doesn't happen today' as you walk through the office door? Why do you question yourself and your success? Where do you lack confidence?"

Joe paused for a moment to think and then confided something I've heard many times: "I often ask myself if it's all worth it. I work a ton of hours and rarely see my family. I live in fear that I'll be seen as a young wannabe executive who's all looks and no substance. I feel like I constantly need to prove myself. I want to be seen as capable and confident, but I wonder if I really am."

"Keep going," I encouraged, knowing there was more. It was all just bubbling to the surface.

"My wife hates me right now. We're at the brink of divorce. She says I spend no time with the family. When she pushes me to do things, I don't want to. Maybe I have a rebellious spirit or something. I love her, so I don't know why I can't just enjoy our time together. If I'm not working, I'm typically thinking about what's coming next.

"My staff members are great, but they're rarely as eager and motivated as I, and I'm not sure how to make them more responsible. I can see people growing resentful and irritated when I try to get them to produce more. When I walk down the hall, I can feel people slipping behind their desks and avoiding eye contact. No one wants to talk with me. One client told my boss that I'm overly aggressive in trying to get new business, and that his firm didn't want to work with me.

"I'm heading up to the top, as that's the goal, but it feels as if I'm pushing a boulder up the mountain. I'm strong, but I'm not that strong! I don't even know if I'll have the energy to enjoy it when I get up there. Is it just me? Do I make things difficult for myself? What's wrong with me, doc, and can you fix it?"

How Does This Compare to Your Story?

Joe thought that there was something wrong with him and believed that he was alone in his inner struggle. He isn't. There are thousands, if not millions, of business leaders, professionals, and entrepreneurs who are successful, yet who share Joe's ambivalence, doubts, insecurities, and desire to go further and do it all. You may be one of them. We all are.

Perhaps you aren't an executive like Joe, or you don't feel an inner turmoil the way he does. What you share with Joe is a desire to be a Confident

Leader and a sense that you could be doing even more, working even less, and feeling even better about it all. Perhaps:

- *Your goal is to be a charismatic, motivational leader.* You make jokes and try to be witty, and you put a lot of thought into what you say and how you present yourself. You are sometimes so involved with thinking about bright quips to say next that you don't hear what other people say to you. Despite your efforts, you've received feedback that you're not a great listener.
- *Your goal is to be more successful as a sales manager.* You worry about how tough things will be if it doesn't happen. So you decide to stay late and work extra hours. To make sure you understand exactly what needs to be done, you ask questions of your boss and your team members. You give zealous sales presentations and follow up with your prospects daily, sometimes multiple times per day. In spite of all this, you are not making the numbers or getting the reviews you want.
- *Your goal is to build your business.* You're afraid that your business will fail the way so many start-up companies do. Because you know that the number one cause of small business failure is financial problems, you try to save everywhere possible. You slash your marketing and advertising budgets and decide not to hire the support team you want until the business is profitable. You take on a part-time job to generate cash flow. Despite all your hard work, your business is floundering, and you're not sure it'll make it.

If one of these sounds like your own situation, you might feel discomfort as you try to achieve your goal. The first example reveals someone who is nervous about being seen as uninspiring or boring and who fights this discomfort by overthinking things and trying to appear charismatic. Because he places so much focus on himself, his efforts backfire. The sales manager is worried about not being successful, so she exhausts herself with work, exhausts her coworkers and her boss with questions, and exhausts her customers with overexuberant follow-up. This overzealousness turns people off. The entrepreneur is trying to alleviate his financial concerns by saving money and taking an outside job. These efforts, unfortunately, are wearing him out and aren't giving the business the resources it needs if it is to take off. The strategies we use to try to reduce the possibility of failure often paradoxically increase our anxiety and the possibility of failure.

The Bottom Line

Your ultimate goal is to be a leader in your field. You may be the leader of a company of 10,000, a company of one, a family, a field of thought, or something else. No matter what you lead, to do so with true confidence, you must first be the leader of one thing: yourself.

All great changes begin with ourselves. I will help you make the changes that have eluded you, achieve new levels of success, and go further than you ever thought possible. But you will have to challenge yourself. Many people are content with being effective. You aren't, and you don't need to be. The bottom line is that exceptional changes begin with recognizing what you avoid because you aren't sure that you're capable, and then doing it.

In Joe's case, he needed some assurance that he wasn't alone and that a solution was easier than he thought. The first step was identifying the problem. Since Joe was asking whether he made things difficult for himself, that seemed like a good place to start. I asked him to tell me about the last intimidating conversation he had had with a client or top executive in his company.

"Well, I was speaking with my boss, and I wanted to make a great impression," Joe recalled. "I told him about the numbers my staff and I have achieved, which are well above our targets. I explained how pleased our clients have been, and I demonstrated a great new technique we've been developing."

With just this brief description, I discovered the reason that success wasn't coming as easily as it appeared.

"Joe, what would have happened if you hadn't been so prepared for that meeting and you hadn't told your boss about all of these great accomplishments?" I asked him.

"I don't know what would have happened, but I know I would have been worried that my boss wouldn't be pleased with my performance," Joe said, thoughtfully.

"There are two issues here," I explained. "First, you're trying too hard. In your eagerness to make a great impression, you overdid it. Your boss couldn't get a word in, and you probably defeated the very goal you were going after. I bet that this happens in other areas of your work and life. I know this because of the second issue—the reason you try so hard is because you are unwilling to experience the uncertainty and uneasiness that come with giving up some control. You've heard of the importance of pushing yourself outside of your comfort zone?"

"Yes, of course."

"Now you need to learn how to do that and much more. You'll need to move into the space where you are uncomfortable, where you take on the right challenges and take strategic risks. Fortunately, this is what leads to things becoming easier, more profitable, more productive, more gratifying, and more genuine.

"Let's face it, you're only operating under the illusion of comfort right now. It's not like you're moving along completely at ease and I'm asking you to get uncomfortable. We know that change without growing pains is unrealistic, and we want to make big changes for you, so we need to be honest about the fact that it gets harder before it gets easier."

Then I asked him the key question: "Are you ready to make some startling changes in your work and your life?"

Joe enthusiastically said yes. He was ready to begin the rocky and exhilarating ride. Are you?

From Knowledge to Action

I began the process of creating a chart for navigating the choppy waters of achieving higher levels of success five years ago when I was on the clinical faculty at the Center for the Treatment and Study of Anxiety at the University of Pennsylvania. I became intrigued by how anxiety can either hold people back or propel them forward toward their goals. Many of us begin with all kinds of great intentions, but find that we don't take action.

I set out to discover a process for taking action when part of us doesn't want to. Whether we tell ourselves that we're too busy to change, too tired, too in debt, or too anything else, the bottom line is that there is a fear there that holds us back. Your fear may be that you'll add more work to your already packed schedule, fail, succeed, embarrass yourself, let someone down, or something else.

To effectively face and actually embrace these fears, you need a process that is proven to work. The GROWTH process that you're about to learn is based on extensive research in the fields of both psychology and business. I've worked through it with dozens of executives, salespeople, and entrepreneurs; have used it myself; and know that it will help you.

In the first half of the book, you'll learn the six-step GROWTH process. To make the steps more concrete and help you through sticking points, we'll apply the GROWTH process to specific areas of challenge in the second section—things like losing focus, having difficulty putting yourself out there, and dealing with difficult people. Throughout, there are interviews with many authors and business leaders who attribute much of their success to pushing themselves outside of what's comfortable, and who provide additional insight and tips to help you do the same. You'll learn how to turn your knowledge into action and make the changes that will enable you to become a Confident Leader.

Your Key to Change

It is easier to avoid discomfort and continue doing what we've always done. When, however, we know how to work with discomfort, we free up energy that we can use to create and achieve valued goals. The key to change is to learn to tolerate—even approach—the discomfort that arises when we make a change. This is how we have optimal anxiety for peak performance, and we take inspired action to reach all of our goals.

You need to have anxiety, fear, excitement, motivation, drive, enthusiasm, passion, and discomfort. These qualities are all various aspects of the same thing: energy. In fact, biological studies show that business leaders with a drive for power experience heightened adrenaline responses. This makes sense because as a leader, you need to put yourself out there. When you do this, you may feel like you are under a microscope. You'll inevitably experience anxiety. Some anxiety is good—with too little, nothing happens; some is bad—with too much, you get overwhelmed or fearful and either nothing happens or you take action, but you do all the wrong things. When I meet with coaching clients at cafes, I often draw this on a cocktail napkin to show how discomfort is linked with performance. This was discovered over a century ago, and it is one of the most powerful change tools in existence. It's called the Yerkes-Dodson Law, and here's what it looks like:

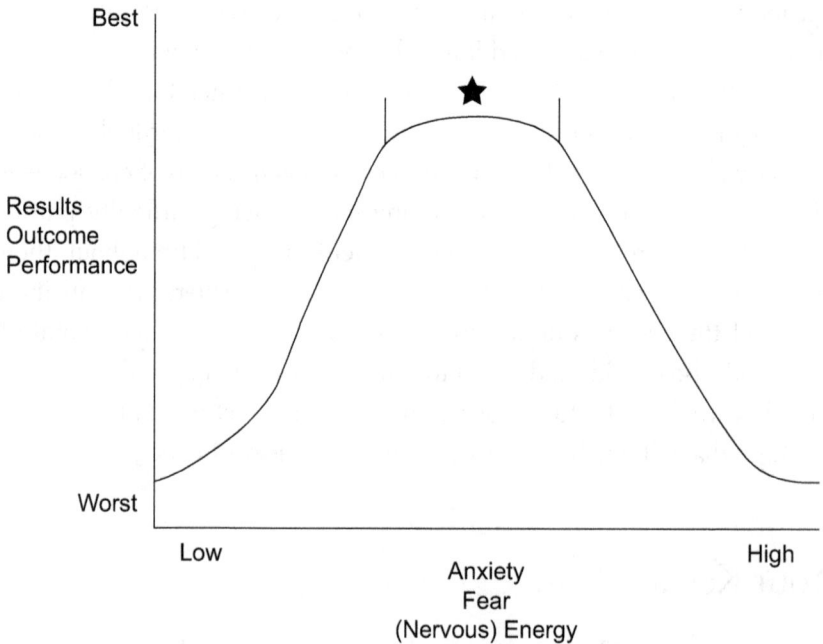

We want to be in the peak performance zone on top. This is the best place to make decisions and take action. It applies to you and to all those you lead. What's at the top of this chart for you? What is the crucial result that you want to achieve?

Going Outside Your Comfort Zone and More

All people speak of the importance of pushing themselves outside their comfort zones, yet no one talks about exactly how to do this and where to go. Unfortunately, simply getting out of the comfort zone does not get you anywhere. It's like saying, "I need to get out of this boring town." Okay, and do what? Maybe you're hesitant for a reason, and neglecting to listen to these worries would be a major mistake. Or maybe you're pushing yourself, but you're not ready for it—you attempt to sink or swim, but you have no idea how to swim, so you sink. You might be trying really hard to be successful, but trying so hard actually backfires and you shoot yourself in the foot. You might get outside of your comfort zone but find that you're still relying on the same old crutches, so you might as well still be there. We'll get to each one of these situations in the GROWTH formula. For now, just know that your vision should be something specific and meaningful that's outside your comfort zone.

As a psychologist and success coach, it pains me to witness someone who's motivated, ambitious, and eager to make changes, but simply doesn't know what to do or how to best do it. Here are the most common mistakes:

1. *You don't go there.* Avoidance is the most common reaction to discomfort.
2. *You take tiny steps,* feel bad, and retreat back to your old ways.
3. *You push yourself* past what you're truly ready for and end up not achieving your goals.
4. *You don't have the skills or support* necessary to propel yourself forward, so you wallow in distress.
5. *You leave your comfort zone and think that's enough,* but you continue to use your old crutches and don't advance forward.
6. *You don't like feeling uncomfortable,* so you try to control yourself and others, but of course that doesn't work.

There's nothing more frustrating than really wanting something and making efforts to achieve it, but finding that your efforts fall flat. Success is often determined not by what you do but by how you do it. It's like making a batch of enchiladas without a recipe. You don't want them to be bland, so you put in several pinches of chili powder and they turn out too spicy. The next time, you cut back on the chili powder and they turn out bland. Optimal challenges are like the chili powder—without them, business is dull and uneventful; with too much or with improper use of the discomfort that arises, you're overwhelmed. If you are going to have the courage to take a risk, you need a system to make sure it pays off for you. That's what the six-step GROWTH formula is for. Let's move to the first step now.

Step 1: What Change Do You Want?

Envision your day with less effort, strain, and stress. Picture yourself living the life you want, continuously growing and achieving new heights in your work performance, business relationships, and leadership skills. Suppose you could face the uncomfortable aspects of your life with grace and poise. You're living in the calm after the storm, and it feels great.

Before, you felt as if you were pushing a boulder up a mountain; you now feel free and light. You stride up the hill, eager to see what's at the top and on the other side. Your personal struggles are no longer struggles; in fact, they're exciting challenges. You make key decisions with ease and confidence, knowing that you've worked through the right process to make the best decisions. You've accomplished something that is significant to you, your family, your business, your community.

What does this change look like? What does it feel like? How are your days different? How is your energy different? What have you achieved? These are some of the questions to ask yourself in creating your exceptional vision for change.

Helping Others Change

If you're a manager, coach, consultant, supervisor, or mentor, and your goal is to develop others and assist them in making important changes, you can use the six-step GROWTH process to best help them. For your clients, supervisees, or direct reports to see significant change, they need to know how to work with the discomfort that arises.

In *Business Psychology in Practice*, Charles Mead and Rachel Robinson, consultants and authors of one of the chapters, say, "In distilling our experience of engaging consultants … we are struck by one over-riding attribute of the best. It is their ability to tell us something normally uncomfortable to accept, difficult to hear, or challenging to our self-concept or our organization in a way that gains our complete attention and ends up creating an opportunity for us or our organization, or both." If you want to be the best, which of course you do, and you want your clients to be the best, you must challenge them effectively.

The Uncomfortable but Powerful Vision

In our busy lives, we often look for the easy road to save our valuable time and energy. Unfortunately, we sometimes do ourselves a disservice with this approach. Over three decades of research have now shown that we are most motivated and get the highest sense of gratification when we seek out optimal amounts of challenge. Too little challenge saps our motivation, and too much becomes overwhelming. In a seminal study, sixth graders solved word puzzles that were ranked either very easy, easy, hard, or very hard. Students showed the most amount of smiling with the hard ones. We sometimes lose our childlike quest to challenge ourselves, but we must recapture it, because it's a key not only to competence and confidence, but to happiness.

When you think of your vision for change, it should make you a bit uncomfortable. This discomfort can be very helpful in the following ways.

Discomfort and Decisions

You're faced with a major life-changing decision, and you can't decide what to do. You feel uneasy, and you see pros and cons on both sides of the issue. You know that it's normal to be anxious about an important decision, but you can't decide whether the apprehension means that it's the wrong move or if it means that you should go for it. (We'll look more closely at how to make the best decisions in life and business in Step 4 of the process.)

Discomfort and Value

If we value something, we want to be sure we attain it, but we naturally wonder if we'll succeed. We doubt ourselves and question our decisions. This is uncomfortable. We worry about the things we care about. *This discomfort illuminates what's important to us.* If we don't go there, we won't fully experience all the things that are important to us.

It is a terrible feeling to regret not going after your biggest, most meaningful goals. And vice versa, when something is important to you, you need to allow yourself to experience the discomfort that occurs with growing toward your goal. You've probably heard that passion and pain are two sides of the same coin. "No pain, no gain," right? To have passion and experience gains, is is often necessary to have a bit of pain. But here's what most people don't know: we don't need to wallow in it, we don't need too much of it, and we *do* need to know how to make it work for us.

Research suggests that three categories of philosophy influence your values and therefore your actions: pragmatic, humanistic, and intellectual. If you're *pragmatic* in orientation, you're achievement-focused, you like benchmarks, and you believe that the worth of an idea or action is grounded in how useful it is. If you have a *humanistic* approach, your guiding value is human relationships. You are loyal and empathic, and you favor a democratic approach. The worth to you of an idea or an action is based on how it will affect your close relationships. If you're *intellectual* in orientation, you're logical, future-oriented, and thoughtful. The worth of an idea or action comes from understanding how things work and creating a secure future. You may have a combination of these philosophies. When you allow your philosophy to dictate your values, vision, and actions, you will experience synergy and growth.

Discomfort and Growth

No matter what your goal, to achieve it, you need to have four things:

1. A desire for change and growth
2. Knowledge about what you need to do
3. A consistent method of doing that which you need to do
4. A process to search for new ways to stretch yourself

All four of these require discomfort. The first requires an openness and honesty with yourself about how much you want to change and how ready you are. If you create a big vision for yourself, you will inevitably have doubts about whether you can achieve it. The second requires a challenging reevaluation of the methods you know to be effective and those that are not working. The third is often the hardest of all. Turning your knowledge into action is not easy. Once you achieve this step, you'll find that what was once uncomfortable is now comfortable. The challenge now becomes the fourth step, finding new ways to grow further or help others grow.

Your Map to the Treasure Chest

You know how kids love movies and books where the characters find a map and use it to discover a buried treasure? The challenge of the journey is worth it when they open that treasure chest. As adults, we feel the same way; part of us longs for a challenging journey toward what's most important. We don't embark on it, though, because we haven't found a map. Here are four powerful questions to help you create your map:

1. *What am I successful in spite of?* This question will reveal your untapped potential to become even more successful. Let's say you say that you're successful in spite of your impatience. The follow-up question would be, "What worries me about being more patient?" You'd realize that you're concerned that you won't get as much done. If you work on being more patient (this will require telling yourself to slow down and not rush things along), you'll find out whether or not it's true that you won't get as much done. Often predictions based on fear are wrong.

2. *If I could change one thing about my work performance, what would it be?* This question is great because it shows what you value. For example, one of my clients answered this with, "I'd be more organized." However, she was concerned that if she were more organized, she'd get assigned more planning and administrative tasks, which she found boring and uninspiring. I challenged her to operate for a week with perfect organization, and she learned that her concern did not turn out to be true.

3. *What is my greatest strength?* Often our greatest strengths are also our greatest weaknesses. When you balance out your greatest

strengths with some of the flip-side qualities, you can become even more successful. If, for example, your strength is unbridled optimism, challenge yourself to play devil's advocate and create contingency plans for what could go wrong. As another example, many successful people are very achievement-oriented. The price for this wonderful strength is that they focus on the solution more than on the process. One of my clients was a college football player, so we used the analogy of scoring a touchdown. If you just saw a player get a touchdown, would that be as exciting as seeing the quarterback convert on a fourth and long situation to keep the drive alive to set up the winning touchdown? Nope.

4. *What drives me crazy about other people?* Our reactions to other people are often a mirror for how we see ourselves. When I'm driving and I get frustrated with the supercautious, slow driver in front of me, deep down I'm really frustrated with myself for getting out of the house late and not leaving enough time to get places. Of course I don't see it this way, but it's true. Let's say you often get annoyed with people for telling you what to do. The discomfort may be about feeling out of control or losing your independence. You would grow if you relinquished control by delegating or asking someone to hold you accountable for certain tasks.

One Person's Treasure Is Another's Trash

Set yourself up to win by selecting the right goals for change. We'll discuss how to commit to your goal and the specific action steps in the next chapter, but now, as you're formulating your vision, make it as personal as possible. A personal goal is more likely to be achieved than one that is framed around someone else's desire.

Don't Lock Yourself In

Our goals change over time, which is part of the beauty of growing. When you use the six steps of the GROWTH process, something that was tough becomes easy. It is then time to look for new challenges and opportunities, and new ways to stretch and grow. Or maybe you want to sit and relax and enjoy all your great accomplishments for a while. That's fine, too—enjoy it; you've earned it!

We can use our contentment in some areas to energize ourselves to grow in other areas. If you're in a stable relationship, decide to challenge yourself in your career. If you have a secure job, choose to focus on developing some of your leadership abilities. You need to have some grounding, and I don't recommend going after everything at once.

Finding Your Vision and Optimal Challenge Action Steps

Answer these questions:

1. *What is your big vision for change?* Thinking big is going to create discomfort for you. It's supposed to.
2. *What's important to you now?* When you think of achieving this goal, it should energize and excite you.
3. *Why do you really care about this goal?* Get clear on the meaning behind achieving this goal. If the meaning doesn't send shivers down your spine, ignite a passion in you, or stir up some energy, your goal may not be powerful enough.
4. *What benefits and major life changes will you see when you achieve this?* What are the incentives and payoffs for going through this process?

The Future Is Unknown, Scary, and Exciting

As you form your vision of the future, remember that as you imagine the future, your brain takes some creative liberties. There is no way that we can really imagine the future without filling in holes. Harvard psychology professor Daniel Gilbert, in his intriguing book *Stumbling on Happiness*, points out that we cannot truly envision the future and that attempts to do so are illusionary. We think it will be one thing, but it turns out to be something totally different. We cannot know exactly what will make us happy in the future. We can manage this by remaining flexible in our visions.

Think of your vision much the way you see a landscape—the further away something is, the smaller, lighter, and less detailed it is. We can get more detailed in our shorter-term visions, but we need to remain broad in our long-term vision because forecasting too much detail can be impossible and not the best use of our energy.

The Next Step—Guarantee Action

After Joe learned what he would need to do, we set out to answer the important question that most people answer incorrectly: are you ready to take action *right now*? Let's answer that in the next chapter.

2

Step 2: Realize Your Commitment

Be Honest. Are You Ready to Make
This Change Right Now?

WE ALL MAKE a fundamental error when we approach change. We assume that we're ready for it. We figure, I want to achieve the goal I decided on in Step 1, so let's go for it. Unfortunately, we are not always as ready for action as we think we are. We start pushing ourselves forward and we feel pushed, so we resist. We get stuck.

We also make inaccurate assumptions about those whom we manage or coach. Thinking that they are fully prepared to reach their goals, we start moving ahead. They are just like us, so they have also made an error in thinking that they're ready. We're moving along, and all of a sudden we realize that they aren't with us. They're resisting. They're stuck.

If you find that you sometimes lose track of yourself or others as you're plowing ahead toward a goal, you've probably skipped this step. A key reason that most people don't achieve their goals is that they never fully commit to achieving them. Instead, you need to take an honest look at where you are and begin there. It's uncomfortable to admit that you aren't completely ready for action, but when you do, you make dramatic strides toward becoming a Confident Leader.

You need to figure out how ready other people are to change, and then meet them where they are. When you do this, a process that previously created a great deal of resistance becomes easy. It's the difference between riding a bike up a hill (the old way) and gliding down an easy hill on a bike toward your destination (the new way that I'll show you).

Is Now the Time for a Change?

As you know, timing is everything. If the timing isn't right, all of your best efforts will fall flat. In deciding whether now is the right time, ask yourself if you have the resources (time, energy, finances, and so on) or can get them with little downside. I don't recommend embarking on a change when you're under considerable stress or duress.

BONUS ONLINE MATERIAL

To help you decide if you are ready for a change, go to www.pascoaching.com/time4change/ and take the self-scoring assessment test entitled *Is Now the Time for a Change?*

The number one problem people face when taking on new goals is that they're not ready to change. We know that we have a problem or could improve ourselves, and we assume that we "should" be ready, but we're ambivalent. We take one step forward and two steps back. We spin our wheels and feel exhausted, but in reality no progress is being made.

Let's say you have an elegant dinner to go to later this evening. If you're sitting in front of the television in sweats with messy hair and taking a shower is still on your list of "things to do today," you're not yet ready for the dinner. If someone said, "Okay, we need to go *right now!*" you wouldn't go. Or if you did, you wouldn't want to be there or you'd feel embarrassed that you looked like you just rolled out of bed (or off the couch in this case). We need to be ready to do things. If we aren't ready, nothing good happens.

So, How Ready Are You *Really*?

When I begin coaching a new client, the first thing I do is figure out how ready that person is to make a change. Once I know this, I can easily propel that person forward.

The goal is to work with your current motivation level. Two influential researchers, James O. Prochaska and Carlos C. DiClimente, developed a model to explain motivation for change. The model was originally developed for addictions, but it has been applied to assess individuals' readiness for change in many areas of life.

Think about a specific goal in your life, and then read through these five stages of change, which are taken from Prochaska and DiClimente's study. Take an honest inventory and ask yourself what stage you are currently in. Then complete the action steps for that stage, which will get you ready for the next stage. Also consider where those whom you manage fall and select the appropriate action steps to motivate them.

Stage 1: "Precontemplation"—Not Even Thinking about It

In the *precontemplation stage*, you are not yet thinking about making a change. The change hasn't even crossed your mind. This does not necessarily mean that you don't *want* to change. You can be reluctant because you don't believe that you can make the change successfully or you just don't have enough information about how it could benefit you.

Can you imagine how difficult it will be to try to start doing something new if you are in this stage? You'll be resistant, especially if things don't go the way you want them to. When you're in an early stage of readiness for change and you face failure or hardship, you're likely to give up, concluding, "See, I knew I couldn't do that." There is a reason that you are in precontemplation. Your fear may be too great for you to move forward. Or perhaps you don't have enough fear (about what would happen if you didn't change) and motivation to take action.

Action Steps for the Precontemplation Stage

1. *Gather information.* Instead of forcing yourself to do something, it is better to learn about the potential benefits of making the change. In the precontemplation stage, someone may think, "I should really work on my anger and temper at work." Instead of trying to change that day, ask, "What's important about working on my anger?"

2. *Strengthen your radar for new ideas* that tell you that a change may be of benefit. Listen to what other people say, and work to hear how a new approach may benefit your life, work, or relationships. Broaden your network, and then strengthen your radar for information that tells you that you don't want to make the change or that you aren't currently ready.

3. *Postpone the change.* It is often better to put your project on hold until you are ready to embark upon it with energy and enthusiasm. Wait to begin something new until you are *ready* to make a change rather than pushing yourself into it and having a negative experience that could turn you off from pursuing your goal then or in the future.

4. *Uncover hidden areas of precontemplation.* You are beyond precontemplation in at least one aspect of your life, or you would not be reading this. Think about whether there are *other* areas in your life in which you're in the precontemplation stage.

Stage 2: "Contemplation"— Thinking about It

The second stage of motivation is called the *contemplation stage.* At this point, you have started thinking about the need for something different, but you are not sure what to do. As you contemplate taking action, you think of the good and not-so-good aspects of doing so. This can be confusing because you want to begin working on your goal, but you also want not to begin. Have you experienced this ambivalence before?

Sometimes people feel unsure but do not readily think of the reasons for or against taking action. If you've found that you have put off something important or have been unsuccessful, it may be that you haven't worked through your resistance. The reasons for the change may be so obvious that you haven't considered the less obvious reasons that part of you doesn't want to make the change. If you don't work through these, either you won't take action or the action you take will be halfhearted.

Action Steps for the Contemplation Stage

1. *Sort through apprehension by making a pros and cons list for pursuing and not pursuing your goal.* For example, someone who is considering working on improving his listening skills might come up with a list like this:

Reasons to Listen Better at Work	Reasons *Not* to Improve My Listening Skills
• Help my direct reports to feel heard and valued.	• I don't have time to hear what everyone has to say.
• Learn more and gain knowledge that can help me.	• If I give someone an inch, she could take a mile and talk my ear off.
• Show that I'm invested in change and improving my leadership.	• People will start to have higher expectations of me.
• Be clear about my boss's specific expectations for me.	• I need to be a decisive leader, and listening to everyone's opinion can make me look weak and indecisive.
• Give more specific and clear feedback.	• If I'm listening, I'm not thinking, and I'm known for always being a step ahead of the game.
	• What if people start sharing feelings and I have no idea how to respond?

As you can see, the wonderful thing about this list is that it uncovers the fears that might hold you back from making a change if you weren't aware of them and didn't address them.

2. *Ask yourself, "Assuming I could achieve my goal, are the pros or the cons more compelling?"* If the pros seem to be more important, then you're ready to move into the next stage. If they aren't, then you can help yourself to make the pros more convincing by gathering information, getting support from others, or picturing how your life would be improved if you were able to make the change. Or it may be that the change is not something that is consistent with your values, and that you don't really want it.

3. *Consider how you will benefit.* If you're pursuing a change for someone else, you won't be successful. Using the example of improving your listening, consider how your career or business will benefit from the reasons to change and listen better.

Stage 3: "Preparation Stage"—Getting Ready to Do Something

When you believe that the reasons to change outweigh the reasons not to change, you become determined to do something. You begin thinking about how you can pursue the change within the next month (if the time frame is longer, you're still in contemplation). You've entered the next stage, the *preparation stage*. You become more and more ready and committed to doing something new.

Action Steps for the Preparation Stage

1. *Work through all your fears and concerns about making a change.* Here's how: take each item on your "reasons not to change" list and consider its validity. Is it really likely to happen? And if it did happen, would it really be that bad? Could something good come of it?

2. *Test out your concerns.* Understand your concerns without being controlled by them. The only way to know if the fear is really true is to try it out. If your worry is, "Listening will take too much time," you can conduct an experiment in which you truly listen to people for a week and see if you are behind in time. Even if it does take longer, is it worthwhile because of the benefits that resulted? And remember that something new takes more time at the beginning until you get used to it.

3. *Make a game plan and timeline.* For most changes, you will not need a lot of time to get ready, but you will need some time. The amount of time needed is related to the size of the change (bigger changes require more preparation) and the investment needed (including your time, money, and energy). If you're planning to buy a house across the country, you'll probably need more time than you would if you were moving down the street. In the preparation phase, you are ready to begin changing within the next month. This doesn't mean taking one month to complete the process; it means getting going within one month. If your goal is to become more organized and you've made no progress toward this goal (for example, you haven't yet started tracking what planning systems work and what don't work) in the course of a month, then you are not actually in the preparation stage.

4. *Ask yourself, "How will things look and feel when my goal is achieved?"* This reinforces Step 1: Get Your Exceptional Vision. The best vision is one that uses emotion and as many of your five senses as possible. Let's say your goal is to become more strategic and organized in your leadership. You want to stop putting out fires and serve as a Confident Leader who knows the big, medium, and small goals and how each daily activity serves to meet those goals. Your motivating vision is yourself in six months, arriving at the office with a clear mind and a plan for the day.

The agenda items on your plan clearly map onto your big vision and your career mission. You feel calm, organized, inspired, and ready for the day. You serve as a powerful role model, and your direct reports are more organized as well. Your employees know exactly what is expected of them, so they have more confidence, which means that they perform better and require less support from you. See how much more powerful this is than what most people do, which is to say, "My goal is to get more organized"?

5. *Create a strategy and steps for achieving your goal.* Once you have your vision, you want to back it up with specific action steps. One of my clients created a vision of moving up to chief operating officer in his company. He knew that he needed to be more assertive to reach this goal, but he was concerned that he'd be seen as arrogant or conceited if he were assertive. Some of his action steps included the following: First, read two recommended books on developing assertiveness within the next four weeks. Second, commit to making at least two opinionated statements on a current topic each day. Third, communicate more powerfully and compellingly by thinking before speaking and speaking for a shorter time. Fourth, do something previously avoided three times per week, such as "working the room" at a networking event.

Stage 4: "Action"—Doing Something

You're now ready to initiate something new. At this point, it's a good idea to publicly announce your commitment to others. You must now take action. If you don't, you're likely to regret it. Recent evidence shows that when people are asked what they regret the most in their lives, they say not acting on something. Interestingly, when asked what they regret the most in the past six months, they say a bad decision that they made or something that didn't meet their expectation. These stages of change help you in both instances. You select the best course of action at the best time in Stages 1 to 3, thereby eliminating the short-term regret for something not going as you'd like. And you take action in Stage 4, eliminating the long-term regret for not having acted on something important.

Action Steps for the "Doing Something" Stage

1. *Figure out how your anxiety and action are related.* Many people find that their fear is highest before the action stage. Do you get nervous when you're anticipating a potentially challenging event? If so, you may actually be relieved when you start taking action. Let's say that someone with a fear of commitment is beginning a new business. Starting a business involves a level of commitment like that of getting married or having a baby, and it can be intimidating. You may become overly nervous before you take the plunge, but once you're in it, you feel great. Others become more nervous after they've committed. The key is not to let anxiety cloud your thinking about the best course of action.
2. *Build a strong support system for lasting change.* There are helpful and less helpful ways to do this. We'll talk about the helpful ones in the next chapter.
3. *Use your discomfort to select the best course of action.* You'll learn how to do this in Chapter 4.
4. *Use your anxiety for motivation and energy.* We'll discuss this in Chapter 5.
5. *Get into the flow by letting go of control.* This is a tough one, but it's powerful, and once you master it, action becomes much easier. We'll go here in Chapter 6.

Stage 5: "Maintenance"—Long-Term Progress and Success

This final stage of change is the one that is often neglected because people figure that they've made progress. Nevertheless, many people then move on to something else, often slipping back into their old habits and their comfort zones. The most important aspect of the maintenance stage is that you recognize what you need to do next. You do not want to become so comfortable with your progress that you are no longer moving forward.

Think of the stages of the change process as being like buying a house. You're going along living in your current house (precontemplation), and you notice some things about it that you don't love, so you start thinking about what type of house you'd want to buy (contemplation). You decide to move, so you start researching housing markets, school districts, financing options, and other things that you need to consider as you begin looking for a new house (preparation). Now you know what price range you would like to focus on, where you want to live, who'll be your real estate agent, and the parameters for the house you want (three bedrooms, a big backyard, move-in ready, and so on). You're ready for action. You call the real estate agent and begin looking at properties. You find a wonderful house and go through with settlement. The exhilarating day comes when you go into your new house for the first time. The process is done, right? Not so fast. You still have the maintenance phase related to the change. You'll need to pay your mortgage, make changes to the house, maintain the fixtures and appliances, mow the lawn, and keep an eye out for good refinancing rates. There is typically a good deal of maintenance if you want to enjoy your house over the long haul.

Action Steps for the Maintenance Stage

1. Ask yourself, "Do I tend to pursue something for a while, but then lose focus and not follow through?" This is the "bright shiny object" phenomenon that the majority of entrepreneurs experience—you see something and are attracted to it … until a new bright shiny object catches your eye. If this sounds like you, you need to pay greater attention to the maintenance phase. This is why I like to present goal achievement as a process and not a destination. If you think that you are done and then change your focus, you'll slide back into your old habits. The maintenance phase is not as glamorous or reinforcing as the process of making the change, but it's equally important.

2. *Create a plan for what to do once you've achieved your goal.* It is all too easy to slip back into our old patterns. Ongoing support and accountability with a peer, executive coach, mentor, or your boss can help you stay on track.

3. *Don't overreact to setbacks.* It is common to have some "slips" where your old habits return. If you're working on your temper and one day you angrily storm out of a meeting, you can get back on track. Know that these slip-ups can happen and don't beat yourself up. Ask yourself what you need to do. You can apologize to your coworker and let her know that you are working on managing your temper and would appreciate her feedback in the future about how you're doing.

You Have the Right Timing and Motivation — Now, Speed

You're now aware of the best timing and motivation. The final consideration in Step 2 is your speed of change. When my clients realize that they need to move out of their comfort zones, they often ask me if it's okay to move slowly. The answer is, it depends.

A good metaphor for approaching a difficult change is that of getting into a pool of cold water. Let's say you dropped an expensive pair of sunglasses into the pool. You dread getting into the freezing cold water. If you move too quickly and you jump in after them, you'll ruin your watch and wallet. Or maybe you don't want to freeze, so you take it slowly, hoping that you'll get used to the cold water. First in goes one foot, then the other ... an hour later, it is getting dark and colder, and you still haven't gotten into the water. At this point, you *really* don't want to get in, and you've come up with many reasons why you don't want those sunglasses anyway. You definitely aren't getting into that cold water, right?

As you can see, the speed of your change is crucial. Consider moving at a speed different from your normal pace. If you are typically a go-getter with a strong sense of urgency, slow down a bit and add to your preparation period. This will be uncomfortable, as you'll want to jump right in. If you are typically a thoughtful planner and a slow, deliberate mover, you can benefit from jumping in, or at least getting in more quickly. You won't feel ready, but that's okay. Let's review a few more considerations about speed.

When to Jump Right In

The best time to do things is usually right now. Get a running start and jump in. A Scottish proverb says, "What may be done at any time will be done at no time." The longer we procrastinate, the more our anxious anticipation builds. One of my clients dreaded making sales calls, so she put them off and they loomed over her for the entire day. She finally made them, but by that time they were extremely unappealing and she caught people at the end of their workday when they weren't focused, so they didn't go well. I like to say that "Worry creates monsters out of shadows." The best thing to do is to turn on the light and see that nothing's there. Just go for it.

It is common to use discomfort as an excuse to overprepare for situations. For example, a perfectionist feels that a report needs to be just right before he turns it in to his boss, so he spends hours going over it, only to get behind on other important activities and become increasingly nervous about whether he missed something on the report. Many of my clients are executives starting their own businesses, and they frequently get stuck in this process. To ensure that they are "really ready" to take the plunge (and it is a big plunge) from their executive suite to ownership of a small business, they buy dozens of books, attend countless seminars and networking events, mull it over, and basically build their fear and risk while never doing something that is important to them. With most things in life, it is impossible to be completely prepared. While some planning and research is necessary, too much facilitates avoidance and inaction.

The Water Will Get Warmer

Once you've thrown yourself into the uncomfortable situation, you need to stay there a while. If my client who didn't like making sales calls tried to get off the phone as quickly as possible and made calls only infrequently, she would not improve. Instead, keep yourself in the situation long enough to ride out the wave of discomfort. Picture yourself as a surfer riding the wave up and then back down. Over time, you will become a Confident Leader, but only if you stick with it. When you jump in and then jump right back out, you are only teaching yourself to escape, and that is the opposite of the message you want to send to yourself. The water that feels cold at first will feel warmer over time once you adjust to it. This process is called *habituation,* and it never fails. You need to get into the situation quickly enough, stay in it long enough, and repeat it enough times to gain mastery and improved results.

When to Jump In Action Step

To decide whether it's best to jump right in, answer the following with yes or no:

- I already have the information I need to take action.
- I know that delaying action is just avoidance.
- I have the skills to handle this situation successfully, but I need more practice.
- I tend to be an overplanner, overpreparer, and overchecker.
- I'm ready and willing to take a risk.
- I know that if I don't do it now, it may never happen.

If you said yes to most of these questions, it is time to go for it and plunge in.

When to Take It Slower and Go Step by Step

In contrast to always jumping right in, it can also be a good idea to begin with something manageable and work your way up to the most difficult step. This is especially true if you tend to be impulsive and someone who acts and speaks before thinking.

You can use the process of knocking out easier goals to build up your confidence and skill sets to ensure that you'll be successful when you get to the most difficult steps. If you find that you've resisted taking action, it may be because you are pushing yourself to move too quickly. Instead of forcing yourself to do the least desirable thing, break up the process into a series of steps. If you play sports, you know the importance of gradually increasing your exertion and practicing before the big game or race day.

Joe, whom you met in the last chapter, was an overplanner and overthinker. It made him nervous to do things spontaneously and not feel fully prepared. While it was best for him to jump in, since he was an overpreparer, going straight into the most difficult situation was too big a leap, so we worked out the following series of steps to give him practice:

1. Spontaneously greet people in the hallway without planning what he would say.
2. When playing golf, simply look at where he wanted the ball to go and hit the ball without extensive strategizing ahead of time.
3. Ask employees questions rather than planning his responses while they were talking.
4. Go into a meeting with his boss with only five minutes of preparation.
5. Give a presentation in a board meeting with only an outline and minimal preparation, allowing himself to improvise.

As Joe was an overpreparer, the key for him was that he progress rapidly between steps. He did all of these within two weeks. These steps were increasingly more difficult for him, but each time he did one and benefited, he became more inspired to do the next one, and he became more and more effective. As Joe went through this process, he began to shine as himself rather than as something he was trying to be, which had come across as not genuine.

One Thing at a Time Action Step

To decide whether it's a good idea to take your change one step at a time, respond to the following with yes or no:

- It would be helpful to me to build up more confidence before doing what feels most uncomfortable.
- I can see a series of steps that I can arrange in order of least to most difficult.
- I need to accomplish one thing before I can move on to the next.
- I tend to be impulsive and have a high sense of urgency, so some more planning and strategy is probably good.
- I do not yet have sufficient knowledge or training on how to go about the task.
- When I try to plunge in, I procrastinate and don't take action.

If you responded yes to some of these statements, the best course of action for moving ahead is to have a specific plan with a series of steps. Draw a ladder and label the rungs 1 through 10, beginning at the bottom. Then assign actions to each rung, beginning with 1 as the easiest and 10 as the most challenging or resource-intensive.

One Hundred Percent Committed and Ready for Action

Once you have committed to a decision, it's important that you do not give yourself an out, because you will take it when things start to get rough, which of course they will. Studies on self-determination show that your commitment is especially important when your goal is a difficult one. We tend to be more satisfied with decisions that we stick to than with ones that are indefinite. In 2002, researchers Daniel Gilbert and Jane Ebert assigned photography students to one of two groups. In one group, students were told that they needed to select one photograph to take home and one to leave on file, and that they could not change their minds once they had decided. The students in the other group were also told that they needed to select one to bring home and one to leave on file, but that they could take a few days to see if they wanted to change their minds. Interestingly, those who were unable to change their minds reported liking their photographs better than those who remained uncommitted.

This finding can be explained in part by cognitive dissonance, a theory developed by the influential social psychologist Leon Festinger, who studied under Kurt Lewin, considered the father of social psychology. This motivational theory shows that it is uncomfortable to hold contradictory thoughts. The concept is that this discomfort motivates us to change our thoughts, attitude, or behavior. Interestingly, if an incentive is involved, people experience less conflict. In one of Dr. Festinger's studies, college students were asked to do a bunch of boring mental tasks. They were asked to tell the next group of study volunteers that the tasks were fun and interesting. Half of these participants were given a $1 bill, and the rest were given a $20 bill. They were then asked if they had found the task enjoyable. The students who were paid only $1 said that they found the task enjoyable because they didn't feel rewarded in dollars (as the $20 group did), so they had to convince themselves that the task was interesting rather than boring to rationalize the time spent. On the flip side, if you commit to something and invest your time, energy, and money into it, cognitive dissonance will help you rationalize your decision as a smart one (which is fine as long as you did the initial work to be sure you were committing to a smart thing).

Most people skip the important step described in this chapter and assume that they are ready for and committed to action. Don't tell yourself, "I'll try," or "We'll see what happens." Don't even promise yourself that you'll do it. Research by Peter Gollwitzer on intentions and what actually gets implemented indicates that vowing doesn't work, but making a specific plan does. Accept the possibility of failure (with the goal of learning from it), and create a specific set of concrete steps that are consistent with your stage of change and vision from Step 1. For example, if you're in action: "Tomorrow morning at 9 a.m., I will call the three prospective customers I met today." Now, we'll move to Step 3, an important step no matter what stage of change you're in: building your team.

3

Step 3: Organize Your Team

Whom Do You Know and What Resources
Do You Need to Help You Make the Change?

THE MOST SUCCESSFUL people know that one of the keys to their success is other people. As with many things, however, it is not what you know but how you do it that counts. Building a supportive team to help you out is challenging for many reasons. You might

- Feel uncomfortable asking others for help.
- Think that you should be able to handle everything on your own.
- Not have the right people around you to give you what you need.
- Think that your success doesn't mean as much if you had the help of others.
- Not communicate what you need in a way that gets you what you need.
- Worry that those you hire or rely on will mess up.
- Overrely on the support of others, thereby doubting your own abilities.

- Feel awkward bringing up business discussions with your personal networks.
- Believe that the "right" people to help you out don't exist.
- Fear that hiring others to assist you will be too expensive.

Any of these sound familiar? Everyone has some worry about using others for support.

I remember when I was building my business and contemplated hiring an assistant. I *knew* intellectually that it was a smart idea and that not doing so would greatly limit the growth of my business. This knowledge, however, did not prevent me from worrying about whether it was the right move at the right time and about the impact that a major monthly expenditure would have on my bottom line. We could group the concerns that I had about hiring an assistant and that people have about receiving support into four categories:

1. *Time.* Others will slow you down or hold you up.
2. *Quality.* Others will dilute the quality of your work.
3. *Money.* It will be expensive to hire others.
4. *Self-esteem.* You'll feel bad about yourself if you rely on others.

Now, think of your own issue. Which concerns stand out the most for you?

Because of these concerns, you may not use your support systems effectively. If you're afraid that using others will be time consuming, you'll be prone to either doing everything yourself, micromanaging, or rushing people along. If you think the quality will not be as good, you'll avoid delegating or you'll try to control others and supervise them. If you think that using others will be too expensive, you'll avoid hiring tasks out or you'll find the least expensive (and probably not the best) people to hire. If you're concerned that you should be able to do everything yourself, you'll either do everything yourself or subtly (or not so subtly) communicate to others that you don't value their help.

If you want to do the tough things that lead to the best results, you need support. Notice my word choice: *need.* It's not that it would be nice to have people supporting you; you absolutely need it. When you're taking on your greatest challenges, you need to have a team behind you. Let's start with the most important part of any team: leadership.

The Team Leader Is *You*

A lot of people dislike the idea of getting support because they feel it makes them weak. They think of support as something that is there to hold them up. In Gothic architecture, tall buildings need buttresses on the side to hold them up. This is one theory of support—that you are the building and your support people are buttresses.

I don't like this theory. I prefer a team-leadership idea. You need to organize, motivate, and guide the team that will make *all of you* successful. The mentality is not, "What do I need you to do and how can you support *me?*" Instead, it's, "How can you support me in my goals that have a clear benefit to you as well?" or "How can we provide mutual benefit and value to one another?" Think of the expression, "A rising tide raises all ships." The higher you go, the higher your team members go.

Think about what type of leader you want to be and need to be for those on your team. Much of this will depend on the type of people you are dealing with. Let's say, for example, that you have your husband on your team, and he doesn't respond well to subtleties. He's willing and happy to help you as long as he knows exactly what you need. In this case, you will have to be an assertive leader who gives clear directions. Don't provide him with a rough sketch and hope that he can complete the picture. Instead, say, "I'd really appreciate it if you would do (insert very specific action)."

Transformational leadership (a style in which a charismatic leader sets an inspiring vision and in which goals are collective and future oriented) has been shown to produce better results than transactional leadership (a style in which the leader relies on rewards and punishments). In 2006, Australian researchers Simon A. Moss and Simon Ngu examined a leadership contingency model to see if leadership style is best determined by the personalities of those being led. Five personality traits known as "the big five" were examined: extroversion, conscientiousness, openness, agreeableness, and neuroticism. Here are some findings:

- Extroverts did well with transformational leaders because they responded well to the stimulation and motivation.
- Conscientious individuals preferred a transformational leadership style as well, perhaps because of the alignment of values and ideals that these leaders demonstrated.
- Individuals who were high on openness, interestingly, did not favor transformational leaders, perhaps because people with this personality type value independence rather than a collective vision. Openness was also negatively related to a preference for transactional leaders, perhaps because open individuals find these leaders stifle creativity.
- Agreeableness was also negatively associated with the transactional style, perhaps because people who are high on agreeableness dislike confrontation, and transactional leaders seek out problems to solve.
- Individuals who were high on neuroticism (anxious, vulnerable, or insecure traits) preferred a laissez-faire leadership style, perhaps because they felt less threatened or scrutinized.

The implications of this study don't necessarily suggest that you need to change your style based on whom you are leading. Just realize, for example, that if you have high-neuroticism people on your team, they may feel threatened, and it's good to help them feel more secure.

Action Step for the Confident Team Leader

Make a list of all of those who you manage directly or indirectly. Then write down your observations of their personality traits based on the Big 5 personality traits: Extroversion, Conscientiousness, Openness, Agreeableness, and Neuroticism. For a week, observe them and write down examples of their responses to situations under the personality trait it seems to fit. Then modify your leadership style as needed to best match each person's personality.

Who's on the Bus?

In *Good to Great,* Jim Collins highlights the importance of having the right team, or, as he puts it, the right people on the bus, before you do anything else. When you have the right people in place, you don't need to spend your valuable energy on motivating them, and you'll get less resistance. In the next chapter, we discuss making important business decisions. You cannot do that until you have assembled and analyzed your key stakeholders.

The first step, therefore, is to recognize who's on your team right now. Do you have all the important seats on the bus filled? Are people in the right seats on the bus based on their strengths and talents? Do you need to bring others on board to make sure that your goal will be achieved? Do you need to get a bigger bus? Do you know how those on the bus feel about where the bus is heading?

Assess Team Members' Readiness for Change

The last question asked is a critical one because it is unlikely that everyone on your bus will have the same degree of readiness for change. You don't always have control of who's on the bus.

In the last chapter, we discussed how to get you ready, and now we need to think about how to get your team ready. It's important to realize that you live in a system. Any change that you make affects those within your system. A change that you perceive as wonderful may not be perceived so wonderfully by those whom it affects. When you realize that people naturally resist change, you'll be able to help people become ready to not only accept change but also to embrace it. Rather than make assumptions about how motivated people are to make a change, ask them. Here are some examples of questions:

- Are you ready to begin moving toward this goal within the next four weeks? (If so, they're in the preparation stage.)
- Are there more positives or negatives about taking action? (If they have roughly the same number of positives and negatives, they are in the contemplation stage.)

- I'd like to get you some resources, such as books and other materials—does that sound good? (If so, they're in the preparation stage.)
- Do you think that we need more or less than six months to start moving full throttle? (More than six months means they're in the precontemplation stage; six months to one month means they're in contemplation; one month to now means they're in preparation. Now means they're in the action stage.)
- We've been making progress toward this goal for a few months now—are you still enthusiastic about it? (If the answer is yes, they're in the action stage.)
- Have you been taking consistent action and, if so, what is it? (If the action is behavioral and has been ongoing for at least a few months, they are in the action stage.)

You can propel people along once you accept where they are. For example, let's say that you have an executive assistant who is a wonderful worker but is not ready for a new technology that you'd like to introduce. If she is in the contemplation stage but you are in the action stage, it won't work. Instead, meet her where she is. Discuss the pros and cons with her, helping her to see how the pros benefit her. Offer to provide her with training and other resources (in the preparation phase) and then reassess to see if she is ready for action.

Remember that the contemplation stage feels comfortable to people because they do not need to commit to anything, but the comfort is an illusion. They're stuck. If people cannot get themselves out of this stage or allow you to help them move forward, then they may not be the right people to be on your bus at that point in time.

Get GROWTH-Oriented People on Your Bus

Confident Leaders learn from watching others. We grow by surrounding ourselves with others who like to take on a challenge. In 2000, researchers Paul R. Nail, Geoff MacDonald, and David A. Levy put forth a model of social influence. One dimension of their model has to do with "disinhibitory contagion." This process begins when we are faced with a decision that feels risky and we're feeling uncomfortable about it. We observe some-one taking a risk. We then feel less inhibited about taking a similar risk. We take action. We end in a state of harmony rather than internal conflict.

The implications of this model, which is supported by previous research as well, show that we challenge ourselves best when we surround ourselves with others who challenge themselves. If, for example, we're hiring a business coach, we should consider one who shows evidence of pushing him- or herself on a regular basis. If we're creating a mastermind group or think tank, a key criterion for entry should be regularly seeking challenges and opportunities for growth.

It's Whom You Ask and How You Do It That Count

When faced with a challenge and asking for assistance, we (often unknowingly) seek out someone who will confirm what we want to hear. This can be great if that is our goal—to get confirmation of our ideas. If, however, we truly want someone who will help us see all sides of the issue and play devil's advocate, then we must choose accordingly. Also, the way that we ask a question makes all the difference. We tend to ask questions in ways that get the answers we want. We can solve this by asking open-ended questions and maintaining a neutral tone of voice.

Handling Objections

It is often the case that people on your bus are great for one thing but not so great for others. I'll illustrate with an example. One of my clients had been happily married to his wife for 20 years. They served as wonderful complements to each other: he was a rebellious, spontaneous go-getter, and she was a thoughtful, practical type. This balance served them well. His goals of luxury items and family vacations were realized—but only after she reviewed the finances and created a budget.

The problem arose when he decided that he wanted to leave his cushy executive suite to enter the unpredictable world of entrepreneurship. An opportunity presented itself, and he knew that he needed to take action right away. His wife was made anxious by this situation. She expressed her concerns and objections by saying things such as these:

- "How can you leave such a great job and steady paycheck?"
- "Now all the pressure will be on me to maintain our standard of living while you get the business up and running."
- "We have three kids in private school, and we need to be saving for college—this doesn't seem like the best time to do something risky."

Obviously he was not going to kick his wife of 20 years off the bus. So what did he do?

Listen to What You Don't Want to Hear

When someone objects to our plans and goals, our first reaction is to feel defensive and hold our ground even more firmly. The problem with this reaction is twofold: first, we won't hear information that can help us, and second, we will not create buy-in. Instead, we must listen carefully because our resisters may have an important consideration that we didn't think of. We often make decisions with emotion before reason. If our objector is not in love with our idea, that is a good thing. He will be able to take a perspective that we don't currently have. If we listen to his objections and information, we may or may not agree, but we're likely to discover new ways of thinking about the situation.

Listening to What You Don't Want to Hear Action Step

Think of a time in the past when you were able to hear someone say something that you didn't want to hear. Remember what got you to listen to it even though you didn't want to. How did you remain open enough to benefit? How did listening to what you didn't want to hear benefit you?

When you recall the benefit of remaining open and perhaps even seeking out negative feedback, you will be able to do so more often. If you can't think of any times that you have done this, you have an excellent opportunity to grow. If you listen only to what you want to hear, you will never learn anything new or challenging. Instead, seek out opportunities to receive difficult-to-hear feedback. Remain open by asking yourself, "How can I become even better at my work and grow with the help of this information?"

Creating Buy-In

When you have resisters, you need to create buy-in. As with most things interpersonal, it boils down to communication. It's not about convincing others that your goal is a good one and they need to support you; it's about asking them whether they can be on your team. The way to balance an emotional reaction is with mild amounts of reason. I say mild amounts because whenever you counteract something with the opposite extreme, you get even more resistance. If it was 60 degrees out and you put on a down jacket because you were chilly, you'd be boiling. If someone was extolling the virtues of down jackets, you would not want to hear her message.

And here is the clincher: don't tell your resister why your idea is a great one. Your temptation will be to share all of the reasons why what you want is a good idea. That won't work. Marilee Adams, author of *Change Your Questions, Change Your Life,* teaches that statements are likely to lead to judgments, whereas questions are likely to lead to learning and growth.

Instead, say, "I can see that this situation brings up a lot of fears for you, and it should; it would require risk that affects our family. What are your main concerns—please tell me as questions."

Let's say that my client's wife said, "How are we going to pay our bills while your business gets up and running?" He could respond with, "What questions would help us to sort that out?" And she would say, "What's our capital investment?" "What's the timeline for projected profitability?" "What if the business is not generating revenue in three months?" and so on. Together, then, they could look for the information to answer these questions. When my client went through this process with his wife, she came up with some excellent questions that he and his business partners had not considered. She became excited about the opportunity, and she provided support that made the business even more successful.

Creating Buy-In Action Steps

1. *Look for situations in your business or life where people have different goals.* Experiment with asking questions and balancing emotion with reason.

2. *Look for situations where you are torn.* We often have resisters within ourselves. Part of us really wants to charge ahead, and part of us says no way. Use this process of negotiating with the resisting part of you and observe what happens. When you begin the questioning process for both sides, you'll find yourself getting unstuck and forging ahead.

3. *Observe others in situations where the people have different goals.* About 95 percent of the time, you are going to see people struggling with the resistance and getting more and more stuck. Learn what not to do. On rare occasions, you'll see people artfully manage the resistance of others. Learn what to do.

4. *Find opportunities to help others do what they do best.* If someone has a role in which he can shine and enjoy the process, not only will he stop resisting you but he will become a wonderful champion for your cause.

Personal vs. Professional Teams

When it comes to getting support from people, it's important to think about who's on what team. I like to think of us all as having two teams: personal and professional. We often make the mistake of either keeping the teams completely separate or making them completely interchangeable.

In the previous example, if my client had been in denial about his need to have his wife on his team, he would have suffered some harsh consequences. If, on the other hand, he had relied solely on his personal support systems as he was building the business, he would not have been as successful as an entrepreneur. In my years as a business coach, I haven't received one referral from a family member. The reason? I believe it has to do with memory and mental priming. Our minds are like filing cabinets, and our memories are like files in the cabinet. We have files for things like, "Family," "Vacations," "Favorite Restaurants," and so on. If my sister were to think of me, the files for personal life would come up first. She'd think of me as being a Sister, Daughter (to our parents), Friend, Wife (to my husband) … and in about tenth place would be Business Psychologist. Therefore, referring people to me simply would not be foremost in her mind.

What works best is to have your primary personal team and your primary professional team, and to allow some degree of crossover. For example, I might talk with my sister about a business situation here and there, but most of the time we're focused on our personal lives. I might talk with my business partners about my personal life, but the majority of the time we're focused on business. The reason that this is so important is that it prevents us from burning out our teams. If we use everyone for everything, we exhaust them. It's like having the two teams on opposite ends of the field and asking them to run back and forth to switch sides all the time. That's very tiring.

Personal vs. Professional Teams Action Step

Think of the key players in your life and in your business or career. What team are they on? Do any of your teams need reorganizing? Do they need new players? Recognize areas where you may have been overrelying on one team member to be part of both teams (thereby exhausting that person). For example, perhaps you're relying on your husband or wife to listen to you vent about work and provide you with advice. If your personal team members are playing on your professional team too much, consider requesting additional support at work via a mentor, an assistant, or a coach.

Once you're clear about each person's team and position, be sure to share her roles with her. Your spouse, for example, may be fine with serving as a fill-in team member on your professional team every once and a while but will be happy to know that her primary role each day is on your personal team, and that you're getting adequate professional support.

Break All the Rules to Get the Best Results

Gallup studies of over 80,000 managers presented in the book *First, Break All the Rules* by Marcus Buckingham and Curt Coffman are revolutionary because they show that relying on conventional wisdom is easy but ineffective. We need to go past what's comfortable and customary to find the truths, and the studies showed that the world's greatest managers actually do things differently from what conventional wisdom assumes.

The research revealed 12 questions that show how to attract, develop, and keep the most talented employees. Of the 12 questions, 6 correlated most highly with strong business outcomes. The questions outlined in the book are these:

1. *Do I know what is expected of me at work?*
2. *Do I have the materials and equipment I need to do my work right?*
3. *Do I have the opportunity to do what I do best every day?*
4. *In the last seven days, have I received recognition or praise for good work?*
5. *Does my supervisor or someone at work seem to care about me as a person?*
6. *Is there someone at work who encourages my development?*

As a Confident Leader, you need to make sure that your employees and other team members answer yes to most or all of these questions. Consistently making sure that these things happen will arouse some discomfort. You may be concerned that you'll need to devote more time to your staff. Remember, this may entail a short-term sacrifice for a long-term reward. When managers help their employees with these questions, it is proven that they get results in the form of top performance and profitability. It appears to be worth the short-term sacrifice.

What if what you think your employees do best is different from what they think they do best? Speak with your team members to find out where you agree, and be sure they're doing those things. The other concern that commonly arises is that you'll have to make yourself vulnerable and express some emotion to provide recognition and encourage the development of your staff. Of course you'll need to do all of these difficult things in order to get your best business results.

Give Everyone the Right Tools

The second question in the list stresses the importance of materials and equipment. Imagine that you were trying to put together a world-class soccer team, but none of your players had soccer cleats, jerseys, shorts, shin guards, or socks. Your team would be at a distinct disadvantage and would be prone to injury and embarrassment. It is essential that you have the right materials if you are to play your best.

Even if you are a solo-preneur, pay attention to this step. You may not have people working for you as employees, but you hire contractors to help you: your Web designer, accountant, copywriter, and so on. If you want people to do their best work for you, be sure that they have the right tools. Make things easy on those around you and they'll reward you with speed and quality. For example, my Web designer has told me that sometimes people get their Web site materials to her in bits and pieces. Her time and energy then need to go toward finding and compiling everything rather than toward staying focused on creating a wonderful Web design.

Be Generous with Praise and Gratitude

You may worry that if you praise your employees, they will become complacent. This is true only if you praise everything regardless of the quality of the work or support, which hopefully you do not do. I've also heard this same line of thinking from people about their personal lives. "I don't want to compliment my spouse because what if he gets a big head and leaves me?" The opposite is *much* more likely to happen—when you don't praise people, they leave you. When you provide genuine positive feedback, you motivate others to best support you and stay with you. When we're recognized, we do our best work and want to support others in their quest for success.

To provide genuine feedback, you must recognize and appreciate it. If you do not, your feedback will be insincere and have the opposite effect. In addition, expressing gratitude can have many beneficial effects on you. Gratitude is linked with happiness.

In one study, Dr. Martin Seligman of the University of Pennsylvania and his team of researchers set out to discover whether "positive psychology" can make people happier over long periods of time. They created five exercises and one placebo exercise and assigned volunteers to each. Over six months, they tracked the participants and measured their happiness and depression. They found that focusing on three good things that went well each day for a week and finding out and using signature strengths every day for a week led to six months of increased happiness and reduced depression.

As the Gallup research showed, using your strengths every day also leads to improved business results, so it is important that you both do this for yourself and provide opportunities for those on your team to do it. Seligman's team also found that conducting a "gratitude visit" created beneficial changes for participants for a month. A gratitude visit entails writing a letter and delivering it in person to someone you appreciate but have not positively told so. Expressing gratitude and praising those around you leads to not only beneficial results for them, but positive results for you. Praise and gratitude fulfill questions 4 to 6 and are key components of a creating a supportive team.

Breaking the Rules and Giving Tools Action Steps

1. *Go through your key players and see if they have the right equipment.* If you are not 100 percent sure, ask them.
2. *Get the best support by giving the best support.* You'll be shocked at how helpful everyone becomes when you provide the right support by making your expectations clear and enabling people to do what they do best.
3. *Focus on at least one positive thing with each of your team members every day.* As Seligman's research indicates, focusing on three good things each day improves happiness. Why not focus on even more by keeping track of at least one great thing about each of your team members every day? Seligman's study had people use the tools for a week, but it also found that prolonged use of the exercises led to even greater happiness.

Put What You've Learned to the Test

You've learned the first three steps in the GROWTH model. You know what you want. You know how ready you and others are to make it happen. You've assembled a powerful team. Now you're ready to use these ideas to help you make those difficult in-the-moment decisions.

4

Step 4: Win with the Right Decisions

*Make Those Tough Choices That
Lead to Your Best Results*

MAKING CRUCIAL DECISIONS is one of the most uncomfortable and important tasks that Confident Leaders face. You need to decide whether to go after a big promotion, take out a business loan to expand your business, hire a new employee, or relocate (which means uprooting your family). These decisions create a great deal of distress. Maybe your discomfort is a red light. It's your intuition telling you not to move ahead, and you should stop. Or maybe it's a yellow light—you're just worried about doing something new. Maybe the discomfort is a green light. It's a sign that you're growing and pushing yourself to achieve more. In this chapter, I'll help you determine how to use these uncomfortable feelings to your advantage.

I recently went through the challenging decision process of whether to invest in a new technology to support my business. There were actually two areas of discomfort in this decision: first, I am a technophobe, and second, adopting the new technology would require a significant investment of resources. The considerations I faced were these:

- Should I listen to the discomfort because it means that the new technology isn't a good idea? Maybe it wasn't a good investment of resources at that time and the discomfort was my intuition telling me to back away.
- Should I get more information about the product before making the decision? Maybe I just wasn't informed enough to make the decision.
- Should I realize that the anxiety was simply the flip side of excitement about a great opportunity and go for it? Maybe it was a perfect opportunity to overcome my technophobia and grow my business.

Decisions under Uncertainty

The most difficult part of making decisions is that the variables and the outcomes are often uncertain. We would do anything to be certain. We'd even pay our hard-earned money, as shown in one study in which college students were asked whether they would purchase a great deal on a trip to Hawaii over their holiday break. They were told that they would receive the grade on their most important exam before they had to decide. Of those who were told that they passed the exam, 57 percent said they'd go for the trip (gotta celebrate), and 54 percent percent of those who were told that they failed said they'd go (gotta recuperate).

However, when the influential cognitive scientists Amos Tversky and Eldar Shafir designed uncertainty into the mix, everything changed. Students were told that they would not receive the exam grade for two days and that they could buy the trip now, pass on it now, or pay five dollars to wait for two days until they received their grade. An incredible 61 percent said that they would wait! They wanted to go if they passed *or* if they failed the exam, but they were willing to pay to wait if they didn't know their grade.

We are often paralyzed by uncertainty and end up basing our decisions on things that aren't even related. Question your attempts to find certainty before making decisions, because you may be lulled by a false sense of security. It may be best to accept uncertainty and move ahead anyway.

Discomfort as a Red Light

Apprehension doesn't always mean that we should proceed. Yes, we need to move beyond what's comfortable if we are to grow and become more successful, but sometimes our discomfort is really a message that needs to be heard. It can be our intuition speaking to us, saying that we need to be cautious about moving forward or we should quit altogether.

One of my clients, Sue, recently told me that she had had a wonderful business opportunity presented to her, but she could feel only nervous about it. On the surface, it seemed like something that she should pursue without hesitation, but she felt overwhelmed, and the idea of adding something else to her plate made her nauseated. Had Sue accepted the new venture, she probably would have worked herself to exhaustion and greatly regretted it. Sue was glad that she allowed her discomfort to warn her not to take further action. As a major go-getter, it was tough for her to put a limit on herself and *not* take action, but it was wise.

Figuring out when your apprehension is about avoidance (and you should ignore it and keep going) and when it is about intuition (and you should listen to it and stop) is one of the most challenging and powerful aspects of decision making. To sort this all out, a question to ask yourself is, "If I could complete this task without feeling too nervous about it, would it be worthwhile?" If your answer is yes, then the discomfort is probably coloring your rational thought processes and making you want to avoid something you actually should do. If your answer is no, then it may be that the situation is simply not the best choice for you at this time. Sue realized that she wasn't nervous about the venture itself, but rather about the impact that it would have on her life. She didn't want to avoid the opportunity because she was afraid of failing or losing money, but because it would have required a significant time investment that she was unwilling to make at that point.

Another question to ask yourself is, "How do I feel about this when I'm in a great mood?" When you're in a negative mood, you think with your emotions and everything you recall is consistent with those feelings. If you're mad at your boss, for example, all you think about is how horrible she is and how many times she's been horrible in the past. Instead, weigh your options when you're in a calm, positive frame of mind. You will approach the situation from a more rational viewpoint. If you still feel a nagging gut sense that this is the wrong thing to do, listen to your intuition.

When Sue was in a great mood and she thought about the new business venture, her energy level went down. This showed us that it wasn't the right decision at that time. I tell my clients, "Let your worries speak to you but not control you." There may be a message there that's worth considering because it sheds light on a new solution. Approach the thought with the objectivity of an impartial jury, and if the argument is compelling, use it to inform your decision.

Listening to Discomfort Action Steps

1. *Think about the times in your professional or personal life when you should have gone with your gut but didn't.* What thought, feeling, hunch, or physical sensation told you to pass on something? Next time you experience one of these things, listen carefully, and proceed with caution, back out, or cut your losses.
2. *Ask yourself whether you have given the situation the benefit of the doubt.* If you've given an employee (who you feel won't cut it) second and third chances, your ongoing concerns are there for a reason.
3. *Get a second opinion.* Ultimately you need to trust your own instincts, but a good way to build up confidence in your abilities is to consult with others. If several credible and unbiased people have the same sentiments as you, you have good support for going with your gut.
4. *Follow your passion.* If you realize that you aren't passionate about making the change and it really isn't important to you, then you're back at Step 1 and you probably shouldn't proceed. Sometimes you don't realize that something isn't that important to you until you're in the in the process of doing it. It takes guts, but it can be much smarter to quit than to stick with something that doesn't fire you up.

Discomfort as a Yellow Light

When they are looking at making a change, most people gather information about what they need to do and assume that this knowledge is enough to be successful. They get an organizer and a daily planner to become more organized. They go to a seminar on improving their leadership skills. They tell themselves that they'll start going to bed earlier to get more sleep. They make a mental note to stop being critical of others. They say that they should stop procrastinating and get more accomplished.

These things sound great until nothing ever comes of them. The planner doesn't get used daily. They persist with the same leadership style. They continue making critical comments and putting things off. Often the problem is not in the knowledge of what needs to be done, it's in the implementation. You know that you need to have an organizational system if you are to be more organized. Or that you have to start things right away if you are to end procrastination. The challenge, of course, is actually doing those things. You need to learn how to *turn knowledge into action*.

There are, however, times when you really do need more information before moving forward. Your discomfort simply tells you that you aren't yet qualified to make a good decision. If you're nervous about giving an employee feedback, for instance, it may be because you don't have enough information on his job performance. Or maybe you aren't skilled at giving feedback and your sessions don't go well, so you need some additional training. If you aren't sure whether someone is a good hire, you need to get more data by checking that person's references, doing thorough interviews, and conducting assessments.

Gathering Information Action Steps

1. *Ask yourself whether you'll be* significantly *more successful* with additional information, training, mentoring, coaching, or other resources. Don't get caught in a perfectionist situation where you feel the need to have every piece of information possible, but do get the right information or training.

2. *Start small with what you can do right now*, and then gather further knowledge as you move along.
3. *Conduct a survey.* Find out what some of your trusted colleagues would do in a similar situation. Observe role models in your workplace and see how they make decisions. Use the information gleaned to help you take action.
4. *Determine whether you have the luxury of time* to collect further information. Done is often better than perfect. If so, get going.

Discomfort as a Green Light

When your apprehension is met with a twinge of excitement and energy about the wonderful results you can achieve, take it as a green light. When I was faced with the decision about adding a new technology, I realized that I was simply experiencing the typical anxiety that results from change. The change was an important one, so it was worth it to me to experience some growing pains. This brings us to the next question.

The Million-Dollar Question That Confident Leaders Ask Themselves

This question is, *"Is it worth it?"* Most people wait until after they've taken a risk to make this assessment. If they risked something and experienced discomfort but came out successful, they say that it was worth it. Instead, be proactive and ask yourself this question first, accepting the fact that you may or may not be successful in meeting your goal. Conduct a cost/benefit analysis to make yourself aware of the costs, challenges, sacrifices, and potential problems with working toward your goal as well as the potential payoffs, rewards, benefits, and wonderful outcomes. We discussed this in Steps 1 and 2. Let's return to it here and consider how to use it for in-the-moment decision making.

One of my clients, Jed, is a global sales manager whose goal for coaching was to improve his communication skills, both at work and with his wife. I had Jed conduct a 360-degree feedback assessment of his workplace performance in which his boss, his peers, and his direct reports rated him on several dimensions. His wife and his oldest daughter also completed the feedback forms. Jed discovered that he had strengths in achievement, confidence, and influence. A challenge that came up in several places throughout the assessment was his "need to always be right." His direct reports felt that he didn't care about their opinions. Jed's wife felt that he often didn't acknowledge her point of view because he was so wedded to his own side. And his peers felt that he always had to have the last word.

If Jed committed to the process, I had no doubt that he would improve his communication and his personal and professional relationships. The key was whether or not he'd commit. We walked through the questions in Chapter 1 to see how motivated he was to change and whether this was the right time to change. Being an action-oriented individual, Jed felt that he was ready for action. Then I asked him the million-dollar question.

"Okay, Jed, we need to figure out if it's worth it to you to take this challenge on."

"I don't understand," he replied. "It seems easy. I just interrupt people less, ask my wife for her opinion more, and give my peers credit for their work."

Jed loved snow skiing, so I gave him the metaphor. "Yes, it sounds easy in theory, but in practice it will be quite difficult. If someone was learning to downhill ski, would you tell her, 'It's easy; just strap on the skis and breeze down the mountain'?"

"No, of course not, she'd curse me as she was out in the cold, wet from falling down."

"Right. What would you tell her?"

"That she has to want to learn to ski. That it'll be cold, and she'll fall a lot. And she'll get frustrated and probably want to give up several times," Jed told me.

"Exactly. This process will be the same for you. It will drive you nuts to bite your tongue while others speak. It will be tough to smile and say, 'Thank you' when someone tells you information you already know. You'll want to correct people if they're not completely accurate. You'll want to get into an argument with your wife because you know that you're 100 percent right and you want her to see the errors of her ways. Instead, you'll ask her questions to understand more of her views, and you'll say, 'Thank you for helping me understand how you're looking at this,' without defending your position. You'll feel like you've 'lost,' which I know you can't stand. So, back to a friend learning to ski, why should she stay out in the cold, fall down a lot, and be sore the next day?" I asked.

"Because flying down the mountain on a sunny day is the most exhilarating feeling of freedom in the world," he said with exuberance.

"Sounds to me like it's worth it to learn to ski! Now the question for you is, is it worth it to you to make your communication changes?" I asked.

"Well, it may be more difficult than I originally thought, and it might get worse before it gets better, but I still think it's worth it."

"Okay, but it's easy to say that because it's the answer you're expected to give. I'll be the jury. Convince me. *Why* is it worth it?"

"I'm not moving to the next level at work because I irritate people. If I communicate better and make people feel valued, there'll be less arguing at home and at work, and my direct reports will feel more independent and confident. I'll have done something meaningful to help them in this way. I'll be closer to my goal of a new executive role, and I'll have more support from my wife. We've been married for 16 years, and it kills me to see her unhappy and know that I contribute to it. I want to be a good role model for my daughter and show her what to expect in her own relationships." I was convinced.

Is It Worth It? Action Step

When you go through a process like I did with Jed, your motivation will skyrocket and your decisions will become easy. Think about the costs associated with your goal and the potential benefits, and then conclude whether it is worth it to move forward. Consider

- *Your feelings* during the process (stressed, anxious, unhappy, embarrassed, angry, shy, hesitant, nervous, frustrated, annoyed, and so on).
- *Your schedule and resources* because a change often requires additional time and resources, especially at the beginning.

- *The things that can go wrong* as you try something new.
- *Other people's reactions.* Others might resist the process or not enjoy the changes in your mood, schedule, and focus.

How compelling are your benefits? Consider

- *Your mood.* Will you feel happier, more confident, proud, courageous?
- *Changes in your schedule and resources.* Will you have more time, earn more money, and have more energy?
- *Improvements in your relationships.* Will you get along better with people? Gain respect? Be more influential? Reduce conflict? Express yourself more assertively?
- *Your work advancements.* Will you be better able to promote yourself? Take on new tasks and challenges? Make a change? Be a better leader? Sell more?

Should You Think or Feel Your Way to the Right Decision?

Participants in a study conducted by Timothy D. Wilson and his colleagues at the University of Virginia and the University of Pittsburgh were asked to choose a piece of art to hang in their homes. Half of them were asked to think rationally about their choice, and the other half were instructed to go with their gut. Those who went with their feelings rather than their analysis were happier with their selection. We can rationalize our way into anything, but our first impressions often tell us how we really feel.

While it's important not to think too much about major decisions, it's also important not to get caught in emotional reasoning. Because emotions color our thought processes, they can have a negative impact on decision making. In the heat of the moment, it sounds like a great idea to tell an annoying customer that we can't help him, but once we calm down, we're able to think of new solutions and express them calmly. Therefore, refrain from making decisions until you are in a normal state of mind, and then trust your instincts.

How to Boost Your Intuition

First of all, you must be able to listen to your gut. This means having some quiet time in your life when you're not on the go, doing a million things, and experiencing constant mental chatter. If you're naturally a doer, you'll find this tough. You can look for simple things to do, such as taking a walk and resisting the urge to take out your phone, waiting in line and letting your mind wander, or spending a few minutes of quiet reflection time each day.

Intuition can lead us down the wrong path, so check it out with other sources of data. This presents a nice checks-and-balances system. In a study of 60 successful entrepreneurs, almost all of them said that they would assess information in combination with their gut feelings—if either was off, they would tread carefully or decide against moving ahead with the new process or project. Data are held and processed in the frontal lobe of the brain, which synthesizes and processes complex information. Another part of the brain also helps us use information to boost intuition. As we learn, often by trial and error, a deep part of the brain called the basal ganglia holds information like a sponge. This is called implicit learning, and it's how, for example, animals learn not to go in certain areas. They don't have a prefrontal lobe and do not think, "Well, the last 11 times I went there, my predator was waiting to eat me; therefore it probably makes sense for me to take a different route this time." Instead, they just know not to go there.

In making complex decisions, the basal ganglia get activated, as does the amygdala, the part of the brain that is responsible for emotional memories. The answer comes to us in the form of a feeling or a "gut" instinct. This circuitry is the gut or deep part of the brain, and it informs us in terms other than words. Confident Leaders listen to it.

When You Think You Know, but You Have No Idea

Our thoughts can lead us astray in decision making because they're affected by many biases. Emotional thoughts and memories stand out to us more than nonemotional ones. If, for example, we read a review for a hotel and someone said that he found a spider in the room, and we're terrified of spiders, when it's time to make a decision about the hotel, we're likely to decide against it despite dozens of favorable reviews.

As another example, which is more common in English, words with *t* as the first letter or words with *t* as the third letter? If you're like most people, you say words with *t* as the first letter because these are easier to think of, so those words are more available. This thought bias is called the availability heuristic, and it's based on how readily something comes to mind and how vivid or emotional the memory is. The way to manage this is to get multiple perspectives. Just as you want to form your intuition on data points, you want to form your thoughts on multiple informants to overcome the natural thought biases that each of us has.

Think or Feel Your Way to the Right Decisions Action Steps

1. *Calm the external and internal chatter* that keeps you from hearing your intuition. Build quiet time into your life—no TV, music, cell phone, and so on.
2. *Hone your intuition by looking at the evidence.* Look at all the data for and against your options—the more data points, the better. Over time, you won't need to go through each data point; you'll just know the right decision.
3. *Beat your own biases by gathering multiple perspectives.* As in Action Step 2, over time, the multiple perspectives will hone your intuition, and you won't need to gather them.

The Biggest Challenge of All: In-the-Moment Decisions

Your action plans can quickly fade away when you're faced with an in-the-moment decision. Jed decided that it was worth it to change his communication, but he was challenged in deciding what to say and how to say it in the heat of the moment. *The short term is always more reinforcing than the long term.* This means that something that can give you pleasure or reduce your discomfort right now is much more motivating than something that will affect you minutes, hours, weeks, months, or years from now.

Anna, a 41-year-old accountant, was beginning her own practice. She was nervous about spending money, as her company was not yet profitable. She hired temporary employees so that she wouldn't have to pay for benefits. She worked like crazy to accrue billable hours. Instead of hiring more CPAs, she did the work herself or sent it to the other CPAs in her company. She worried that everyone would quit after the insane tax season. Clearly Anna's business model was burning her out and not creating profit. Yet she was reluctant to hire the right people because they were more expensive. To solve this quandary, I suggested that Anna ask herself the million-dollar questions:

- "Is it worth it to me to take on more expenses because they could pay off greatly in terms of productivity, morale, and client satisfaction?" (Yes!)
- "Is it worth it to me to continue on this path I'm on and keep feeling overworked, overwhelmed, unsupported, and resented by my staff?" (No!)
- "Is it worth it to take a short-term risk for the long-term rewards?" (Yes!)

Anna decided to hire a high-level receptionist who would also serve as her assistant and to hire another CPA. No one quit that year, and the firm had the best tax season ever. Anna even enjoyed a relaxing vacation on the beach without worrying how the work would get done.

In-the-Moment Decisions Action Step

Think of a time in the past week when you experienced tension because your in-the-moment desire clashed with an important success goal. How would asking yourself, "Is it worth it?" have been helpful in that situation? What would you do differently? Then, the next time you're faced with a decision, ask yourself, "Is it worth it to me to do this, knowing that it may be intimidating and I may fail?"

Uncommon-Sense Decision-Making

Three more thought patterns influence our decisions: whether we're accepting or rejecting something, the amount of choices we have, and our time frame.

How We View Positive vs. Negative Attributes

We tend to overlook what's not there, selecting things for their positive features and rejecting them for their negative features. In one study, researchers asked participants if they'd rather go on an average island vacation or a vacation on an island that had amazing weather and beaches but not great nightlife or hotels. At first, participants selected the second choice because they were attracted to the positive features. If, however, they already had reservations for both and needed to cancel one, they were more likely to cancel the second one because in rejecting a choice, they were looking for the negative attributes. People can come to a totally different decision depending on the way the information is presented to them. For example, if you need to choose between two ads for your company, you would probably select the one with more positive features. If you were running two ads and had to cancel one, you would cancel one based on its negative features (even if it was outperforming the other ad). Be aware of these mental biases when making decisions.

Choice Is Good—Or Is It?

In 2000, Sheena Iyengar of Columbia Business School and Mark Lepper, chairman of Stanford's psychology department, conducted a study in which two tasting displays of gourmet jams were set up in an upscale supermarket. They had 24 jams arranged for tasting in one display, and just 6 jams in the other. They found that more people were attracted to the table with 24, an equal number tasted at both tables, and a huge difference in purchasing resulted: only 3 percent of those who had tasted at the table with 24 jams bought a jar, whereas 30 percent of those who had tasted at the table with 6 jams bought a jar! To make decisions effectively, you want to limit your options. If you sell products or services, help buyers make choices easily by limiting the number of choices.

Making Decisions for the Future

An interesting psychological process happens when we think ahead: we make our decision based on *why* we want to do something. Let's say that one of your business partners asks you to manage a couple of client accounts while he's out of town next month. You say sure, answering the question of "why?" with "because it is a nice thing to do to help him out." Fast-forward a month, and you're knee deep in his client accounts, unable to find his clients the resources that they need, and totally behind on all of your own work. In the short term, you answer the question "how?"—in this case, "How the heck am I going to get out of this mess?!" Be aware of this process when making decisions for the future.

Another Way to Use the Million-Dollar Question

A habit works like this:

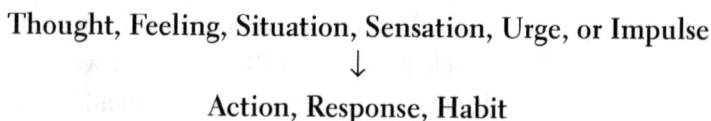

Thought, Feeling, Situation, Sensation, Urge, or Impulse
↓
Action, Response, Habit

Inserting "Is it worth it?" helps you to reverse your habit. There are two ways to do this.

The first way encourages you to assess whether your old, familiar habit is the most helpful way of behaving in the current situation. It reminds you of your broader goal and forces you to consider whether your typical response is the best course of action. That looks like this:

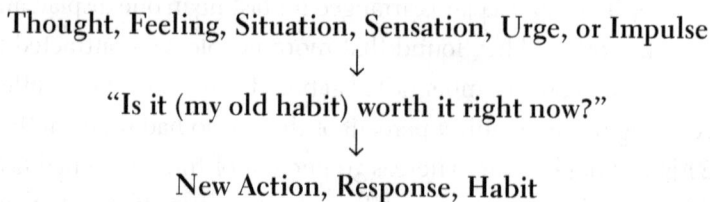

Thought, Feeling, Situation, Sensation, Urge, or Impulse
↓
"Is it (my old habit) worth it right now?"
↓
New Action, Response, Habit

The second method is similar but slightly different. In this method, you ask yourself whether doing something new and therefore uncomfortable is worth it. This helps you not do your old habit and purposefully insert a more productive action. This looks like this:

Thought, Feeling, Situation, Sensation, Urge, or Impulse
↓
"Is it worth it to me to get uncomfortable to achieve my goal?"
↓
New Action, Response, Habit

Habit Reversal Action Step

Think of three habits that you want to change. They can be bad habits that aren't serving you well, or they can be desirable habits that you want to do more often.

1. *What are the thoughts, feelings, sensations, urges, and impulses* associated with this habit?
2. *What are your typical behavioral responses?*
3. *Ask yourself, "Is it worth it to me right now to do my usual thing?"* Answer with more than a yes or no, honestly stating your case with no excuses.
4. *Ask yourself, "Is it worth it to me to get uncomfortable to get a step closer to my goal?"* Again, answer with more than a yes or no, honestly stating your case with no excuses.

You're Right on Track; Now, Keep the Momentum Going!

You've now mastered the first four steps in the GROWTH model: Get Your Exceptional Vision, Realize Your Commitment, Organize Your Team, and Win with the Right Decisions. You're growing into an even more Confident Leader than ever before, and with these changes come anxiety. How do you turn this anxiety into optimal energy? We'll cover that in the next step.

5

Step 5: Turn Anxiety into Optimal Energy

*Keep Yourself Moving Ahead Even
When You Want to Stop*

"WHEN YOU TURN *over rocks and look at all the squiggly things underneath,
you can either put the rock down, or you can say, 'My job is to turn over
rocks and look at the squiggly things,' even if you what you see can scare the
hell out of you.*" This quote (from Fred Purdue, a Pitney Bowes executive,
cited in *Good to Great*) exemplifies the essence of this chapter: Confident
Leaders confront their fears and use them to propel themselves. When we
stay within our comfort zones, we don't experience much anxiety, but we
also don't experience much growth. Knowing exactly how to make the best
use of our worries is something that inevitably comes up as we get closer to
our goals.

When Anxiety Is Good

We need some anxiety if we are to succeed. Anxiety has a purpose, and it's
not just to keep us from doing things that are uncomfortable or feel dangerous. There are, of course, occasions when this is anxiety's primary purpose.

If we're walking somewhere at night and have an instinctual reaction to get into a taxi because the neighborhood doesn't feel safe, we should listen to the fear and take a taxi home.

Other times, however, as I like to say, "Worry creates monsters out of shadows." The key is to listen to our worries, to know how to respond, and to allow them to energize us toward success. People often misunderstand the message their fear sends them—they feel the physical sensations (racing heart, shortness of breath, sweaty palms, and so on), and they think their bodies are saying "fight or flight." If they stay in the situation, they'll find that their bodies were sending a false alarm of danger and were really giving them the energy to do well. This is good anxiety.

One of my clients is afraid of public speaking. In one of our meetings, she told me about the butterflies she gets when she needs to speak in public. We discussed how that anxiety serves a purpose and helps her. It won't hold her back if she doesn't let it. Now, before she has to give a brief presentation, she reminds herself, "I have energy, and I'm doing something important. It will get easier as I get more practice." And her presentations are great.

Good Worry Action Step

Think of a time when you experienced helpful anxiety. What happened? How did you handle it? Jot down some times you noticed that your worry worked for you.

The Right Balance

With no anxiety, you get no results. With too much, you get poor results. But with the right amount, you get great results. Anxiety improves performance—up to a point. Most people think that this point is lower than it actually is. The power of a moderate level of anxiety can be seen in most areas of life—from investing in the stock market (with too much anxiety, you play it too safe and hurt your chances of great returns, and with too little, you put your hard-earned money at too high risk) to relationships (if you're too comfortable, you probably don't care much, and if you're too nervous, you're likely to be overcontrolling or jealous).

Where do you fall on this spectrum? Think of different areas of your life where you'd like to achieve greater success. If you'd love a new job but you haven't started a serious job search, you may have too little anxiety. If you're terrified to put yourself out there for a new position because you fear failure, you may be paralyzed by too much anxiety. Do you need to tone down or amp up your anxiety and energy to reach your goals?

How Anxiety Is like Cholesterol

Do you remember when research first indicated that cholesterol is bad? The medical community realized that cholesterol clogs arteries and advised people against eating food high in cholesterol. As a result of these warnings, people stopped eating food with high fat content, and new medical problems developed. Medical researchers then learned that not all cholesterol is bad. There is good cholesterol (HDL) and bad cholesterol (LDL). Good cholesterol can help lower your risk of cardiovascular disease. Anxiety is like cholesterol. Good anxiety helps you by lowering your risk of underperforming and getting stuck in life. Whatever your goal, good anxiety is the key to the change you want.

As we discussed in the first chapter, anxiety almost always latches on to something that you care about, something that's important to you. If you value being a kind and thoughtful person, you may worry about being rude to others. If it's important to you to have financial freedom, you'll worry about money. If you want to be fit and healthy, you may be nervous about food choices. Keep in mind, however, that *the message that your anxiety gives you is not necessarily right*. This is because it engages the emotional part of your mind, which is less rational and objective. If, for example, it tells you that you must be completely nice all the time or you'll be a rude person, this is unlikely to be true.

The idea, therefore, is to listen to your worries and let them show you what you value, but not to take them at face value. Take them with a grain of salt. I often say, "Let anxiety speak to you but not control you." You don't need to do what it suggests. But listen to the message it gives you because there may be a strong clue to the path to success. Often the thing you resist doing is the very thing you need to do for an optimal outcome.

Anxiety and Values Clarification Action Step

What do your worries say to you? How are they showing you things
that you value? Consider how your values (integrity, relationships,
honesty, growth, compassion, giving) are related to the worries that
arise when you think about making a change.

When Anxiety Is Bad

Confident Leaders recognize when apprehension is useful and when it's
harmful. Anxiety often results from trying to have complete certainty,
control, predictability, or stability, which of course is impossible and, in
my view, not desirable. It is difficult to experience these things *and* grow,
but the opposite of stability is instability, which connotes mental unrest.
The trick, then, is to recognize anxiety when it is helpful and keep it there
without allowing it to go bad.

Bad Anxiety Is Usually Obvious

One of my clients, Steven, had obsessive-compulsive disorder (OCD). He
was afraid of getting sick from ingesting chemicals and pesticides. He lim-
ited his diet to a few specific foods and refused to eat at restaurants. It is
clear that your anxiety is disruptive when your diet is restricted to pasta, fish,
water, nuts, and rice, as Steven's was. He worried that fruits and vegetables
would be contaminated with pesticides, and he could not eat animal products because the animals might have been fed food that contained pesticides or other chemicals. Bovine growth hormone terrified Steven, so dairy
products were out of the question. He used only paper plates and plastic
utensils and threw them out after each use because plates and silverware
that were washed in a dishwasher could have some detergent residue left on
them. He and his wife hadn't been out to dinner in years, and she had given
up trying to prepare any food that he would eat. He was an investment
banker who worked about 70 hours per week, and he spent about 3 hours

per day on careful food preparation and other rituals. Steven's anxiety was destroying his life. His OCD was clearly an example of unhelpful anxiety.

Some other examples of bad (i.e., too much) anxiety include the following:

- An executive who doesn't take an incredible promotion because he is scared of being in a senior leadership role
- A woman who has panic attacks (a sudden rush of physical symptoms) and won't go to work because of her fear that she might panic in front of colleagues
- A marketing director who has to do everything so perfectly and meticulously that he doesn't leave his office until 10 p.m. and gets only about five hours of sleep a night
- A salesperson who dreads making sales calls and giving presentations and who is highly anxious and not making her numbers

If you experience excessive fears like these, it's clear that this level of anxiety is bad. It can certainly be problematic in less dramatic circumstances, too. If you find that you're up at night worrying about the next day, feel distressed when doing new activities, wonder whether you can "make it" in your career, or have not been successful in relationships, your anxiety may be problematic.

Bad Worry Action Step

The first step is to be self-aware: go through the past couple of weeks and ask yourself, "How have I experienced too much worry?"

How Good Anxiety Morphs into Bad Anxiety

Most people assume that anxiety is bad because it feels bad. When you're anxious, you feel worried, overwhelmed, nervous, afraid, distressed, and unhappy; in short, you don't feel well. You may have physical symptoms like muscle tension, racing heartbeat, feeling out of breath, feeling shaky or dizzy, or stomachaches. You *really* don't feel well. But, as we've discussed, anxiety on its own is not bad. It can, however, go bad.

There is no bad dog or bad child—it's more about how they're raised. The same is true with anxiety—it often begins as good anxiety but turns into bad anxiety because of how we treat it. It's well intentioned, but it can go astray when we respond to it in the wrong way, which unfortunately is the way most of us respond.

My husband is a marathon runner. He's inspired me to attempt running even though it does not come naturally or easily to me. I'm just beginning to run, and I've realized that running is a whole different ball game from the exercise I've done before—it is painful! I ran a few blocks, and I felt as if my heart would pound out of my chest. I had an awful side stitch, I was burning hot and sweaty, and I couldn't catch my breath. What does this sound like? Fear! If I never ran again (which is tempting, but I'm still working on it), I would be left thinking, "I can't run. I hate running. Running is miserable!" Running, which is a wonderful thing, feels bad, so I could interpret it as such. I could end up making it much harder on myself than it has to be. I could avoid running, only to have it become more difficult each time. I could put it off and end up running when I'm tired, thereby making it more difficult to do. I could tell myself that I should just deal with it and force myself to run when it's 90 degrees outside or push myself to do too much and get hurt. If, however, I accepted the discomfort and instead pushed myself to do just a little bit more each time, I would build up my endurance and I wouldn't think that running is bad; it might even be fun.

Anxiety is simply energy with an unfavorable interpretation. A classic study conducted by Donald G. Dutton and Arthur P. Aron showed that anxiety enhances attraction to others. A shaky suspension bridge swayed 230 feet above a river in Vancouver, and researchers had an attractive woman approach men as they walked across it or after they had crossed over the bridge. She asked them to fill out a questionnaire and gave them her number, saying that they could call and she would explain the study. More of the men whom she approached on the bridge than those whom she approached after the bridge called her. The men on the bridge experienced symptoms of adrenaline due to anxiety, but interpreted them as arousal because they were speaking with an attractive woman. This shows us that the anxiety is not the problem; it's how we interpret it that counts. If we think it's bad and avoid it or handle it in ways that make it escalate, it grows, gains control over us, and becomes problematic. *We turn good anxiety into bad anxiety by how we respond to it.*

Take the example of Don, a 50-year-old business owner who worked incessantly. When he began his business, Don experienced normal levels of distress. Most business owners worry about whether their companies will succeed, how they'll pay the bills, and whether they have what it takes to be business leaders. Don found this anxiety unpleasant, so he worked harder. He felt out of control when he delegated, so he didn't delegate or he micromanaged. Over time, it became more and more difficult for him to relinquish control, and his anxiety and stress both increased. Don's normal anxiety had morphed into bad anxiety.

Or take the public relations executive who works under a demanding boss and makes efforts to avoid contact with her, thereby increasing his discomfort when he does see her. Or the busy executive who is worried about losing time, so she rushes an employee along, only to stress the employee out and cause him to take longer to fix mistakes. Or recall Joe, who was nervous about being seen as an imposter, so he tried to speak eloquently, yet he came off as artificial. This list could go on and on. We all do things to turn everyday little fears into problematic situations.

Even Extreme Anxiety Did Not Begin Bad

Even extreme anxiety like Steven's is not bad in and of itself. You can learn a great deal from a typical OCD cycle—even if you do not have OCD yourself. When you understand how a severe anxiety disorder forms and sticks around, you can easily understand how to manage everyday levels of anxiety. Steven did not become scared of all those foods and chemicals overnight. At the beginning, he noticed that he felt nervous when he saw a film or a waxy substance on his fruit. Back then, he washed his fruits and vegetables a little extra, but he ate them anyway. Then he began eating only organic fruits and vegetables. He and his wife ate at a few select restaurants. However, after seeing a television special on the chemicals and bacteria that lurk in restaurant kitchens, he stopped going out to eat.

What happened during this process was that Steven experienced some anxiety and backed away from it. Instead of allowing himself to be anxious and eat anyway, he tried to control the anxiety by carrying out a ritual, like not eating at a restaurant or scrubbing his fruit for five minutes before eating it. Each time his anxiety came up, he pushed it down. The harder he tried not to experience the anxiety, the more he experienced it.

Carrying out a ritual or avoiding anxiety is like trying to push a beach ball down in a swimming pool. The ball is the worry or obsession you try to get rid of by pushing it down. What happens when you try to push a beach ball down in a swimming pool? It pops back up. Likewise, anxiety pops back up when you try to push it down or avoid it. What started as a little innocuous anxiety became severe anxiety (OCD for Steven) because of the way Steven responded to it (with rituals). My cocktail napkin drawing of this process looks like this:

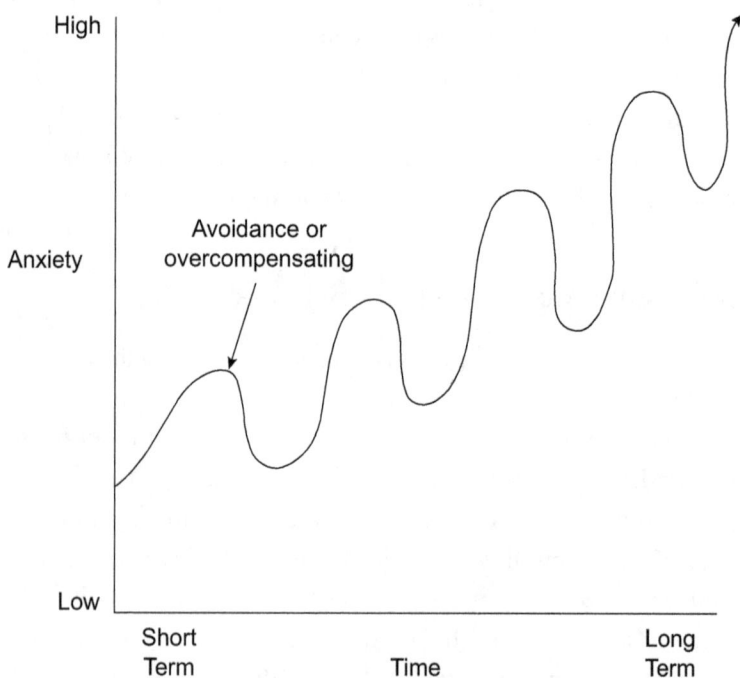

So you see, anxiety rises when we encounter a challenge, and when it's artificially pushed down with avoidance or rituals, it comes back up with even greater force. Normal anxiety becomes bad anxiety because of how we respond to it.

Unhelpful Responses to Anxiety Action Steps

1. Identify the ways in which you've pushed distressing thoughts or feelings down, only to have them pop back up.
2. When you notice discomfort, interpret it as helpful energy rather than a hurtful hindrance.
3. When you're tempted to avoid something, challenge yourself to do it. The more you avoid it, the more difficult it will become.

Good or Bad Anxiety—The Solution Is the Same

Whether the anxiety that arises with change and growth is minimal and not disruptive or so severe that people like Steven can barely function, the solution is actually the same: *allow yourself to experience anxiety and it will work for you rather than against you.* This solution is amazingly effective. Steven no longer had symptoms of OCD after just 12 treatment sessions. He followed a plan in which he confronted the situations he feared, beginning with the easier ones and working up to the most difficult ones. He stayed with the uncomfortable situations until his anxiety subsided, and he repeatedly confronted his fears until he was no longer fearful. Most important, he didn't allow any rituals or subtle forms of avoidance to creep in. The solutions in this chapter can work for you, too.

When anxiety is too high, the way to bring it down looks like this:

High

Allow yourself
to experience and
get used to anxiety

Anxiety

Low

Short
Term

Time

Long
Term

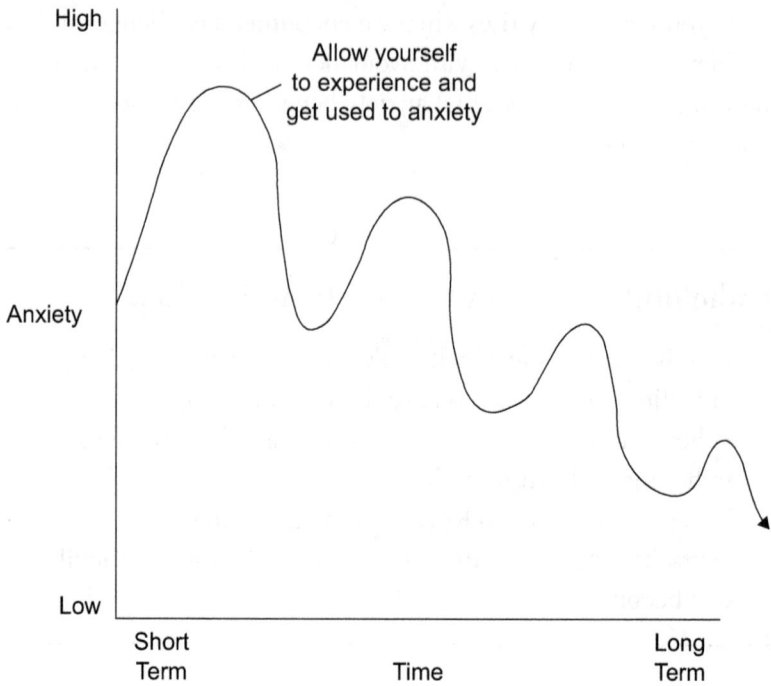

Each peak is a time when you purposefully confronted your anxiety and rode it out, just like being on a roller coaster. What goes up will naturally come down. This process is called habituation.

White Bears and Pink Elephants

In *Winter Notes on Summer Impressions* (1863), Dostoyevsky asked the question: "How do you stop thinking about a white bear?" Researcher Dan Wegner and his colleagues set out to investigate this issue in 1987. They asked college students to not think about a white bear. What do you think happened? The students couldn't stop thinking of a white bear. The researchers concluded that trying to suppress a thought actually produces more of that thought. Wegner went on to repeat the experiment, asking students to purposefully think of a pink elephant. What happened? The opposite—the more you try to think of something, the less you actually do think of it.

These pivotal studies on thought suppression show that every way to deliberately banish a thought (by trying not to think about it) is wrong. If you find yourself dealing with someone who is anxious and stressed out and you say, "Just don't think about it," your well-intentioned advice is going to make the person feel worse. If you want to get rid of a thought, you actually must allow yourself to experience it.

Research by Stanley Rachman and Padmal de Silva shows that 80 percent of people experience intrusive thoughts just as people with obsessive-compulsive disorder (OCD) do. The reason that people with OCD experience more of these obsessive thoughts and more distress is that they try not to have the thoughts. If someone is worried about an important project, she should let the thoughts be there. She shouldn't focus on them, but she also shouldn't put a lot of energy into distracting herself and trying not to have the thoughts. As with the pink elephant, eventually her brain would tire of the thoughts, and they'd drift off. What this means for you is that it is critical that you accept and not judge or push away your thoughts. If they are distressing or distracting, don't worry; they will eventually go away once *you stop trying not to have them.* You don't have to stop what you're doing and listen to them; just proceed with your work, almost as if the thoughts are songs on a radio at a low volume.

What happens when someone tells you to relax or calm down? Do you become more relaxed? Most people tend to get more irritated and less relaxed. This is because our minds inextricably link things like nervous and relaxed or hot and cold, like two sides of a coin. Trying to force one of them brings up the other one. This may be why people who are prone to having panic attacks find that relaxation actually brings them on.

You don't have to force the anxiety down artificially; if you do, it pops back up like the beach ball in water. Instead, stick with the uncomfortable thing until it gets easier. As you can see by the graph, the more you confront your fears, the less anxious you will become, and pretty soon you'll have optimal anxiety for peak performance. And rather than telling someone else to relax, encourage that person to stick with it and remind him that he is strong and can handle whatever the challenging situation is.

Acceptance Improves Work Performance

Acceptance entails two things: first, a willingness to experience all feelings and events, and second, the ability to use the energy (which would normally be invested in trying to control the thoughts and feelings that you find disturbing) toward acting in accordance with your values. This means that acceptance can help energize you to pursue your exceptional vision. In London in 2003, investigators measured the job performance of 412 customer service workers in a financial institution. Using a scale that measured acceptance as one's willingness to experience undesirable thoughts and feelings, they found that acceptance was significantly related to work performance. Other studies have shown that having a sense of control in your job leads to improved performance, and the results of this one suggest that acceptance further enhances the benefits of job control.

The Art of Acceptance Action Step

When you notice an undesirable thought or feeling, observe it without making a judgment about it. Think of it as a fly buzzing around—while it can be distracting, it will eventually fly away. Accept its presence and choose to focus on something else. This is subtly different from purposefully trying to distract yourself (which implies a lack of acceptance). Distraction can work like pushing a beach ball down in water. Master the art of acceptance and your self-leadership skills will skyrocket.

Using Habituation in Business

In 1995, psychology and economics researchers Daniel Read and George Loewenstein conducted an experiment in which they offered volunteers snacks each time they came into the lab. Some of the volunteers were asked to select all of their snacks ahead of time; when they did so, they selected a variety of snacks. This shows us that we think we want variety. Another group of participants was divided in half. Part of the group came in weekly and had no variety; the volunteers just got their favorite snacks each time. The people in the other part got either their favorite or their second favorite snacks. Satisfaction was highest in the group that had no variety, which shows us that while we think we want variety when we are planning ahead, when it comes down to it, this isn't always true.

It's important to realize that the study was conducted just once a week for several weeks. If they had come into the lab every day or every week for a year, the participants might have gotten sick of a single snack. Or if the variable were more intensive, such as watching a three-hour movie each time, they might have habituated to that. We get used to great things just as we get used to anxiety. You know how when you go to your favorite restaurant, you sometimes order something other than your favorite dish because you feel like you should branch out, and then you're disappointed? Well, if you went to this restaurant three times a week, it might be a good idea to add some variety, but if you go only once every few months, stick with your favorite.

Here's how to use this all in business. Let's say that you have a direct report who is anxious about a new activity. You want to support him to engage in that activity as much as possible so that his anxiety declines. You want habituation to occur. Let's say that you have an e-mail newsletter that you use to market your company. You don't want habituation to occur, because then people will get sick of your newsletter and never open it. Depending on the frequency of your mailings, you want more or less variety. If you mail every day, you want more variety to keep people from getting bored. If you mail just once a month, you should stick only to the most loved topics. How can you use the principle of habituation to help yourself or others turn anxiety into positive energy or keep positive energy from waning?

The Sixth and Most Important Step

Now that you're facing the things you dread that will get you ahead, you're ready for the final step. Your success depends on it, so read it carefully.

6

Step 6: Harness Your Strengths and Release Control

Make the Change Stick by Using Your Natural Strengths
Instead of Overcompensating for Your Weaknesses

WITH ALL THE energy you've created in the last step, you're now ready for the sixth and final step, and it's the most important one. Before jumping into it, let's review the other five steps in the GROWTH model for Confident Leadership:

Step 1: Get Your Exceptional Vision.
Step 2: Realize Your Commitment.
Step 3: Organize Your Team.
Step 4: Win with the Right Decisions.
Step 5: Turn Anxiety into Energy.
And now ...
Step 6: Harness Your Strengths and Release Control.

Most people encounter difficulties in making important changes because they become focused on their weaknesses or "areas for improvement." This focus on weaknesses creates two serious problems. First, we attempt to control these weaknesses by overcompensating for them. This approach typically backfires. Second, we forget about our strengths. Our strengths are what make us most successful. When we neglect to focus on them, we prevent ourselves from reaching our Confident Leader potential.

Remember Joe, who feared that he was all façade and no substance? He was very successful, but he was exhausted and frustrated. Because Joe was focused on his perceived weakness, he tried so hard to make a good impression that he pushed himself and his employees to the limit. He over-prepared for meetings and came across as lacking the spontaneous, charismatic, humorous, kindhearted characteristics that were actually his greatest assets. They were hidden under his "professional" demeanor. This process is a common one: something is important to us, so we go after it overzealously. Unfortunately, this enthusiasm results in our overcontrolling the situation, and success eludes us despite our greatest efforts. Joe worried about being seen as a young imposter, so he overcompensated and ended up feeling like an imposter.

How Control Works and Doesn't Work

Control is extremely important in life. When we feel in control, we experience less stress and more confidence. I'm sure you know this from your own experience—think of the times when you have felt relaxed, happy, and assured. You felt in control during those times, right? And how do you feel when you don't feel in control? If you're like most people, you probably feel nervous, uncomfortable, apprehensive, frustrated, or irritable.

Research backs up your experiences. In 1971, David Glass conducted a seminal study in which college students listened to extremely loud noise while they completed mathematic and verbal tasks. One of the groups was told that they could signal someone to turn down the noise by pushing a control button. Two of the groups did not have a control button, and the fourth group had a control button but couldn't signal the person to stop the noise. While all the groups performed equally well on the tasks, after 24 minutes the noise was turned off and the participants were asked to complete a proofreading task. The first group (the one that had control over the noise) experienced less tension and performed significantly better than the other groups, indicating that a sense of control is helpful and necessary for reduced stress and improved performance.

Harvard professor Ellen Langer conducted several classic studies in the 1970s that showed that we want control, but having it is often an illusion. She found that people thought that they'd be more likely to win the lottery if they picked the numbers and more likely to win a dice toss if they threw the dice themselves. In another study conducted by Langer, an extreme effect resulted from feeling out of control: death. She teamed up with Yale professor Judy Rodin to discover how control affected residents in nursing homes. The results were dramatic and disturbing: residents who had control over when volunteers visited them showed greater signs of health, activity, and happiness after two months than those who did not. A few months after the study, something equally dramatic and disturbing happened: a disproportionate number of the residents who had had control had died. The reason? Their control was taken away.

Control is important, and losing control after you have had it can be devastating. Strategically relinquishing control (especially if we're likely to lose it) is a smart decision. And whatever you do, do not give control to your direct reports or others, only to take it away. They're not likely to die, as the nursing home residents did, but the effects cannot be good.

The Habit of Struggling with Control

As ambitious, achievement-oriented people, we sometimes get caught in vicious cycles of trying to control situations, and often what we think works is the opposite of what actually does. Dr. Steven C. Hayes, the founder of Acceptance & Commitment Therapy, likens struggles with control to being caught in quicksand. A person in quicksand will thrash about or try to step up to get out. The quicksand will pull the person in deeper if he lifts his leg because there will be more force downward. He must actually become flat, parallel with the ground. He then will stop sinking and can roll out. It is, however completely counterintuitive to maximize contact with the quicksand when trying to get out of it. Instead, the person tries to control the situation using an ineffective method, maybe because he didn't know the method that would work, or maybe because that method sounds too unusual to be true or too scary to try. *Control is paradoxical, and letting go of ineffective control is the key to change.*

Let's explore some true stories and see how people were using control as an ineffective means of achieving their goals. As you read through these examples, ask yourself if there's anything that sounds like what you do.

Jada was a self-proclaimed "professional procrastinator." She spent a lot of time organizing, cleaning, and making lists, which made her feel like she was taking action. In reality, she was just spinning her wheels. If you are a procrastinator like her, you know that it's easier to put something off than to actually do it. You feel better at the moment, but you feel much worse when you need to do it later. Do you engage in paper shuffling like Jada? You move some things around to feel better, but really you haven't done anything.

Do you worry about what people think of you? If so, you may be like Olivia, a bright, ambitious attorney, who worried about whether people would like her. Thoughts about impending embarrassment frequently floated through her head. Olivia tried to make sure she didn't offend people, but, sadly, her fears became her reality. She apologized a lot, and her never-ending apologies drove others nuts. Olivia carefully monitored her statements before uttering them out loud and ended up sounding robotic, uninterested in her conversation partner, and less likable than she naturally was. She bent over backwards to please others, yet people felt uncomfortable with her and stopped taking her seriously. Her actions turned her fear into reality.

One of my clients was worried about money. When his stocks started to go down and his fear went up, he'd sell his stocks. He frequently lost money because he acted out of fear and sold his stocks when they were low (despite his financial advisor's recommendation to wait) because he worried that they'd continue to go down. His attempts to control his fear led to poor decisions, and he often did lose money. This is another example of how the more we try to control the things that make us uncomfortable, paradoxically, the less control we have.

Paradox of Control Action Steps

1. How has controlling important situations not led to the results you wanted?
2. Challenge yourself to think of subtle ways in which you may attempt to control yourself or others, but the control backfires.

Be Willing to Have What You Don't Want

And be willing to not have what you do want. As we discussed in Step 5, the feelings that you do not allow yourself to have are the very ones that you are more likely to end up experiencing. If you're unwilling to experience discomfort, you'll probably have more discomfort because you'll try to control it with actions that end up increasing it. If you try to make sure that something will *not* happen, it is more likely *to* happen. If you want to make sure that your direct report stays on top of all his activities and does a phenomenal job on a project, you tell him precisely what you want done. You then check up on him to make sure he's doing it. You e-mail him with reminders of the pending deadline. You give him a lot of constructive criticism to help him improve his report. What happens? He doesn't do a phenomenal job on the project. Your unwillingness to let go of control deprived your report of his motivation. He didn't get to develop a sense of ownership of and personal accomplishment from the project. You must be willing to lose in order to win.

If You've Ever Had a Sleepless Night . . .

Have you ever lain in bed at night trying to fall asleep? You think, "I really need to go to sleep. I have a big day at work tomorrow, and I don't want to be exhausted." This is the paradox of control. The hidden cause of insomnia is control. You worry that you won't get to sleep, and that you'll be a basket case the next day and fall asleep in meetings. When you worry about being a walking zombie the next day, you try to make yourself sleep, which of course, doesn't work. The wonderful thing about being an ambitious, motivated person is that you want to create excellent outcomes for yourself in your life. You care about things like doing well at work the next day, having the energy to go out with your friends, and looking your best. Unfortunately, your achievement orientation can make you force outcomes on yourself or others, which makes it less likely that you'll achieve them.

Trying to sleep doesn't work. The cure for insomnia is to let go of control, so much so that you do the opposite and try to stay awake. In fact, one of the proven treatments for insomnia is sleep deprivation! This breaks the negative association between being in your bed and being awake. If you find yourself up at night, remind yourself that you'll sleep eventually and stop trying to force it. Ironically, you'll soon be sleeping like a baby.

Similarly, trying to make yourself have or not have a feeling will backfire. We've discussed how pushing down anxiety only makes it pop back up. Similarly, trying to make ourselves happy has the opposite effect. In one study, participants listened to a classical music song; half were told to listen to the music, and the other half were told to listen while trying to feel happy. The result? The ones who tried to be happy felt worse than the ones who simply listened.

Consider how the above affects your business. You need to create experiences that help your customers or clients discover favorable feelings, rather than stating that the goal is to have such a feeling. For example, if I were selling spa services, I would not say to the client, "Focus on relaxing and feeling calm during your massage." Instead, I would say, "Notice the feel of the pressure on your back, breathe in the aromatherapy, and listen to the music." When the client does these things, she will feel more relaxed than she would if she were sitting there trying to relax.

Not for Control Freaks Only

The process I'm describing is something that everyone does. It does not mean that you're a "controlling" person, that you're a "control freak," or that you have "control issues." All of these control-seeking reactions occur naturally. When you experience discomfort, anxiety, or doubt, your first reaction is to make it go away. Think about how parents respond when their child is crying. They typically say, "Don't worry, everything will be okay." And how do parents generally respond when their child is afraid? The most common response is to take the child away from the feared object. If a child is afraid of being away from his parents, his parents stay in the room with him while he goes to sleep. If the child is afraid of spiders, parents kill them so that the child doesn't need to see them. There is nothing wrong with these parents; they are simply doing what comes naturally to comfort their child. Unfortunately, however, the child could remain afraid of these things and learn that negative emotions are not good, which undermines confidence. The child will get caught in the vicious cycle of trying to control experiencing troubling feelings and situations, and it will be harder for him to change as an adult because he will have had so many years of the ingrained habit of avoiding distress.

Doing It Anyway Is Good, but Not Enough

Sonya, a successful management consultant, sat in my office one afternoon, looking uncomfortable as she discussed her fear of her boss. "I don't understand," she told me. "I deal with my boss every day, but I'm still terrified of her." At first, I didn't understand either. She talked with her boss all the time, so she should be less nervous. The best way to beat your fear is to do it anyway, right? Yes, it is, but doing it is actually only half of the equation. The other half is to stop the controlling and overcompensating behaviors. It turned out that my client dealt with her boss only when her boss came up to her. Sonya often avoided her boss. She chose to walk down the hallway that didn't go by her boss's office. When speaking with her boss, she was very careful about what she said, and she tried to escape from the conversation as quickly as possible. For meetings with her boss, Sonya overprepared and felt too rehearsed and artificial. While Sonya did speak to her boss, she sent herself the message that she couldn't handle it well (by her overcompensating strategies), and she therefore remained uncomfortable.

Overcompensating behaviors are like crutches. We come to depend on them. Let's say someone felt nervous about walking on an injured leg, so he used a crutch. His leg healed, but he got into the habit of using the crutch. Using a crutch reduced his uninjured leg's strength and muscle. He walked, but he did it in a way that made things worse rather than better.

You might also have had the experience of having an injury, over-compensating for it, and then injuring something else. This is very common, and it shows just how natural it is to counterbalance a problem. Overcompensating behaviors keep you from being the most Confident Leader. You rely on your old habits, subtle avoidances, and crutches, so you aren't able to develop true confidence. So, it's not just about facing your fear, it's about *how* you do it.

Identifying Your Crutches Action Step

When you get uncomfortable, what do you do to make it easier or to try to make your discomfort unnoticeable to others? These are your crutches. It's time to start boldly walking without them.

Compensating vs. Overcompensating

Let's say that your goal is to increase your sales numbers. You overcompensate with these behaviors:

- Scripting all of your sales calls and rehearsing them to exhaustion
- Spending a ton of time researching your prospects and then acting overly knowledgeable instead of finding out what *they* think their needs are
- Asking your sales manager endless questions to be sure you have everything just right
- Changing your outfit 10 times until your find the perfect outfit to wear to customer meetings (when 9 of the 10 outfits would have been great).

As you can see, these things could be useful in moderation, but at this level they are overkill. This is the difference between compensating and overcompensating.

Another example is overthinking. We engage in a comprehensive analysis of the situation to be sure we understand every angle. Ultimately, we get stuck in analysis paralysis and don't make progress toward our goal. Some thought may be necessary, but too much makes us lose the forest for the trees. Frequently, high achievers try to appear intelligent. They want to appear to be the experts, so they use big words, try to speak with commanding voices, avoid getting assistance, and sound like they're trying to convince us of their ideas. But this backfires. They may sound unintelligent, or perhaps they sound smart, but at the cost of coming across as insincere or obnoxious.

Most people don't realize that they do this. If you feel that you're working too hard, you're exhausted and nervous, you aren't getting the best results despite your efforts, or you feel insincere, there's probably some overcompensating to blame. The opposite strategy (and the more effective one) is to be inquisitive and take the approach that anyone can offer you some feedback that's of value. Don't overprepare, overanalyze, or overdo it.

Compensating vs. Overcompensating Action Step

Think about a key challenge you face or a change you want. If you continue to be uncomfortable or unproductive, you may be using crutch behaviors. What are they?

Do the Opposite

When you find yourself exerting a lot of effort, but not getting the results you want, you may be trying too hard. You may have activated the law of diminishing returns and be just spinning your wheels. Or perhaps you're not taking the most effective approach. In fact, you may be doing the opposite of what works best.

When you're outside your comfort zone, you'll be tempted to do what you've always done, which will get you the same results that you've always gotten. You want exceptional results, so you need to do something radical. For example:

- If you're uncomfortable with giving up control to your employees or direct reports, you'll be tempted to not do it or to micromanage. Instead, give them full responsibility. Accept that they may mess up, but that mistakes are necessary stepping-stones for growth.
- If you feel like you're always chasing leads and trying to land new customers, do the opposite. Draw customers to you by focusing on getting quoted in industry magazines and writing articles to showcase your expertise. Your perceived value will skyrocket, and customers will be calling you and asking to hire you.
- If you're being driven nuts by a coworker because he talks too much and tries your patience, instead of rushing him along, do the opposite. Listen. Perhaps he has something important to say, and the reason he talks so much is that he knows he has a good point and he doesn't feel that you typically hear what he has to say.

Doing the Opposite Action Steps

1. Think about something that's important to you and ask yourself how you've been trying too hard to achieve it. Is it possible that your best efforts have been leading to the worst results?
2. Do the opposite. If you find yourself trying too hard, try the opposite approach. The radical change will break you free of being stuck and just might produce an incredible result.

3. Do the 90 percent experiment. Select a task that doesn't require complete precision, but that you typically devote 100 percent effort to. Purposefully slack off a bit. Complete the task at 90 percent and see what happens. Does anyone notice? Do you get just as much done in less time? Does it feel easier?

Focus Is Important *and* Problematic

Your focus is extremely important, but there is such a thing as being too focused. When you're overly focused on what you want, you're more likely to become even more nervous and then overcompensate. In his bestselling book *The Attractor Factor*, author Joe Vitale points out the importance of focusing on what you want, but being willing not to have it. Similarly, it isn't helpful to focus on what you don't want. When you do, you're more likely to get what you don't want. A race car driver who is focusing on the wall in an effort to avoid it is more likely to drive into it. Where you look is where you go. If you're focused on what you don't want, you'll probably get it.

One of my clients was a professional golfer. He was very talented, but he frequently found golf to be stressful, and he was often disappointed because his playing did not live up to his standards. We were working on achieving optimal focus, and I realized that he was actually *too* focused on his game. He thought that there was no such thing as "too focused" and was skeptical of my assessment. I explained that his fear of letting himself or others down drove him to try to focus all of his energy on the game. As a result, he burned himself out during the course of the 18 holes.

Nobody can stay 100 percent focused for hours on end. Our minds are simply not equipped for that. We end up putting pressure on ourselves that sets us up to be less successful. I asked my client to give up focus during noncritical times in the game. I even asked him to pull back some of his intense concentration during critical moments. To his surprise, his performance and his contentment with his game both improved. "This way is easier, and my game is better!" he exclaimed. He became a Confident Leader in golf.

Too much focus creates an obsession. And an obsession is fueled by, and fuels, anxiety. Because you want to have the right level of anxiety for optimal performance, you'll want to have the right level of focus.

Optimal Focus Action Step

Ask yourself if you have been under- or overfocused on your goal. The way to find the right amount is to experiment. If you think you are capable of greater results than you're currently achieving, play around with your focus level and see what works best. The process is much like an artist learning how to use the right amount of paint and colors to achieve the finest results, or how a chef knows the right amount of spices and salt and pepper to use to make her food delectable. Experiment with optimal levels of focus and take note of your results.

Once You Master This, It All Becomes Easy

You've heard the expression "If you can't beat them, join them." This is what I'm suggesting that you do. Instead of struggling with and trying to control your concerns, join with them. If what you've been doing to deal with things like your employees, your work performance, business growth, insomnia, and workplace conflicts hasn't worked as well as possible, why not adopt a new approach? The idea is to "join" with the difficulties you've experienced and regain control by giving it up. When you start to use the ideas in this chapter, you'll initially feel less comfortable. This is good. You need to stick with this approach because once you get used to it, everything becomes easier.

One senior executive in an insurance company with whom I worked was desperately afraid of failure. He controlled his career and his direct reports to be sure everyone was successful. Ironically, his exertion of control (as an attempt to assuage his fear of losing his financial and professional status) was exactly what held him back from greater success. He sat in my office one day, beaming from ear to ear. "It's like I've stopped pushing the boulder up the mountain," he said to me. "Everything that was so hard before is now so easy—I wish I had discovered this secret years ago. I'd have fewer gray hairs and more cash in the bank." "And what exactly have you done?" I asked as if I didn't know the answer. "I've let go of control," he told me.

Use Your Strengths for Support

This final step in the GROWTH process is challenging because, as we discussed, it is human nature to try to control things. The way to give up some control and therefore achieve optimal control is by harnessing your strengths. Remember that we overcontrol when we feel threatened or intimidated. When, on the other hand, we focus on our talents instead of on what we lack, we no longer have a need to overcontrol. In *Now, Discover Your Strengths*, author Marcus Buckingham points out extensive Gallup Poll research that shows that we are most successful when we use our strengths every day.

The problem is that we're all focused on our "areas for improvement" rather than on our strengths. One of my clients told me that his team has gone from making 105 percent of its sales numbers to 200 percent over the first quarter. He had hypothesized why, and I agreed, but I found this less important than how his team members had been harnessing their strengths. I told him to ask his team members how they are currently using their strengths and doing what they do best. This way, we can have them do more of what's working rather than trying to control their weaknesses. He found out that the improved performance was due to an increased use of their strengths and increased attention and feedback from him, their manager.

Do you know what your natural strengths are? You can take the StrengthsFinder assessment (published by the Gallup Organization and available on www.strengthsfinder.com) to find out. You can also ask people what they think you're great at and what they consider to be your natural

interests and talents. These are things that are relatively consistent throughout your life

A Counterintuitive Way to Harness Your Strengths

While it's important to focus on your natural talents, it's equally important to remember that if you overrely on your strengths, you may not grow
and improve. You definitely want to capitalize on your innate abilities, but
not become complacent and dependent. I like the phrase "harness your
strengths" because you want to be aware of your strengths and capitalize
on them, but also not let them run rampant.

There can always be too much of a good thing, and our strengths
often have a downside. Someone who has the strength of empathy can
become easily saddened when hearing about other people's problems.
Someone who has the strength of action orientation can be impulsive
and rush into (or out of) things without thinking. Someone who has the
strength of future thinking can lack the ability to live in the moment and
be spontaneous. Someone who has the strength of achievement may be
unable to let himself relax and just be. Someone whose strength is humor
can use it at inopportune times and offend others. You get the idea—
every strength has a downside.

Confident Leaders capitalize on their talents and use them to
develop new competencies. Push yourself to try some things that don't
come naturally to you.

Harnessing Your Strengths Action Steps

1. *Write down your top five strengths.* If you are not completely sure
   what they are, do the research recommended earlier to find
   out.
2. *Strategize specific ways in which you can focus on your strengths* and find
   more opportunities to use them every day.
3. *Write down the flip side of each of your strengths.* Think of how relying
   on each strength can create problems for you.

4. *Hone your strengths by practicing the opposite.* Do the things that don't come naturally to you, and observe the results you get. Use this process to find the optimal balance between your natural strengths and the uncomfortable opposite. In general, this balance follows the 80/20 rule—80 percent strength and 20 percent opposite—but it can vary widely depending on the strength and the situation.

Moving On to Greater Levels of Mastery

Now that you know the six steps of the GROWTH process to get out of your comfort zone and become a Confident Leader, we're ready to dig deeper and apply these ideas to key areas in business. You'll learn to master key challenges and achieve more than you ever thought possible. Let's go there now.

PART II

HOW CONFIDENT LEADERS TURN PROBLEMS INTO DYNAMIC OPPORTUNITIES

7

Focus on What's Important

"I Get Caught in the Daily Grind and Lose Sight of the Bigger Picture"

YOU KNOW WHAT it's like to be busy but not focused? You're constantly putting in effort, but your efforts are scattered. You don't feel that you're connected with what's important. You have so much to do that you don't even have time to figure out what matters most. Or perhaps you aren't even sure what activities are meaningful. Or maybe you don't know what's *not* important—everything feels critical, so you have a hard time saying no and forgoing certain activities.

Finding Your "Big It"

The first step in getting focused is figuring out what my friend Sam Rosen calls your "Big It," or what's most important. This may seem obvious, but it's not always readily apparent. It's difficult to recognize when you aren't pursuing what truly matters and then to change your course. It's easiest to continue doing what you've always done.

It is critical to determine your "Big It" because *that* is where you need to concentrate your effort. We've been discussing how to challenge yourself, but you do not need to force yourself out of your comfort zone all the time. You need to do so only in those areas that are significant to you. If something is intimidating but mastering it is likely to lead to your greater success and happiness, then *that* is an area in which you should push yourself.

Another challenge arises when you don't know what you really want. You make choices based on what you believe you want to have happen, which is influenced by your memories. You think, "The corporate retreat was amazing; I want to do more of those," forgetting that two-thirds of it felt boring and useless. Or you think, "That speech I gave went horribly," because you remember especially difficult questions that you were asked.

Daniel Kahneman, a psychologist who won a Nobel Prize, found that our memories are dictated by the peak and the end experiences, known as the "peak-end" rule. The corporate retreat may have been boring, but if there was one powerful peak experience and a great ending, we remember it as fabulous. The speech may have gone brilliantly, but if one grumpy person grilled us and it didn't finish with a bang, we think it was horrible. The length of the experience becomes irrelevant—we'd prefer a wonderful 10-minute lunch over a nice 60-minute lunch. It sounds impossible, but this is a proven mental bias. So, when you are deciding what's most important, recognize that you'll be basing much of the decision on the peak or end of a past experience.

Sometimes we're operating on the basis of what we "should" care about, such as achievement, money, or prestige. These "shoulds" can disguise what we truly value. As a result, we end up pursuing "success" and never finding it. Where do these "shoulds" come from and what can we do about them? My colleague Dr. Max Vogt, who coauthored a book with me called *Immediate Personal Power*, teaches a fascinating concept about an "Internal Committee," or IC. Our IC, he says is a panel of people that we carry in our minds. Over the years, we internalize the voices and ideas of our family members, friends, teachers, and other people, and they affect our thought processes and decisions. When we're faced with a decision, our IC meets and gives us its perspective. One member of our committee may speak up and say, "Forget about that—you need to focus on being more successful," or "If you do that, you'll neglect your family and not be a good mom," or "Good dads provide for their families," or "You should forget that big dream; you'll never be capable of achieving it," or "You need to work very hard to become wealthy—success can't be easy."

As you see, your IC influences the way you create and pursue your Big It. It may hold you back or make you doubt your ability to achieve everything you want. The first step is to recognize who the people on your IC are and what they say to you. Once you're keenly aware of this IC-influenced internal dialogue, you can start to modify it. The idea is not to be harsh or to argue with the members of your IC. The idea is to accept that they are part of you, and probably always will be, and to help them to be on board with what you truly want. Their objections are important, so you want to be grateful for their perspective and resolve their objections. You want to negotiate with them, just as you would in an important business meeting, and help them to be aligned with your Big It.

True Success

The "shoulds" often lead us down the path of defining success as achievement. We believe that if we achieve, we'll be successful. Yet, even when we do achieve, we feel unfulfilled. I believe that the definition of success as achievement is limiting.

Instead, I like to use the definition put forth in the book *Just Enough: Tools for Creating Success in Your Work and Life* by Harvard professors Laura Nash and Howard Stevenson. They define success as a combination of achievement, significance, legacy, and satisfaction, and I believe that Confident Leaders achieve all four. Let's go through them:

- *Achievement* is what you accomplish in your career or business, usually as measured by your job title, promotions, accolades, and business bottom line. It may also be measured by such things as how many employees or customers you have, the percent growth of your department or business, movement into new markets or countries, or development of new product lines.
- *Significance* is the sense of meaning you get from the work that you do. Does it have personal importance to you? Do you feel

that you have a reason to be in business? It boils down to why you are passionate about your work and business.

- *Legacy* is the contribution that you make to the world. It is the mark you will leave. It is how you make things better for your children's generation. As people move through life, a sense of legacy becomes increasingly essential.
- *Satisfaction* is the enjoyment that you get each and every day from your work. Do you get up in the morning and look forward to at least some (and preferably most) of the activities you'll do that day? Do you get energized by your daily activities, interactions, and responsibilities? If you're a business owner, recognize that you will be working both in and on your business, so you must enjoy the role that you create for yourself.

When you develop your vision for success, be sure to include the four elements achievement, significance, legacy, and satisfaction. These goals are great, but are often lost in the midst of a busy lifestyle. In fact, it is easy to get microfocused on the things that aren't important and that create discomfort. Let's explore how to spot and stop this unhelpful tunnel vision.

Tunnel Vision

One of the hallmarks of anxiety is tunnel vision. This means that when we become nervous about going outside of our comfort zones and making strategic changes, we are likely to narrow our focus of attention. Do we focus on what makes sense and is important? Typically not. Instead, we focus on the thoughts and behaviors that are associated with our fears rather than on the big picture.

Let's say that your goal is to get promoted in your company. You have a big project at hand, and you fear that if you do not blow everyone away with it, you will be passed over for promotion. Every decision feels like a huge deal. You worry that the wrong decision will lead to failure on the project and no promotion. As a result, you work extremely hard and push your team. You obsess about the details and lock yourself in your office and plug away. As a result, you do great work on your project, which is good, but it comes at a cost: you lose visibility in your company. Because you were holed away in your office working day and night, you missed out on opportunities to network and get exposure. You neglected to meet with your boss and other important decision makers. Promotions often go to those who are well connected, well liked, and well respected. If you had not gotten into tunnel vision about all of the details of your project, you would have had a better eye for the big picture and focused on what's important: showing yourself as an interested and competitive contender for the position, promoting yourself, and so on.

Examples of tunnel vision come up every day. Whenever we are outside of our comfort zones, we are prone to obsessing over details and forgetting about what really leads to big-picture results. Another way that tunnel vision operates is by focusing us on a negative outcome. When we are uncomfortable, we focus on a potentially catastrophic outcome. We get immersed in the possibility of a negative outcome and lose perspective. We become prone to making thought errors, such as overestimating risk and minimizing resources.

One of my clients, for example, was an executive who wanted to be a business owner. She felt ready to make the big move out of her executive suite and into her own business. She no longer felt intellectually stimulated at work and she had money saved, so she was ready for a change—well, part of her was ready, and the other part was concerned. She focused on the statistics that most small businesses fail, and she thought about how horrible it would be to not have the financial comfort she was used to. "How would I pay for my kids' college tuition?" she wondered.

A characteristic of tunnel vision is all-or-none thinking. My client was thinking that either her business would be successful or it would fail. One of my goals was to help her see that even if failures occurred, she could handle them. She had overcome all kinds of adversity in her life and had risen through the ranks to be a successful executive—she was strong and resilient. When she worked through these fears and began her business, she ended up being highly successful (including achievement, significance, legacy, and satisfaction). She taught other women how she did it, and she was proud of the positive role model she set for her daughters.

Joe's Challenge

Let's return to Joe's situation and explore his difficulty with staying focused. Joe was concerned that if he did not present his most polished, professional, assertive, powerful self, he would not be taken seriously and would lose respect. As a result, Joe felt that he was constantly working to prevent being "found out."

The Problem of Overcompensating

Joe's discomfort led to his focusing too much on himself. He constantly evaluated himself to see how he was coming across, and he overanalyzed his every move. As a result, he was unable to truly connect with his employees, boss, customers, and family members. People picked up on the fact that he was focused on himself rather than on them. They looked at him, saw someone who was attractive and very successful, and assumed that his self-focus was egoism. The most unfortunate part was that one of Joe's greatest strengths was his ability to connect with people. He was charismatic and showed wonderful listening skills. He was empathic and understanding. When he was comfortable, he made you feel that you were the most important person in the world, and he focused 100 percent on you. Joe's overcompensating behaviors (analyzing his word choices; planning what to say; trying to gesture and come across appropriately; trying to appear strong, confident, and powerful) were crutches that backfired. They disguised his true social eloquence and ability to connect with others. His fear that his star would start to fade led to his working too hard and becoming addicted to work-related activities (checking his BlackBerry, calling his assistant for messages, and so on). He did not enjoy the fruits of his labors because he was so focused on preventing failure.

The Big-Picture Solution

I taught Joe one question that he should ask himself whenever he was focusing on his concerns in an unproductive way: "Is it really that serious?"

When you ask yourself this question, you regain perspective. You see that just because something feels critical in the moment, that doesn't mean that it actually *is* critical. This allows you to take pressure off of yourself, engage your strengths, and focus on what really is serious.

Others also put pressure on us. When they are not good at perspective taking, everything feels critical to them. They then pass this pressure on to us. The solution to falling prey to others' anxieties entails three steps. First, empathize with their situations. Be careful not to get into a judgmental mindset—recognize that their situations feel serious to them. Second, be emotionally detached from their reactions. Let their pressure, stress, and anxiety roll off you. Third, do your best, but also be assertive and state realistic limitations on what they expect. If they are in tunnel-vision mode, they are likely to be more perfectionistic or demanding, so you need to be assertive about what you can and cannot do and the additional resources you need.

An Uncertain and Flexible Vision

A vision is a wonderful thing, but it can limit you. If your vision is static and you feel that you aren't achieving it, you become frustrated and lose confidence. Confident Leaders actually keep their vision flexible and cultivate uncertainty. Phillip G. Clampitt, Robert J. Dekoch, and M. Lee Williams, the authors of a 2002 article in *Ivey Business Journal* titled "Embracing Uncertainty," recommend asking yourself questions that increase uncertainty. This is the opposite of what most people do in business (they ask questions to create certainty, which is often an illusion), but it is a key for growth. These are questions such as:

- Do I really need to know everything before moving ahead?
- Am I jumping the gun here?
- What certainty level makes sense for this goal?

They advise leaders to frame challenges rather than specific solutions, helping people to take a realistic viewpoint that includes uncertainty and the big picture. The fine line to walk is maintaining focus, which creates direction and motivation (we discuss these in the next few chapters), while remaining flexible in terms of vision and actions, which allows for rapid responses to continuously changing situations.

Urgency Addiction

An achievement mindset and the latest technology combine to make it easy for us to get caught in urgency addiction. Everything seems urgent and important. We all know what it's like to be addicted to our "crackberrys," our cell phones, our voice-mail messages, and so on. We're constantly interrupted throughout our workdays, and we feel scattered, out of control, and unfocused. Our productivity declines, as does the depth of our work. We find ourselves working hard but accomplishing little.

Think about it; if you are interrupted when you're just getting into the flow of something, you lose your train of thought and need to start over again. After 10 minutes, instead of being in the midst of a brilliant brainstorm and flood of ideas, you're still stuck at a surface level. Creativity, insight, and breakthroughs often require time and energy—you have to wade through the shallow waters before you're in deep where your true talents emerge.

The art in prioritizing where your attention gets directed rests on deciding what is truly both urgent *and* important. Often urgency is like a wolf in sheep's clothing. It wants you to think that it is there to help focus you on what's important, but really it leads you astray. The best way to sort it out is by asking yourself questions such as these:

- Do I need to tackle this before I can take on the next part of the task? (If the answer is yes, it is probably both urgent and important.)
- Does this fit with my big-picture vision, values, and goals? (If the answer is yes, it is probably important, but it may not be urgent.)
- Do I feel that I must do this now because it's stressing me out and I want to get it out of the way? (If the answer is yes, it may not be truly urgent.)

- Do I have everything I need to do a good job with this right now? (If the answer is no, it is not urgent until you get the proper resources.)
- Is there a clear time frame, and is it soon? (If the answer is yes, it may be urgent.)
- Are others depending on me to get this to them as quickly as possible? (If the answer is yes, it is probably both urgent and important.)
- Am I the right one to do this job, or can I delegate it to someone who could do it better? (If someone else can do it better, it is not urgent or important for you.)
- Does this utilize my strengths, talents, and passion? (If the answer is yes, it is important.)

These questions give you a decision tree to determine what is both urgent *and* important. There are dozens of other questions that you can ask yourself—the key is that you're taking a few seconds (most things are not *that* urgent that you don't have 30 seconds, and if something is, please don't start asking yourself a bunch of questions!) to sort it out.

Think Before Acting

I believe that urgency addiction results from being unable to resist the impulse to do something. We see that an e-mail message has arrived, have the impulse to check it, and immediately do so. We act before thinking. The way to handle impulse-control issues is to use stimulus control and reverse the habit.

Stimulus control means setting up your environment to make it impossible for you to engage in the behavior you're trying to eliminate. A shopaholic would not go into expensive stores. She wouldn't even walk by the shops because it would be too tempting to stop in. Someone who is trying to lose weight would not go near fast-food restaurants or have pints of ice cream in the house. (This doesn't mean that you need to deprive yourself—you can always stop in at Ben & Jerry's for a small cone.)

If you struggle with the most common type of urgency addiction, e-mail, stimulus control means not having the pop-ups that tell you that you have mail, turning off your BlackBerry, and not checking e-mail when you're engaged in an important project.

Habit reversal is the second strategy. It means doing something that is incompatible with the habit that you are trying to break. For example, if someone is trying to quit smoking, a habit-reversal strategy would be chewing gum (to keep his mouth busy) or completing crosswords (to keep his hands busy). Think about what you can do that is compatible with your big-picture goal and incompatible with your urgency addiction. Remember that it typically takes around three weeks to break a bad habit, so be consistent.

Confident Leader Action Steps for Changing Habits

The goal is to break your urgency addiction. Using the six GROWTH steps, here's how:

- *Step 1: Get Your Vision and Intention—ask yourself big-picture questions,* such as the ones given earlier in this chapter, to sort out what is truly urgent and important.
- *Step 2: Realize Your Commitment—sometimes action is not good.* Typically you need to take action, but in this case you need to stop taking your normal course of action. Use the stimulus-control and habit-reversal strategies as your new actions.
- *Step 3: Organize Your Support—create a system of checks and balances.* When you have a team or a coach, you can run your ideas by them and get a different perspective from a fresh set of eyes. Listen carefully to their ideas.
- *Step 4: Win with the Right Decisions—choose what's most important.* Ask yourself, "Is it really that serious?" or "Is it consistent with my values and goals?" when deciding what to focus your resources (time and energy) on.
- *Step 5: Turn Anxiety into Optimal Energy—have fun.* In Richard Branson's autobiography, *Screw It, Let's Do It* (Virgin Books, 2006), one of his lessons is to have fun. It sounds simple, but for most people, it is one of their greatest challenges. Many

executives and entrepreneurs are so serious. Remember why you are doing what you are doing. The goal of having fun satisfies all the components of the success model (achievement, significance, legacy, and satisfaction).

- *Step 6: Harness Your Strengths and Release Control—ask yourself what maintains your urgency addiction.* It's often a way to control a hectic schedule. Of course, it doesn't work. An even greater problem is that it prevents you from capitalizing on your greatest strengths. I'm sure that responding to e-mail right away is not your best natural talent. What is it? Be sure you are doing what you do best first and foremost.

The Courage to Think Big

Because of our fears of both failure and success, our comfort zones typically have only safe goals. For example, a professional service provider might say that she wants to increase her annual income from $100,000 to $115,000. Why such a modest increase?! Or a human resources executive might say that her goal is to improve retention. Why just improve retention—why not help her people shine at work so that they experience true success and not only want to stay, but want also to recruit their bright, talented friends who are a great match for the company? Or a sales manager might say that he wants to improve communication and reduce conflict on his team. Improve communication? Why not help all sales representatives gain dozens of new clients and refer business to one another?

Of course, it is much easier to see someone else's unlimited potential. When it comes to ourselves, however, thinking big triggers fears of failure ("Who's to say that I can do all of that?" and "How horrible it would be to commit to a big goal and then fail miserably in front of everyone") and of success ("What if I do get there—how would my life change?" and "Once I'm successful, everyone will have high expectations of me, and I could let them down"). In the expert interview with Michael Port, you'll learn from a thought leader who began the Think Big Revolution.

Expert Interview

Michael Port

Michael Port is the bestselling author of *Book Yourself Solid* (Wiley, 2006) and *Beyond Booked Solid* (Wiley, 2008). He is known as "the guy to call when you're tired of thinking small," and is the founder of the Think Big Revolution, which helps you think bigger about who you are and what you offer the world. Learn more about Michael at www.michaelport.com.

Why is big thinking challenging for people?
I can't speak for most people, but I can speak for those I've met and for myself. It seems to me that there are different reasons that big thinking is challenging. With big thinking come big things, and with big things comes big responsibility. It is often intimidating to think about what comes next when you achieve your big vision. For example:

- You want to be on TV to share your ideas, but you wonder if you can get or stay thin enough to be on TV.
- You want to move up in your career, but you know that you'll be in charge of more and have less free time.
- You need to bring in new employees or take your company public to grow your business, but then you'll be responsible to more people (contractors, shareholders, and so on) other than yourself.

Essentially, the responsibility of all businesses is the fulfillment of commitments. The bigger you play, the bigger your promises will be.

It is scary to make big promises because we become afraid that we can't or won't fulfill them. When people first come to the Think Big Revolution, I see this problem—they get into an internal battle between small thoughts and big thoughts. I heard Tony Robbins call this an "internal civil war." The small thoughts pop up as a way to manage our ideas of ourselves. They serve as a reference point to the person we've known ourselves to be and the ideas we were raised with. We then try to battle the forces outside of ourselves (the financial challenges, career development difficulties, and so on) while we battle the small thoughts in our heads. It is often easier to stay small because this all feels like so much.

So how do we win this "battle"?
Once we commit to our big vision, we need to follow through, and that's intimidating. I often feel this way, too; I'm not sure that the battle ever goes away completely or that we even need it to. We need to be aware of how natural it is to have small thoughts, and that we increase our capacity to do big things *as we do big things*.

I see increasing your capacity to do those big things as the only way—that's how you build confidence. Every time you overcome a challenge, your capacity to do big things grows; it's a generative process.

Where does the journey to increasing your capacity begin?
I don't have research to back this up, but I believe that it all starts with desire. For many of us, it's a feeling that we want. It can also be a feeling that we want to get away from. For example, we feel bad about our work performance, and we want that to change. A desire to create something new can be more inspiring than a rebellion or a desire to get away from something.

When possible, be "a-historical." Being rebellious and moving away from something keeps you tied to your past. Instead, incorporate your past into your future. Integrate your past with your future rather than depending too much on it.

And how can we continue to make progress, especially when those fears come up?
I think it's best to do this with others. You can do it alone, but that's harder. Sometimes the thoughts you're battling are so intense that it's best to work them out with a professional therapist. Other times, work with your peers. In selecting the way to work with others, consider what works best for you—a one-on-one professional relationship, a group dynamic, business partnerships, or some other

arrangement. You need to choose wisely and think about who will help you create the future you want. We often choose those who represent the person we are now, not where we want to go. This is what keeps us stuck.

How else can we expand our big thoughts and actions?
I like to incorporate both psychology and ontology. In terms of psychology, it helps to be comfortable in our own skin. We all need to look inside and work on ourselves. In terms of ontology, we also need to pay attention to how we're *being* as we're behaving. I see three steps to this process, which I originally learned from reading the works of the Chilean politician Fernando Flores. Ask yourself:

1. What do I want to do?
2. What do I have that can help?
3. What can I get from other sources to help me?

The first step is to articulate what you really want. The second step is to reconfigure what you already have that can help you. And the third step is to cross-appropriate by looking at environments outside your own.

What is a practical way to grow by cross-appropriating?
Read a lot outside of the space where you live and work. Continue to read the things that help you achieve mastery in your domain, but include things outside as well. I read books on things like philosophy and martial arts that you'd think have nothing to do with what I do professionally, but these things show me other worlds. If you read the same newspaper or magazines or blogs every day, you're likely to continue thinking as you have been thinking. When I travel on planes, I often chat with flight attendants and hear them say that they want to make a major life change. Then I see them reading gossip magazines and I wonder how they'll change. Read and take action outside of what you're used to, and you'll think and act bigger.

Now that you're thinking big and focused on what's important, you're ready to take the actions of a Confident Leader. To do that, you'll need energy, so in the next chapter you'll learn how to get and keep your energy flowing throughout the workday.

8

Keep Your Energy Flowing

"I Often Feel Like I'm Spinning My Wheels—I End Up
Exhausted with Little to Show for It"

PEAK PERFORMERS IN BUSINESS, sports, relationships, and life share several characteristics. The two most important qualities are knowing how to regulate their energy and focusing on results. Olympic athletes, for example, often need to finish just fractions of a second ahead of their competitors to win. This means that their energy, attention, and actions all need to be focused, efficient, and deliberate. Winning at business is like winning in sports.

Try Easy

It's an unfortunate irony that sometimes the more we try, the worse we do. We think that we're putting in our best efforts, and we can't understand why we aren't getting the results we want. In *Accidental Genius*, author Mark Levy shows readers how "trying easy" creates genius moments. We can't just make ourselves have a genius moment. He describes a story he learned from mental coach to athletes Robert Kriegel, who helped sprint-ers get ready for Olympic trials. The runners were putting pressure on themselves to make certain times, so Kriegel astutely asked them to run at 90 percent of their normal intensity. Guess what happened—the runners ran much faster this time; in fact, one runner set an unofficial world record. We often make things more difficult for ourselves, thereby limit-ing our potential, and when we try easy, we achieve our full capabilities. For optimal energy in sports and in business, we must throw ourselves into the game, fear and all.

My husband and I were on Maui last spring, and we did the excur-sion where one goes to the top of Haleakala volcano and then bikes down. There were 10 people on our tour, and when we were getting ready to ride down, I noticed two women becoming nervous. Our guide told us that we had to ride down at a minimum of 25 miles per hour. Many groups were riding down the volcano that day, so there was pressure to go quickly on the bike despite the curvy, winding road. The guide astutely pointed out that it was important to lean into the turns, even though the temptation was to lean away. He also said that we should not put our feet down because the road was made of volcanic rock and was "sticky," so it could pull us over. I was concerned about one of the women who continued to be nervous because I know how people tend to react to their fears (i.e., they overcompensate). Of course it wasn't really my place to counsel strangers, so I bit my tongue.

We began going down the hill, and the ride was fast. The woman who was afraid of heights and speed was biking in front of me. As we went around a steep, winding turn, I saw her attempt to slow herself by putting a foot down. This overcompensating behavior led to her falling. Unfortu-nately she got entangled in her bike and sprained her ankle. She did what came naturally to her to deal with the fear, but as in most situations, her response was much worse than the fear itself.

Too Much Focus

In business you can become too focused on the results you want. Here are a few examples:

- The hard-sell approach to landing a new deal with a client.
- The hit-them-over-the-head marketing copy—with eight different colors, tons of exclamation points, lots of capital letters and underlined words, and an overly generous sprinkling of words like *killer, mind-blowing,* and so on.
- Explaining only the end goal to your employees or direct reports (without helping them realize how to get there).
- Marketing *all* of the results that you're able to get. (If you don't highlight the most relevant ones, your key point gets lost in the data.)
- Telling prospective clients or customers exactly what you can do to help them without first understanding and recognizing what they need.
- Focusing on income without regard to expenses. Or focusing on gross income without acknowledging what is sitting in accounts receivable.
- Being sold on what a new technology *could* do for you without regard for the opportunity cost of your time to learn how to use it.
- Getting swept away in the ego gratification of short-term results without careful consideration of the long-term impact.

Confident Leader Action Steps for Optimal Energy

- *Step 1: Get Your Vision and Intention — use strategic visioning* to be clear on how you want to perform. This process is described later in this chapter under "Visioning and Mental Rehearsal."
- *Step 2: Realize Your Commitment — are you willing to accept where you are?* One of the things that leads to trying too hard is not accepting where you currently are in your skills and abilities. Put your ego aside and realize where you currently are. Then you'll take off and become even better.

- *Step 3: Organize Your Team—get help.* Once you acknowledge your current abilities, you can look for opportunities to grow by learning from others.
- *Step 4: Win with the Right Decisions—recognize when discomfort means that you should stop.* Your need to try too hard or to overcompensate may indicate that you're in over your head or that you're in something that is not of true interest to you.
- *Step 5: Turn Anxiety into Optimal Energy—stop trying so hard and boost your energy.* Overcompensating drains your energy and keeps you from focusing it where it needs to be. When you try easy, you'll automatically have more energy.
- *Step 6: Harness Your Strengths and Release Control—instead of focusing on what you lack, focus on what you have.* Focus on your courage, passion, enthusiasm, and other character attributes to propel yourself ahead.

In Favor of a Favorable Outlook

An optimistic outlook and positive expectations do not always come easily because we don't want to expect the best and be let down. Optimism is a pattern of looking at the favorable side and expecting a positive outcome. Dr. Martin E. Seligman's research on optimism shows that our explanatory style is related to our career success. Our explanatory style involves how we interpret events in our lives, including three key elements: the event's permanence (how long we think a result will last), pervasiveness (whether we see a situation as specific or global in scope), and personalization (whether we see a situation or result as caused by us or by external factors).

To assess explanatory style, Seligman created the Seligman Attributional Style Questionnaire (SASQ). This instrument has been used in thousands of research studies and has shown a strong connection between an optimistic mindset and success. When optimists experience setbacks, they see those setbacks as external, unstable, and specific. This means that the explanatory style of Confident Leaders helps them to view failures as specific to a certain situation (rather than as a pervasive pattern of defeat) and as being caused by external forces. As a result, optimists are more resilient and able to recover from setbacks. On the flip side, optimists see successes as internal, stable, and global. The result looks like this:

Optimists' Explanatory Style	Permanence (Time)	Pervasiveness (Scope)	Personalization (Cause)
Good Events	Stable	Global	Internal
Bad Events	Unstable	Specific	External

When you move out of your comfort zone and into greater success, failure is possible, even probable. Failure is one of the keys to growth. I believe that it's helpful to be optimistic and expect to succeed, yet recognize that failure can be useful. When we face failures with an optimistic mindset, we're likely to be more successful. Optimism as defined by results on the SASQ has been shown in studies to promote success in sales. For example, optimistic insurance executives outperform their pessimistic counterparts by 38 percent. Extremely optimistic insurance salespeople outsell extremely pessimistic agents by 88 percent.

The reaction I've heard is, "You want me to see the world through rose-colored glasses, but I'm a realist." I think *realist* is a euphemism for pessimist. An optimist views bad outcomes with a less personal focus. This doesn't mean that optimists don't learn from their mistakes. On the contrary, optimists first take responsibility for their role in creating the outcome and then factor in the roles of others and external circumstances. Optimists see setbacks as temporary ("I'm having a hard time with this now—I'll come back to it later when I'm fresh") but do not ignore a pervasive pattern of results indicating that a new tactic is in order. Finally, optimists see the scope as specific ("This one project is challenging, but my overall work performance is excellent"), which helps them to keep an eye on the bigger picture. Research has shown that mild forms of positive distortions of reality (looking on the brighter side) can be beneficial, especially following stressful events.

Visioning and Mental Rehearsal

Charles Garfield is a computer scientist who led the team of the *Apollo 11* project (the first time humans landed on the moon) and made monumental discoveries about the dynamics of peak performance. In the late 1980s, Garfield interviewed top business leaders to ascertain the psychology of peak performers. He found that top business performers are both consolidators (focused on improving and also on not changing what has been shown to work) and innovators (constantly looking for opportunities to change). They have an internal sense of mastery, or the ability to act based on their knowledge, which creates true self-confidence. Peak performers are driven by a mission and are engaged in the act of visioning.

Visioning, or the mental rehearsal of achievement, has shown to be nearly as effective as actual real-life practice with Olympic athletes. Yes, this means that sitting in your office picturing yourself giving a stellar presentation can be almost as effective as standing up and practicing on stage. Many people attempt to use mental rehearsal but find that it doesn't work. This is typically because they didn't do it in the right way. The way to mentally rehearse a performance of any type (from writing a book, to marketing a business, to introducing yourself in the boardroom) is to follow these steps:

1. *Be clear about your objective.* Let's use the example of writing a book. Your objective is probably not to write a book. Your objective is to favorably influence people with your words, get on Oprah, receive letters from readers expressing their appreciation, and so on. The objective is your ultimate destination.
2. *Be clear about the process.* Garfield found that peak performers focus on both the journey and the destination. A lot of my high-achieving executive and entrepreneur clients are great with the destination, but less great with the journey. How do you want

the process to go? Let's say that you are using mental rehearsal for delivering a great speech. You could say that you want the audience to be engaged throughout your entire speech, to participate, and to laugh and smile. You want to feel at ease, poised, and energized. A focus on the process even more than the outcome can help to alleviate performance anxiety.

3. *Use your five senses.* The more vivid your image for visioning, the more powerful it will be. You want to see, feel, taste, smell, and hear the situation going exactly as you would like it to go.

4. *Connect your image to your mission.* As you see yourself performing exactly as you'd like to, feel the energy and enthusiasm that come from connecting the activity to your life and work purpose.

Are You a Human Being or a Human Doing?

If you are working very hard, experiencing discomfort, *and* not getting the results you want, then you have not found flow. I'll explain the concept of flow in a minute, but first let me explain what it is not.

Activity Addicted

Answer these questions to see if you are addicted to doing. Check off all that sound like you:

- ☐ Do you get impatient when people pause to collect their thoughts?
- ☐ Do you feel that your sense of worth is connected to your productivity level?
- ☐ Do you always have multiple activities on your plate and fill every spare moment?
- ☐ Does anyone notice or complain that you put in a *lot* of hours at the office?
- ☐ Do you feel guilty or less worthwhile when you take time off?
- ☐ Have you forgotten or have you never known what downtime is?

If you checked off several of these, then you're what I call activity addicted, and you are at high risk for becoming a workaholic, if you aren't one already. The difference between workaholics and peak performers is that *workaholics seek out activities, whereas peak performers seek out results.*

In the Flow

Flow is a concept that has been researched for decades, spearheaded by a former psychology department chair at the University of Chicago, Mihaly Csikszentmihalyi. A flow state is one in which you are completely immersed in an activity. It is so enjoyable, rewarding, and consistent with who you are that time passes quickly and you lose track of the outside world when you're engaged in the activity. Flow is the opposite of activity addiction and is the essence of a human "being" rather than simply doing.

Getting into a flow state requires a degree of mindfulness, or being fully present in the current moment. You are using your five senses to get wrapped up in what you're doing. You lose self-consciousness and a sense of time. You are not preoccupied with what you're doing and how you're coming across. You aren't worrying about the past or the future. You are so engaged with the activity, conversation, or situation that you don't even notice it, even if you are doing something that is anxiety-provoking.

Turn Down or Amp Up Your Energy

Remember that energy, excitement, and anxiety are all the same thing biologically—the only difference is your interpretation of the feelings. Here we'll explore how to use your thoughts and actions to control your energy level.

Activation Control

Activation control entails recognizing the discrepancy between your current energy level and your ideal energy level. If you are exhausted, but you need to deliver a high-impact presentation, you need to amp up your energy. If you are anxious, but you need to deliver a calming presentation and show a relaxed demeanor, then it's time to turn down your energy level. There are two ways to modulate energy: your thoughts and your behaviors.

Amp Up Energy with Your Thoughts

Experiment with tools like these to see which of them energizes you most:

- Focus on the part of the situation that you are passionate about.
- Think about how wonderful you'll feel when you perform at your best.
- Think about a time when you excelled in the past.
- Picture yourself as energetic, charismatic, engaging, and entertaining.
- Envision resoundingly positive feedback from your colleagues, clients, and audience.

Amp Up Energy with Your Behaviors

- Get active. Go for a brisk walk or climb up and down the stairs a few times. Do this right before you need energy.
- If you're an extrovert (extroverts tend to be energized by others), partner with colleagues or build a team to create the best results.
- Avoid being around those whom I call "energy vampires," those people who suck the life energy right out of you. Be assertive and limit your involvement.
- Consult a nutritionist or dietician to create a "high-performance" diet that helps you eliminate the sugar roller coaster, which can drain you of energy.
- Drink more water. Dehydration is a common cause of fatigue.

- Listen to your favorite energizing music—*loud!*
- Eliminate the activity-addiction types of tasks from your schedule, and do what you love and what's truly important.

Turn Down Energy with Your Thoughts

- Envision a peaceful, calming scene—a time when you were completely relaxed and happy. Use your senses to really experience the moment.
- Ask yourself how likely it is that your fear will come true (it is probably unlikely), and in the event that it could come true, ask yourself how you'd handle it. You'll probably see that you can handle the situation.
- Picture yourself performing with poise, grace, ease, and effortless confidence.
- Think about all of the times when you've been successful in similar situations.

Turn Down Energy with Your Behaviors

- Breathe deeply from your diaphragm—four counts in through your nose and four counts out through your mouth.
- Exercise—but do it at least 90 minutes before you want to feel calmer.
- Use progressive muscle relaxation. Tighten your muscle groups (such as by making a fist, flexing your feet, and so on), and then notice the deep relaxation as you loosen them.
- Spend time with people who have a peaceful, calming presence about them (especially for extroverts).
- Take some quiet time for yourself (especially for introverts).
- Eliminate the possibility of additional stress by building time into your schedule to get to where you need to be and to have time to focus before you're "on."
- Listen to relaxing music that triggers positive memories and makes you smile.

Confident Leader Action Steps to End Activity Addiction

- *Step 1: Get Your Vision and Intention—envision your day filled with flow.* Think about how you'll feel, what type of energy you'll have, what you'll be doing, and what you will need to give up to make this happen.
- *Step 2: Realize Your Commitment—commit to free time.* Those of us who are prone to activity addiction fill every second of our calendar with something. We think that a blank space equals being unproductive. This is not true, but the habit will be hard to break, so begin with something small, every day. For example, walk your dog without talking on your cell phone, drive without listening to the radio, or cook dinner while mindfully noticing the sights, sounds, smells, tastes, and feel of the food you are preparing.
- *Step 3: Organize Your Support—get rid of energy vampires.* Surround yourself with people who boost your energy. If you can't eliminate relationships with energy vampires, work to modify them (a mediator, therapist, or coach can help) or limit them to small amounts of time.
- *Step 4: Win with the Right Decisions—base your decisions on their impact on your energy.* Ask yourself, "Will this invigorate me?" If the answer is no, find something that will.
- *Step 5: Turn Anxiety into Optimal Energy—practice activation control.* Use the strategies for turning down energy and experiment to find some of your own that can help you focus your nervous energy and use it to your advantage.
- *Step 6: Harness Your Strengths and Release Control—delegate energy-draining activities.* You will need to relinquish some control to reduce your time spent on activity addiction rather than high-performance activities. Ask yourself, "Is this something that only I can excel in?" If the answer is no, outsource it. Remember that your time and energy are your most precious resources, and you can only afford to invest them in the areas that you are best in and most enjoy.

Gratitude and Energy

Another pathway to greater happiness, energy, and business results is focusing on what you appreciate rather than focusing on what you don't want. Research by psychologists such as Robert Emmons shows that gratitude is a strength that can create a higher level of energy and well-being. A grateful focus helps you not become disappointed when you habituate to happy experiences in life. Just as anxiety goes down over time as you get used to something uncomfortable, happiness and excitement can decline as you get used to something wonderful. Gratitude keeps you focused on what you do have, which helps you stay energized.

The positive psychology research of Dr. Seligman and his colleagues shows that acts of gratitude can improve a person's outlook, optimism, health, and mood. For example, one activity these researchers have found to be helpful is for people to write a letter of gratitude to someone to whom they have not fully expressed their appreciation in the past—and then to hand-deliver the letter.

Many of us achievement-oriented types have difficulty focusing on what's going well because we always want to be doing and achieving more. Ironically, the more we focus on what we don't have, the less well we will perform. In his bestselling books such as *The Attractor Factor*, Joe Vitale explains that when we get stuck on what we don't want, we end up attracting more of it. This means that if you frequently have thoughts like, "I don't want to be so busy, tired, stressed, (fill in the blank) all the time," you are too focused on what you don't want, and you are likely to continue attracting that very thing. Instead, focus on what it is that you do want. Gratitude is a great way to do this.

I've incorporated gratitude into my life to tame my natural urge to focus on everything that is yet to be achieved by taking a few moments to focus on what I appreciate each day. These things include my work, dogs, relationships, health, lifestyle, and so on. I've found that the more I notice and appreciate these things, the more of them I seem to have to notice and appreciate. In the expert interview, you'll hear from Joe Vitale himself about how he views and uses these energy-boosting ideas.

Joe Vitale

Joe Vitale is the bestselling author of many books, including *The Key*, and is one of the featured contributors to *The Secret*. He uses his positive energy to focus on what's important, and he is one of the most prolific and influential marketers, educators, and writers of our day. Read his articles and blog at www.mrfire.com.

What is the key to getting your positive energy flowing?
Doing what you love. I am passionate about my work, so it is easy for me to be energized about it. If there is something I don't enjoy doing, such as taxes, I find someone who thinks it's fun and hire that person to do it.

Why is it challenging for people to change their focus and energy?
Most likely fear. They are afraid of either success or failure, so they find it better to not act or not complete a project. I've learned to do what I fear. There's energizing power in that. I also know that I can still love myself, whether I succeed or fail.

What happens when people change their energy toward what they most want?
More good things! A fundamental truth in psychology is that you get more of whatever you focus on. Focus on what you want, and you'll get more of it.

Has being outside of your comfort zone and taking on important challenges led to your success?
Yep. Playing it safe will keep you where you are or even let you slip back a few steps. You have to keep growing, stretching, and evolving. My basic rule is to do either what excites me or what scares me, as both have energy in them.

> One of the things that is remarkable about you is your love of learning—is this related to your energy and productivity?
>
> Absolutely. I'm always reading, attending seminars, listening to audios; I know I don't know it all, and there's so much I want to achieve by learning more.

You now know how to exert optimal effort, get into a flow state, regulate your energy level, end activity addiction, and maintain an optimistic and grateful mindset. You're ready for the next step: motivating yourself and others, even in the face of uncertainty and challenge.

9

Build Supreme Motivation in Yourself and Others

"I Want to Motivate Myself and My Employees to Take Inspired Action"

As a Confident Leader, you motivate yourself to move outside your comfort zone to get better results, but you also inspire others to move outside their own comfort zones. And as a leader, your goals are to motivate people the right way, have the courage to encourage your people, and express your emotions.

Lessons from Basketball Dribbling

You know that goals are important, and you may have heard that the best goals are SMART: Specific, Measurable, Actionable, Realistic, and Time-limited. What you may not know is how important the language you use to frame your goal is. In 2002, motivation researchers from Rochester, New York, and from France learned something interesting from how teenagers dribbled basketballs. Students were randomly assigned to one of three groups. In the first group, called "performance-approach," the students were told that their dribbling would be filmed to select those with the best dribbling, and the video would be shown to other students to teach them how to dribble. The second group, called "performance-avoidance," was told the opposite, that tapes of students with the worst dribbling would be selected to help other students learn what errors to avoid. A third group of students, called "mastery group," was told that the purpose was to assess the teaching of dribbling, and that the group members would have two attempts to work on improving. The only difference among the three groups was these 30-second instructions. Intrinsic motivation was measured by how long students continued to dribble when the evaluator told them that they had free time.

The results showed that students in the performance-approach group and in the mastery group had equally high levels of intrinsic motivation, and that those levels were significantly higher than the levels in the performance-avoidance group. Three variables explained this: competence (how capable you feel), state anxiety (how nervous you are at the moment), and task absorption (how much you're concentrating on the activity). When you focus on the prospect of failure, you feel less confident, become more anxious, and are not engaged in the task. While mastery goals can be quite motivating, there are times when they aren't a good idea because they can encourage you to keep going down dead ends, rather than strategically moving on. Now, you're probably not a 14-year-old basketball dribbler, but if we were to generalize these findings, we'd consider how you should set your goals and your attitude for both fun and challenging tasks. Create performance-mastery goals for yourself or others to build optimal motivation and effort. Keep yourself and your direct reports focused on success rather than on the prospect of failure. Recognize people for what they do well rather than publicly pointing out mistakes. If you find yourself going into the performance-avoidance mentality, bring yourself back by getting absorbed in the task.

Multiple Motivations

There are two types of motivation: explicit (goals in our conscious awareness) and implicit (unconscious and emotional goals). A recent study conducted by Johannes Michalak and colleagues at Ruhr University in Bochum, Germany, confirmed that there is surprisingly little connection between the two, and that avoidance tendencies in both the explicit and the implicit motivational systems are linked with increased psychological symptoms. People tend to be motivated by one of three things: affiliation, power, and achievement. You may be motivated by all three, but there is probably a primary source of your ambition.

- Affiliation motivation means that you're primarily motivated to enhance your relationships.
- Power motivation is linked with leadership, and those who are high in the power motive tend to profit most from leadership development programs.
- Achievement motivation is associated with the drive to succeed and perform at your best.

Which are you most motivated by? The answer to this question shows you your explicit motivation. Figuring out your implicit motivation can be more difficult, but you can find clues in your feelings—do you experience the most positive reactions in affiliation, power, or achievement situations? Once you know what motivates you most, you can create inspiring goals and seek out situations that maximize your motivation. For example, if you're motivated by affiliation, you can frame your goals around your personal and professional relationships. If you're motivated by power, your goal can be to attain a new title or more direct reports. If you're motivated by achievement, your goal can be to maximize your performance on key measures by which you're evaluated.

Mood and Mindset for Motivation

Two of your most powerful motivational tools are your mood and your mindset.

Mood Is Contagious

In the last chapter, we discussed how to stay upbeat, positive, and energized. A 2000 study by Sigal G. Barsade, Andrew J. Ward, and colleagues showed that energized CEOs led to motivated and high-performing employees. The group studied 62 CEOs from Fortune 500 companies and top service firms and their management teams to see how upbeat they were. The results showed that the better the energy level and mood of the team, the better the work performance. Mood is contagious, and a harmonious climate leads to both inspiration and productivity.

The Power of a Growth Mindset

Your mindset is also a source of enormous motivation. In *Mindset*, researcher Carol Dweck describes two types of mindsets: fixed and growth. The key to growth and success is a mindset that is focused on learning. A fixed mindset entails the belief that you have a specific set of skills and talents that are relatively unchangeable. It is more outcome-focused. A growth mindset entails the belief that you are constantly evolving, learning, and changing. It is more process-focused. With a growth mindset, you stay motivated even in the face of failure, whereas with a fixed mindset, failures are devastating because they are taken as a blow to who you are as a person.

Those with fixed mindsets have roughly the same amount of self-confidence as those with growth mindsets. The difference is that self-confidence in fixed-mindset people is vulnerable. When employees taking a computer training course were put into a fixed mindset (by being told that their results were due to their ability), they lost confidence when they made mistakes. In contrast, those put into a growth mindset (by being told that they'd develop computer skills by practicing) showed an increase in their confidence in the face of mistakes. The fixed-mindset people probably thought, "I'm not good at computers," while those with the growth mindset probably thought, "I'm really learning a lot about computers." Keep in mind that both groups started out with equal levels of confidence. This shows that when the going gets tough, growth-oriented people get going in a positive direction, while fixed-mindset people get frustrated and disappointed and move in a negative direction or not at all.

The way to keep your momentum with a growth mindset is by looking at your life as a continuous learning experience. This is key to being a

Confident Leader. Remember that Step 6 in the GROWTH model is about capitalizing on your strengths and not overcompensating for your weaknesses. If you don't get something, don't be in denial about it, and don't think it's symbolic of a personal defect. Remember that some strengths and talents are inborn and part of your personality, but you develop many over time. I believe that we cultivate the strengths that interest us. For example, I love to share my ideas with others through writing, coaching, and speaking, and I have cultivated my strength of communication. I may have been born with some of it, but much of it I've studied and practiced.

Marilee Adams, author of *Change Your Questions, Change Your Life*, advocates question-thinking to keep yourself in a "learner" mentality and to keep from falling prey to "judger" thinking, which thrusts you into a fixed mindset. Stay out of judgment by asking yourself questions like, "What resources do I already have that can help me solve this problem?" "What resources do I need?" "What strength can I call upon or cultivate that will help me?" "What have I learned?" "How can I take this a step further?" When you get into the habit of question-thinking, you are more likely to stay in the growth mindset and to remain motivated, even in the face of problems, setbacks, mistakes, and failures.

Locus of Control: Your Key to Success

The way in which you attribute success or failure is your locus of control. If you have an internal locus of control, you see yourself as being responsible for your successes and feel that you can make decisions and manage situations effectively. If you have an external locus of control, you attribute your successes to forces beyond your influence, such as luck or fate. Studies have shown that an external locus of control is associated with increased distress and reduced motivation and productivity. Develop your internal locus of control for success by asking yourself: "How did my actions contribute to the positive result?"

A related concept is that of self-efficacy, developed by Albert Bandura, which entails your belief concerning your ability to create the performance that you want. A strong sense of self-efficacy keeps you motivated and helps you to see difficult tasks as challenges to be mastered rather than as stressful threats. Bandura posits that we develop self-efficacy by

1. Mastering tough experiences.
2. Observing others whom we can relate to successfully navigating challenges.
3. Letting others persuade us that we are capable of handling various situations.
4. Interpreting our moods accurately. It is important that we don't think that just because we are nervous, we are incapable of handling something.

According to Bandura, the greatest source of motivation comes from our thinking about what we expect to accomplish. When we attribute the result to our efforts, we develop an internal locus of control and a strong sense of efficacy. Additionally, we boost self-efficacy by setting challenging goals for ourselves and persisting even in the face of failure. We learn that we can achieve more and develop positive expectations for success in the future.

Confident Leader Action Steps for Motivating Yourself

- *Step 1: Get Your Vision and Intention—picture yourself achieving a goal that is in line with your primary motivation.* Create a clear vision of what achieving your affiliative, power, or achievement goal would look like.
- *Step 2: Realize Your Commitment—get yourself ready for great things by getting into the growth mindset.* Before taking action, ask yourself, "What can I learn?" and if you make a mistake or fail, stay committed to action by asking yourself, "How can this new information help determine my next step?"
- *Step 3: Organize Your Support—surround yourself with encouragers and top players.* Seek out those who encourage your development and provide honest feedback. Select people

who motivate you because they are bright and successful, and who motivate you to play the game of business at their level.

- *Step 4: Win with the Right Decisions — choose challenges.* Whenever possible, choose the activities that will challenge you at a level of at least 4 out of 5. This will tap into your internal motivation and help you to excel.

- *Step 5: Turn Anxiety into Optimal Energy — get and give feedback to get more energy.* Go out of your way to attend to and recognize the efforts of others. Give genuine compliments. Recognize accomplishments. When you encourage others, you want to achieve more yourself. You activate the Law of Reciprocity, which shows that people can't help but reciprocate kind deeds. All the positive energy you put out there comes back to you.

- *Step 6: Harness Your Strengths and Release Control — go with your mood and your talents.* Your motivation and your results will be best if you go with what comes naturally to you. Don't try to force yourself to use strategies that don't work for you. For example, you may have heard that starting the day by checking your e-mail isn't a good idea because it puts you in the mode of following what comes up rather than proactively tackling important projects. This may be true for some, but if it isn't for you, don't force it. If you're a morning person, take on your most difficult tasks in the morning, when your natural motivation is at its peak. If you're half asleep until 10 a.m., schedule something that is more reactive (such as checking e-mail) than proactive first thing and take on your challenges when you're naturally at your highest point.

Are You Motivating People the Best Way?

We often do things that we think will motivate others and then can't seem to figure out why those people aren't changing. Let's figure out why that happens.

External Rewards Can Drain Internal Motivation

Whether your goal is to motivate yourself, your employees, or your family members, you need to be careful about engaging extrinsic motivation, which results from external criteria or rewards (whereas intrinsic motivation capitalizes on our natural desire for growth). Your goal as a leader or manager is to have people feel inspired rather than pressured. You think you're doing a great thing by dangling carrots in front of your employees, but their focus on the carrots deprives them of the biggest reward of all: an internal sense of growth, creativity, and accomplishment. Recall that the questions from the Gallup research that were closely linked with results (presented in Chapter 3) focus on capitalizing on internal strengths and motivation. Another interesting point: we think that *we* are most motivated by self-esteem needs, whereas *others* are motivated by money and materialistic items. Don't fall prey to this bias.

In another study, Susan Harter explored intrinsic and extrinsic motivation with sixth graders completing challenging tasks. She assigned the children to two conditions: in the first, the students were told that they were playing a word puzzle game; in the second, the students were told that it was a school type of task and that they would be assigned grades. The students in the game condition chose challenging difficulty levels, and they enjoyed it, as evidenced by their smiling and their verbal reports. In the grades group, something different happened. Students were fearful about making a mistake, and they chose much easier tasks.

This shows us a couple of things. When we don't feel that we are being judged, we push ourselves further. And when we tap into extrinsic motivation (such as receiving grades), we don't challenge ourselves. To go from effective to exceptional, we need to engage our intrinsic motivation and our natural proclivity for challenge. When growth is the goal, extrinsic rewards *can* undermine the goal. However, certain types of extrinsic rewards, such as social reinforcement or recognition, have been shown *not* to have this demotivating effect in the way that grades, money, and externally imposed deadlines do. Extrinsic rewards, therefore, are not all created equal. When possible, ask yourself or others to create the deadline by saying, "When can you get that finished?" This subtle difference in framing the task can engage intrinsic rather than extrinsic motivation.

> **BONUS ONLINE MATERIAL**
>
> How intrinsically motivated are you? Take the free assessment at www.pascoaching.com/motivation to find out.

Growth-Minded Leaders Develop Others

In 1989, graduate students in business participated in a study in which they were put into a fixed or a growth management mindset. The researchers Robert Wood and Albert Bandura gave the business students a computerized task of running a simulated company. Fixed mindsets were created in half the business students by telling them that their task performance would be based on their abilities. The growth mindsets were induced by telling the other half of the students that the task performance would be based on practice. The results showed that the fixed-mindset leaders were not able to profit from their mistakes. A dramatically different pattern was seen in the growth-mindset leaders. They were able to look at their mistakes and create new strategies for motivating their employees. They showed greater productivity, and they maintained their confidence levels. Mentoring and developing others is a characteristic of growth-minded leaders because of the philosophy that we can all continuously grow and change, especially when we are given good practice and feedback.

What Language Are You Speaking?

Be sure you give feedback in a language that others understand and are best motivated by. Gary Chapman wrote the bestselling book *The Five Love Languages* about how to express feelings and commitment to our significant others. Chapman posits that everyone is different in what makes him or her feel most cared about, and that the best way to have your feelings heard is to speak in the language of your mate—at work, this translates to the language of your colleagues and employees. The five languages are quality time, words of affirmation, gifts, acts of service, and physical touch. The way to figure out your mate's language is to assess what makes your mate most happy and what he or she wants more of. If, for example, your spouse or partner often says, "We never spend time together!" then his language may be quality time. If she says, "I wish you'd tell me that you appreciate me more often," then her language may be words of affirmation.

We can apply this concept to business. Behavior that is rewarded gets repeated, so you can select the right language in which to reward your own and others' efforts. If, for example, your coworker's love language is quality time, you can take him out to lunch to celebrate the completion of a project. If your own language is acts of service, you can celebrate the project's completion by taking yourself out to dinner and letting someone wait on you.

Reward others in the language that's most rewarding to them. Pay attention to what makes them light up and how they recognize others. We tend to make the mistaken assumption that what speaks to us also speaks to others; like being a fish in water, it's what we know. So if your business partner gives people gifts, it's likely that his language is gifts. Once you have an idea of the language of others, use that language it to motivate and reward them. Keep in mind our earlier discussion about external rewards if you think someone's language is gifts. If you think someone's language is physical, proceed with caution, such as a pat on the back or an appropriate hug.

The Courage to Encourage the Heart

James M. Kouzes and Barry Z. Posner, authors of the bestselling book *The Leadership Challenge*, have conducted over two decades' worth of research that shows five qualities that are displayed by leaders who function at their personal best: Model the Way, Inspire a Shared Vision, Challenge the Process, Enable Others to Act, and Encourage the Heart.

Encourage the Heart is a particularly tough one because it doesn't always come naturally, but it is crucial in motivating others. We make the assumption that people don't need feedback or encouragement, as they can tell when they're doing a good job. We worry that we'll be wasting time if we go out of our way to acknowledge people. We get preoccupied with the daily grind and forget to provide feedback. In their book *Encouraging the Heart*, Kouzes and Posner point out that managers and leaders worry about providing encouragement because they're concerned that

- They'll be seen as playing favorites.
- It entails expressing emotions, which makes them feel vulnerable.
- It takes up a lot of precious time.
- It takes away from one's independence and individualism.

Learn more from Kouzes in the expert interview.

Confident Leader Action Steps for Motivating Others

- *Step 1: Get Your Vision and Intention—picture your staff members achieving all of their goals.* What you expect is what you get. If you have a strong vision of your staff members succeeding plus a belief that they can do it, encouraging the process becomes easy.
- *Step 2: Realize Your Commitment—ramp up your encouragement.* You don't want people to wonder if aliens have invaded your body when you are suddenly highly encouraging. For encouragement to work, it must be genuine, and if you do too much too fast, it won't feel genuine. Work your way up to make it work best for yourself and others.
- *Step 3: Organize Your Support—give public displays of satisfaction.* Instead of taking someone aside, celebrate together as a team or department. Tell the story of the great accomplishment, including the process, not just the outcome.

Don't worry that others will be jealous; the more powerful takeaway thoughts will be, "My manager really cares about us," "My department supports individual and collective wins," and "I want to do what she did for that great acknowledgment—it will be me next time!"

- *Step 4: Win with the Right Decisions—establish priorities for what to encourage* and what *not* to encourage. If you go around praising everything, the feedback will become meaningless. Similarly, you don't want to overdo it just because you feel that you "should" be more encouraging. Come up with a list of five criteria that tell you when something deserves acknowledgment. Don't forget to encourage those things that you want to see changed. The best way to change behavior is to reinforce the small changes in the direction that you desire. It is uncomfortable to overlook the things that aren't going well and focus on any small thing that is, but it is a very effective way to change.

- *Step 5: Turn Anxiety into Optimal Energy—when presenting something new, tell people that they can learn it.* Your employees will be most motivated when they are in a growth mindset. Create a growth mindset by saying that a new technology, technique, or approach is something that everyone can learn (rather than stating or implying that it is something that people are naturally good or bad at, which encourages a fixed mindset).

- *Step 6: Harness Your Strengths and Release Control—don't use feedback to overcontrol people.* This is not to say that you can never give negative feedback. If someone didn't perform the way you wanted, first ask yourself whether you gave that person everything she needed (clear standards, tools, and materials) to be successful. Don't use feedback to make others feel bad or to manipulate people into agreeing with you. Focus on recognizing people's strengths and providing them with the opportunity to showcase their talents.

Expert Interview

James M. Kouzes

James M. Kouzes is the award-winning cocreator of the Leadership Challenge. He is also a preeminent researcher and highly sought-after teacher in the field of leadership. Kouzes's groundbreaking studies, pioneered in 1983, led him and cocreater Barry Z. Posner to create a model of leadership that has been embraced by more than 1 million people around the world. Learn more at www.leadership challenge.com.

What are some of the problems that occur when leaders continue to do what is comfortable for them rather than what is needed for growth?

When we asked people to tell us about the times when they performed at their personal best as leaders, every single case was about a time when they were seriously challenged. The challenge may have come from the external environment, or it may have been something that they initiated, but personal bests were always associated with searching for opportunities to grow, change, innovate, and improve. These situations presented serious risks of failure, but they also presented exciting opportunities for growth and learning. Our personal bests—those times when we are performing at our peak—are never, ever about keeping things the same. They are *always* about changing the way things are. Our research shows quite clearly that extraordinary things get done only when we step outside our comfort zones.

How has being outside of your comfort zone advanced your own career?

My first "job" after university was as a Peace Corps volunteer. I spent two years in a country whose language, customs, religion, and way of life were totally foreign to me. It certainly wasn't in my comfort zone at that time. Yet I wanted to do it. I was inspired to stretch myself by John F. Kennedy and by my parents. I look back on that experience as one of the turning points in my life. My entire career has followed that kind of path. From directing a university executive center to being the CEO of a training company to venturing out on my own as a speaker, I've always been attracted to things that test me and teach me. And my work as an author is the same. Each new book is a challenge. Each new book is about something that I've wanted to explore. And talk about being outside one's comfort zone. When you publish a book, you're "dancing naked on a table," to quote an author colleague. You're out there in all your glory, fully exposed to the world and open to criticism as well as praise. I just love it, though. As another colleague, Rick Culley, said to me the other day, "If you're not on the edge, you're taking up too much space!"

Why is providing encouragement challenging but so important?

When we were doing our research for our book *Encouraging the Heart*, we asked people if they *needed* encouragement to perform at their best. The key word in this question was *needed*. Only about 60 percent of our respondents said that they needed encouragement to do their best. This wasn't the answer we expected, and it wasn't particularly encouraging to us, either. After all, we were writing a book on the subject, and nearly half of the people we were addressing didn't seem to think it was necessary. We were curious, however, so we asked a second question, "When you get encouragement, does it help you perform at higher levels?" To this question, 98 percent said, "Yes, it helps." Well, if it helps, then we need it! We just won't admit it.

We seem to be in denial about our own need for positive reinforcement. Perhaps it's because our culture worships individualistic achievement, so we try hard to maintain the appearance of not needing anyone's help. Perhaps it's because we don't want to be seen as weak. Perhaps it's because we are just ignorant of the power of recognition. Whatever it is, it's tough for folks to admit to needing encouragement, although we do recognize in retrospect how helpful it is.

Encouragement is an essential practice of leadership because the very essence of leadership is mobilizing others to want to struggle for noble aspirations. We aren't leading if we aren't energizing others to strive for higher goals. After all, what is a leader supposed to do: improve performance, keep it the same, or cause it to decline? This is a rhetorical question, obviously, but it makes the point. If leaders are expected to improve performance, whatever the measure, and if encouragement helps people do that, then leaders are obligated to express encouragement. It's just part of their job.

How can leaders express affection?

This is another thing that leaders have a tough time admitting. It's another one of those things that leaders think will make them appear weak. We hear it all the time. "I don't care if people like me; I just want them to respect me" is a common phrase that you hear in business and politics. What is this, a binary choice? Can I only have one of these? Can't I both like you and respect you? Of course there are some people in significant management roles who clearly don't care what other people think of them, but they're also the ones who destroy value and destroy lives. As Irwin Federman, a former high-tech company CEO and now a partner in a venture capital firm, said to us once, "I contend that people will work harder and more effectively for people they like, and they will like them in direct proportion to how they make them feel." There is a positive correlation between how much we like our leaders and our performance. Irwin's right. We perform better for those leaders who we like.

Leaders must show that they care about their constituents, and they can express their affection for others in numerous ways. As leaders, we can listen more attentively. We can say thank you more often. We can be positive about other people's contributions. We can sit down and talk with them about what's going on in their lives. We can brag about them to others. We can stand up for them when they are wrongly criticized. We can admit we're wrong. We can take their advice. Any time we make someone else the center of our attention and not ourselves, it's an expression of affection. It shows that we care.

For leaders who are uncomfortable delivering feedback (positive or negative), what are some skills to practice or develop?

Before you can give anyone feedback, there first has to be an agreed-upon *model* of excellence. What does success look like? If the leader and the constituent don't first have a common understanding of expectations of excellence, then it'll be tough to get agreement on what was done well and what was done poorly. The first step is creating a shared understanding—a model—of exemplary practice.

Second, you need to develop the skills of accurate *observation*. You have to be able to see what the other person is doing relative to the model of exemplary practice.

Third, you have to be able to *describe* with precision, as well as compassion, what the person was doing relative to the model. John Gardner—the founder of Common Cause, former secretary of H.E.W., a man who served five U.S. presidents, and a Stanford professor of leadership—once said, "Pity the person caught between unloving critics and uncritical lovers." Leaders need loving critics—people who will honestly describe their performance, but do so with a caring heart.

Fourth, you then need to be able to offer some positive suggestions of *techniques* to try ... things to do to improve performance. Feedback by itself is of little value. If you're going to give feedback, be prepared to offer recommendations on what someone can do differently to perform at a higher level.

Fifth, leaders have to be willing to detach themselves from outcomes in order to allow for mistakes and *learning*. Trying something new means that there are likely to be many errors in execution. No one ever did anything perfectly the first time, and the expectation that someone will "get it right the first time" can destroy effort. The focus should be on learning and not on results in the early stages of the improvement process.

We've covered strategies for motivating yourself and others, including framing goals in the best way, using your mood to motivate others, creating a growth mindset, responding to failure in a way that builds rather than drains motivation, building intrinsic motivation, and encouraging others. In the next chapter, we'll cover how to stay motivated and on track when you want to procrastinate.

Overcome Procrastination and Boost Your Productivity

"I Put Things Off and Can't Seem to Get or Stay Organized"

You KNOW HOW IT GOES: You're going to begin something important, but you squeeze in "just one more" e-mail. You have a key project to work on, but you wait until you have a good chunk of time, which, of course, is never. Let's talk about how Confident Leaders approach procrastination.

Procrastination as Your Comfort Zone

It's easiest to keep doing what we've been doing. Making a change, starting something new, or doing a difficult task requires us to enter uncomfortable territory. As a result, we are tempted to procrastinate. Ironically, procrastination is more often the result than the cause of anxiety. Putting something off creates a vicious cycle:

You're uncomfortable with a task, so you avoid it. The more you avoid it, the worse it gets. → The worse it gets, the less you want to do it. → The less you want to do it, the less you do it.→ The less you do it, the more anxious you get. → The more anxious you get, the more you avoid it. → The more you avoid it, the worse it gets, and so on.

Another way in which procrastination can be part of your comfort zone is that it's a habit. To break any habit (even a bad one) requires initial discomfort, and you might not be willing to make yourself uncomfortable right now. In addition, people often procrastinate because they are more comfortable with a specific task, so they continue with that task to the detriment of others. While the most common form of procrastination is putting off something that you don't want to do, it can also come up as not wanting to stop something that you enjoy.

My biggest procrastination challenge is getting myself to exercise at the end of a busy workday. To manage this, I tell myself that as soon as I sit down on my couch, I can just forget about getting myself to the gym that day. Newton's first law definitely comes into play—a body at rest stays at rest! So if I intend to go to the gym, I know that I cannot lie down on the couch with the excuse of "I'll just rest for 10 minutes and catch the news."

Putting Off What Makes You Uncomfortable

Clearly we put off what's uncomfortable, and, in turn, we limit our ability to grow and excel. There are four categories of uncomfortable situations that we tend to avoid:

1. *Social situations.* These are things like office holiday parties, difficult conversations, making phone calls, or asking the boss for a raise.
2. *Undesirable work projects.* We don't want to do these, but unfortunately we have no choice. It can make sense to delegate, but that's not always an option.
3. *Challenging work projects.* These are important and could be enjoyable, but because they are crucial, they are intimidating, and therefore we put them off.
4. *Ending something comfortable.* This is my gym example. I don't find going to the gym undesirable, but there are many things that I find more relaxing.

Putting Off What You Love

Interestingly, it is also common to put off things that we really enjoy. This may sound ridiculous, but for us high-achieving types, it is often the case. Doing something that is purely enjoyable and relaxing can be tough because we are sacrificing work time. It may be that we are waiting until we feel we have the time to do what we love. Or it may be that doing what we love feels unproductive and arouses guilt or "the shoulds."

One of the most challenging things is to prioritize yourself. It is easy to prioritize everyone else. Ask yourself what you would love to do for yourself (take a Spanish class, learn how to paint, travel to Africa, learn how to play tennis, and so on) but are putting off. Then ask yourself, "Down the line, as I look back over my life, what would I regret?" I'm willing to bet that it won't be giving yourself permission to pursue some of these ambitions.

Is It Smart to Put It Off?

In the GROWTH model, Step 2, I recommended that you ask yourself how ready you really are to do something. There are times when you must listen to your procrastination—perhaps there's a reason for it. Maybe you aren't ready. Have you ever said:

- "I'll begin tomorrow."
- "I just need to prepare a bit more."
- "As soon as I get organized, I'll get going."
- "I need more information before I can make a decision."

These are very common excuses, but they can also be valid. It's best to be honest with yourself and not pursue something if you are not ready to do it (i.e., if you are not yet in the preparation phase) because you are likely to be unsuccessful and falsely conclude that you aren't capable of doing it when the true reason is that you are not yet ready to do it.

It is *not* procrastination to recognize that you are in the contemplation phase and that you need to propel yourself into preparation and eventually action. It is smart to realize where you truly are and *why* you aren't ready for action. Is it because your gut tells you that you are in the wrong job? Is it because you need mentoring? Is it because what you really want is to be an entrepreneur? Is it because the task doesn't utilize your strengths and talents?

When you get to the bottom of why you aren't doing something, you often identify (and can therefore resolve) a core issue. When you resolve a core issue, you free yourself up to accomplish so much more because you no longer need to push yourself. Recognize, however, that identifying these core issues and aligning your work with your values and strengths can initially be a great deal more work and effort. This is similar to the other things we've discussed where you need to approach the hard to get to the easy.

Here are some key questions to ask yourself to identify the core issue:

1. How would I continue to be dissatisfied even when I have accomplished this task?
2. What do I need to successfully complete this project?
3. How could I approach this differently to get inspired and start taking action?
4. What support do I have, and what do I need?
5. What fears may be keeping me stuck?

This last question is an important one—let's go there now.

Face Your Fears and Procrastination Disappears

Procrastination can help you realize the things you're nervous about. You normally don't think to yourself, "Wow, it's really important that I face my fear of failure." But if you find yourself putting off key projects, you're motivated to solve the problem. Let's review some of the common fears that keep us stuck.

"If I Fail, I'll Be a Failure!"

Most people are afraid of failing. We want to do our best and succeed. As much as we know that we can learn from our failures and mistakes, failing isn't something that we typically want. As a result, we play it safe, try to do too much, or avoid taking action.

The solution, ironically, is to fail. When we allow ourselves to fail, we see that it is not as horrible as we had anticipated and that the effects are not as pervasive and long-lasting as we had feared.

A few years ago I started providing free monthly teleseminars for my mailing list. I remember the first one like it was yesterday. I had an incredible guest booked, and over 300 people around the world were registered. A few minutes into the call, I noticed that I was getting a ton of e-mails with subjects such as, "I can't get on the call!" I couldn't stop the interview, so I couldn't do anything about it. Afterwards I realized that I had given out the wrong password. I felt absolutely horrible. All these people had blocked valuable time out of their schedules and were looking forward to the interview, and instead they experienced the frustration of not being able to get on. Upset, I spoke with my wonderful virtual manager, Cindy Greenway. "Don't worry, Larina," she told me. "People will realize that it was an honest mistake, and they'll forgive it. Those who truly value what you offer them will return next month." They did return next month, and I learned that even a large screw-up like this one can be forgiven and does not necessarily have a long-term negative impact.

"What Will Happen When I'm Successful?"

Interestingly, the fear of success is almost as prevalent as the fear of failure. There are many reasons why you may fear success. Here are some common concerns:

- How will I change? What if my values change?
- How will people's views of me change?
- There's a longer way to fall from the top!
- There'll be higher expectations of me, and I'll be under greater scrutiny.
- What if I get even busier and have no time with my family?

The way to manage this discomfort is to bring your fears out into the open. Write them down. Then ask yourself two powerful questions:

1. How likely is that to happen?
2. How would I handle it if it did happen?

You'll see that what you fear is unlikely to occur, and that even if it did, you could handle it.

"I Don't Like Uncertainty or Feeling Out of Control!"

We often would rather live with a difficult situation that is familiar than face uncertainty. This is the fear of the unknown. And it is one of the biggest reasons that people get stuck. It keeps us from finishing projects because we worry about what's next. The solution is to accept and embrace ambiguity and unpredictability. Realize that without uncertainty, life would be dull and boring. We need to approach it rather than avoid it.

"What If Everyone Thinks I'm an Idiot?"

The fear of rejection is similar to the fear of failure, but it's social in nature. The fear of failure is about messing up, whereas the fear of rejection is about being unworthy or unlikable. Deep down, many of us wonder if we really are worthy or likable. The way to handle the fear of rejection is twofold. First, be prepared. Present yourself well. Practice some conversation starters. Don't rely on alcohol to become at ease. Second, take some risks. Once you're ready, you need to go for it.

One of the ways I built my business was through joint venture partnerships. I called people and proposed ways in which we could help each other out. One guy I called was a real jerk. "That's crazy. Why would *I* want to cross-promote with *you*?!" he rudely said. As horrible as this felt, I learned that you can get over rejection if you choose to. It's typically not about you so much as it's about the other person. This guy was clearly an egomaniac, but rejection is not always something bad. Someone who rejects you for a date may simply have a different preference. Someone who rejects you for a job may think you're overqualified.

"What If I Commit to This and Then I'm Stuck with It for the Rest of My Life?!"

Ah, the fear of commitment. It keeps you from moving forward because you're nervous about making the wrong choice. Ironically, you worry about being mired (in something forever with no way out), yet this fear keeps you stuck in place. Many people experience significant discomfort before a major life commitment such as getting married or switching career paths. You wonder whether your anxiety is a sign that you're doing the wrong thing (and you should get out of it) or simply cold feet (and you should keep moving ahead). Here are some questions to help you sort this out (they're specific to marriage, but you can modify them for your situation):

- Did I have doubts about this person before my fear of commitment set in?
- If I wasn't nervous about commitment, would I still have doubts?
- Are my feelings toward this person at least 80 percent resoundingly positive, and are the other 20 percent things that I can live with?
- Based on how things are right now (you don't want to try to be a fortune-teller or try to change someone), do I get my needs met in the relationship?

You're trying to look at the situation with rational thought processes rather than emotion. If you take the fear out of the picture, how do you truly feel?

A Scattered Focus

Confident Leaders stay focused on what's important, as we discussed in Chapter 7. A scattered focus can also be a cause of procrastination. You may not qualify for a diagnosis of attention deficit/hyperactivity disorder (ADHD), but you may suffer from shiny bright object syndrome. You think, "What's this new and exciting thing?" (Then, five minutes later) "Oh, wow, what's *that* new and exciting thing?!" This is you if you

- Work with 10 windows open at once on your computer.
- Have 10 books that you've begun but haven't finished.
- Get a rush from starting something new.
- Have diverse interests and hate to be locked into one thing.
- Are extremely busy, but often unaware of what you complete.
- Are easily bored and often looking for something that will interest you.
- Have been described as "well-rounded," "a Renaissance type," or "ADD."

In *Refuse to Choose*, Barbara Sher creates a profile of what she calls "Scanners." A Scanner is someone who meets the previous criteria and who has difficulty limiting himself to one field. The difficulty is that Scanners believe that they need to limit themselves, so they continuously feel disappointed in themselves and believe that they are letting others down. This is why Scanners frequently experience discomfort. Instead, Sher recommends embracing your Scanner ways. Carry a notebook like da Vinci did so that you can write down all your brilliant brainstorms and disjointed thoughts.

Scanners often have commitment phobia, which might be expressed as, "What if I need to spend the rest of my life in one job, and it's not really the right one?" The reality is that you do not need to spend your life on one path (most people change paths several times), and you don't have to make a career out of all your loves—you just have to make room for them in your life. Scanners can have a difficult time getting started because so many things are interesting and because of their fear of commitment. Sher recommends backward planning. Start with your end goal and write it in a circle on the right-hand side of a horizontal piece of paper. Then ask yourself, "Could I achieve that goal right now? If not, what would I need?" Write the answer in a circle to the left and ask yourself the same question again. Keep doing this until you get to an action that you can take *right now*, and then circle it and say, "Now!"

Confident Leader Action Steps for Plunging In, Not Putting Off

- *Step 1: Get Your Vision and Intention — picture how you'll feel when you're done.* It can be exciting to start new things, but instead envision the wonderful feeling you'll have when you get something done and check it off your list.
- *Step 2: Realize Your Commitment — are you really ready?* Reread the section "Is It Smart to Put It Off?" to figure out how committed you really are.
- *Step 3: Organize Your Team — get more done.* Ask your colleagues and set up joint venture partnerships to hold you accountable for doing what you say you're going to do when you say you're going to do it. This accountability will help you form new habits.
- *Step 4: Win with the Right Decisions — decide what* not *to do.* Productivity is about prioritizing and often about what we won't do in the moment because it could distract us.
- *Step 5: Turn Anxiety into Optimal Energy — overcome your fears.* Go through the fears listed previously and select one to work on.
- *Step 6: Harness Your Strengths and Release Control — engage your strengths in every task.* When you are faced with something you don't feel like doing, challenge yourself to use your strengths to do it.

Hidden Procrastination

There are two Ps of hidden procrastination: perfectionism and preparation. Perfectionism is a hidden form of procrastination because you think that you're polishing something, but you're really putting something else off. Many perfectionists don't actually do the tasks they worry about doing a substandard job on. They wait until they have enough time to begin or figure that they won't be able to do a great job, so why bother? Perfectionism is characterized by unrealistically high standards combined with a sense of inadequacy. You set the bar high and then feel like you're never getting there. The solution is to either set the bar lower or change your interpretation of where you end up. If you reach 90 percent, reframe that as excellent. Done is often better than perfect.

The second P is preparation. You tell yourself that you're taking action, but really you're stuck in the preparation phase. There are times when a great deal of preparation is necessary, but often preparation is used as an excuse for not doing the more difficult things. The key is to ask yourself: "Am I learning or earning?" Learning often leads to earning, but not always. Sometimes you need to accept you can't know it all and just jump right in.

Five Steps to Overcoming Procrastination

It comes as no surprise that the most common time to procrastinate is when getting started. The five steps in the STING model by Rita Emmett, the author of *The Procrastinator's Handbook,* can help you get started and end procrastination.

- S = Select just one thing to do. Anything that is important to you is fine.
- T = Time. Set a kitchen timer for 60 minutes and work on the activity. You may think that you can keep track of an hour in your head, but it is really helpful to set a timer because it gives you a sense of urgency and limits you to just one hour.
- I = Ignore everything else. During the time that your timer is set, make sure that you aren't doing anything else. Don't say, "I'll just check messages first."
- N = No breaks. We can easily turn a 10-minute task into a two-hour, two-day, or two-week task by taking breaks. You'll be amazed at what you can accomplish in just one hour.
- G = Give yourself a reward. It must be a reward that is realistic and enticing. You can withhold something that you normally have (such as a big mocha) until after your hour is complete, or you can add something that you want (such as a massage or time to read a great book). Emmett recommends including others in

your reward because it makes both you and them feel good. You can say to your kids, "I accomplished a challenging task, and I'd love to take you to the park to play as my reward."

BONUS ONLINE MATERIAL

Listen to the 60-minute audio interview with Rita Emmett at no charge: www.pascoaching.com/procrastination/.

Too Much on Your Mind

According to David Allen, author of the bestseller *Getting Things Done: The Art of Stress-Free Productivity*, if something that you want to change is on your mind, you haven't

1. Clarified your intended outcome.
2. Decided on the first or next physical step.
3. Put reminders of Steps 1 and 2 into a system.

Allen, whom you'll learn more about in the interview at the end of the chapter, states that the primary cause of mental stress is that we constantly have in our minds a running list of all the things that we need to do. These things weigh on us, and we worry about them. We worry that we'll forget them, and we wonder when we'll get to them. Unfortunately, we remember these things at the most inopportune times, when we can't or shouldn't act on them. So we continue to be stressed out by them.

I'll share briefly how attention and memory work to help you understand this process. When we pay attention to a piece of information, it enters our short-term memory. Typically we can only hold between five and nine pieces of simple information in our short-term memory. If this information is not acted on or encoded, it goes away. To keep information available, we need to get it into working memory. Working memory is like a vehicle that transports information from short-term memory into long-term memory. Working memory will transport something that fits into an existing memory.

Our minds are like filing cabinets, so if there is already a file for a new piece of information, working memory can deposit it there. Working memory also transports information that is rehearsed or manipulated. For example, let's say that you want to remember the name of someone whom you meet at a networking event. If you meet an executive named John and you try to remember "John," you're likely to forget. If, however, you think, "His name was John and he's wearing a blue shirt—that reminds me of my husband, who is named John and has blue eyes," then you're likely to remember his name because you engaged working memory. Working memory files information in long-term memory. These files are not easily accessed—you often need reminders. And it's easier and more efficient to recognize something than to try to recall it from scratch.

There are two important lessons to learn from the way our memories work. First, we can't expect to recall something when we need to. We may not have gotten that piece of information into long-term memory, and even if we did, recalling it can be tough. Second, getting ourselves to take action works in much the same way that memory works. Just as we can remember only so much, we can do only so much, and we can't rely on ourselves to remember what we need to do when we need to do it. Memories need filing, and behaviors need a filing system. The only way to be productive is to take action, and we need a method for doing so.

Allen lays forth an excellent behavioral organization system that he calls the Five Stages of Managing Work Flow. First, *collect* information outside of your head. If 100 percent of your information is not collected externally and appropriately, it will continue to nag you. There are many ways to collect information, such as notepads, e-mail, pocket PCs, Black-Berries, and so on. The keys are that you use your collection buckets consistently and empty them regularly (for example, you could use e-mail every day, but if you never empty your inbox, you'll soon have a million unorganized messages). This means that you don't want dozens of Post-its and pads cluttering your desk.

Second, have a *process* for moving information through the system. David Allen recommends asking yourself two key questions: "What is it about?" and "Can it be acted on?" If it cannot be acted on, then it goes into the filing system, and if it can, then he recommends taking action if it requires two minutes or less. If it requires more than two minutes, defer it or delegate it.

Third, *organize* where your information or project will go. This step has to do with prioritizing. Does the item get done as soon as possible? Does it go to someone else to do? Does it go on your calendar to be done at a later date? This process helps you not to procrastinate, but to be smart about what you do and when you do it. And if you put something off for later, but you have deemed it an important task, then you need to create a reminder system, which brings us to the next point.

Fourth, *review* your plans. This entails taking a step out of the daily grind (using some of the strategies we discussed in Chapter 7) and reviewing your options and actions. David Allen recommends a weekly review, which gives you a great time to gather your information, review and update your systems and lists, and get caught up. This gives you that clean slate feeling that you so often crave but never achieve.

Fifth and finally: *do*. Productivity is about doing what needs to be done when it needs to be done. At this point, you can trust your intuition. Remember how earlier in this book we discussed how discomfort can color your intuition and make you feel confused and unable to trust yourself? Well, using the first four steps in Allen's model of Managing Work Flow reduces all your stress and discomfort.

Expert Interview

David Allen

David Allen is the founder and chairman of the David Allen Company, an in-demand international speaker, and the author of the international bestsellers *Getting Things Done: The Art of Stress-Free Productivity* (Viking, 2001) and *Ready for Anything: 52 Productivity Principles for Work and Life* (Viking, 2003). He is called "the Productivity Guru" by *Fast Company*, and he has helped over a million people improve the quality of their work and lives by becoming more productive. Learn more about his books and his company's services at www.davidco.com.

Why is it so difficult to get organized and improve time management?

In a way, people are as organized as they ultimately want to be. You're as organized as you need to be to maintain the comfort zone that you're willing to tolerate. If there was a fire and you saw the smoke, you'd quickly be organized and time management wouldn't be an issue. People don't have a problem being organized with what they love. If you love golf, your clubs are probably in great order.

In my work, I have the strange challenge of solving a problem that most people don't recognize that they have. The problem is not necessarily disorganization; it's where you set the bar for yourself. You have a bar for how many e-mails you're willing to tolerate in your inbox—whether it's 30, 300, or 3,000. It's not about the number. It's about how many things you're comfortable with. The key is to find the standard for yourself and then shift it.

How does this relate to workplace stress?

It's easy for all of us to get caught in the busy trap where we work harder and harder. But we can't work harder and harder to get rid of stress. The stress comes from cognitive dissonance between our desired outcome and the bar we set for ourselves, which may not allow us to achieve the outcome we want. The stress comes from avoiding what we need to do. For example, neat and organized are not the same thing. We may have a very neat desk as a way to control all the mental clutter in our heads, but still not actually be organized. The stress comes from having a backlog (mental or physical). We can handle daily stress much better when there's no backlog. It's about finding out if we're doing the wrong thing. It is better to know our options and look at them from outside of the process than to get caught up in the loudest and latest.

What is one of the most significant productivity problems you've seen?

Most people haven't a clue about what they've committed to. Most of the people that we've worked with need one to six hours just to collect all the agreements they've made with themselves. We don't realize what we've committed ourselves to. It is easy to get sucked into this because we haven't been trained to keep track of all of our agreements. If you already have enough to do (which is the case for most of us), and you take on a new project or commitment, as soon as you make this agreement, you must drop off another or you have a formula for burnout.

The first step is to recognize those 43 things that you're not doing. Our stress comes from breaking agreements with ourselves. Once you realize what all of these things are, the second step is to make it okay to not do all of them. This is tough. You have three choices: you can unmake the agreement, complete it, or renegotiate it. This is how you get to stress-free productivity.

Are any of the stages in your five-stage model more challenging than others?

I haven't researched this empirically, but anecdotally, for many sophisticated people, it's about figuring it out to begin with— being aware of all the information in your head (stage 1: collect). Of course, once you do that, new challenges arise. I had a client who was shocked by all of the information he was getting down. But he was writing it all down on Post-it notes, and his office was getting cluttered with them. You've figured out what you need, but you don't know how to process it (stage 2: process) and organize it into projects and steps for the next action (stage 3: organize). Many people get hung up on reviewing (stage 4: review) because they don't get into the habit of doing a regular weekly review. If you don't have a weekly review, you'll start relying on your head again rather than your system because your system isn't current. And, of course, the biggest problem that people have is that they don't start. They don't take action (stage 5: action). So really you can encounter challenges at any stage of the process, and that's why all the stages are necessary, because they're so important together.

If someone is uncomfortable with a task, when is it a good idea to put it off, delegate it out, or say no?
It all comes down to what you are trying to accomplish. If your goal is to build your dream house, but you're uncomfortable because you don't know how, that is different from needing to call a client who is going to unhook 50 percent of your business revenue because he isn't happy. With building your house, you do some research and hire contractors and people to help you. With returning the call, you may be the only one who can do it. In this case, consider what outcome you want. Then think of the next positive action that will help you achieve that outcome. This is important because if you don't do this, you get focused on all of the negative things that *could* happen. You can't hold these negative fears and focus on your positive next step in your head simultaneously, so focus on that next step. One of the reasons Getting Things Done has been effective is that it has helped people define what that next step is. Engage your resources to figure out and take that next step of action.

How does your Getting Things Done system help people to end workaholism?
If you're addicted to being stressed and busy, my system won't fix those things—you'll still find a way to do them. But what can help a lot is to know that there is a result that is achievable. It's very motivating to know that you could get there. You don't need fancy software or the latest program. We can't get rid of the stress of work, and we don't necessarily want to because some of it is good, but we can see that you can make your vision happen by resolving the inner conflict between where you want to be and where you are. And when you reduce this stress and start achieving your vision, you can be more productive and work less.

Can you share a couple of your quick tips?
Absolutely:

1. Write everything down. Leave nothing as clutter in your head.

2. If something can be done in two minutes or less, do it now.
3. Have a great filing system. Without this, you will experience a backlog like a clogged pipe.
4. Create an in-basket and have it right in front of you at all times.
5. Once a week, sit down and clean everything up. Get back up to the top of the mountain every week.

You are now able to trust your gut and take inspired action. Next we'll address how to be likable and authentic no matter what.

11

Be Authentic and Project Likability and Confidence

"I Sometimes Feel Like an Impostor and Want to Show My True Self"

ARE YOU LIKABLE? If so, others perceive you as warm, genuine, empathic, and an excellent listener. Many leaders possess all these characteristics of likability, but they do not come across as being as likable as they could. How come?

The Impostor Syndrome

Deep down, even the top leaders in the world feel that they have something to hide, that they're not worthy, or that they could be doing a better job. I call this the impostor syndrome. You feel as if you're "on," as if you are acting and not truly being yourself. Acting requires a great deal of energy and is draining and exhausting.

Remember Joe, whom you met in Chapter 1. While he was an excellent leader and a high performer in his organization, he was headed for burnout, and he had the sneaking suspicion that his employees were not as eager to follow his lead as they let on. Joe tried to present himself as

165

capable, likable, confident, and charismatic, but his efforts didn't pay off. He felt insincere, and he feared that he'd fall out of character and the charade would be over.

The impostor syndrome is both a cause and a result of not being a Confident Leader. Here's what happens. Leaders become uncomfortable when situations require them to do things that are outside their comfort zones. Instead of effectively converting the discomfort to optimal energy, they control the discomfort by avoiding, overcompensating, or relying on crutches or old, unhelpful habits. These fixes serve as Band-Aids, and even if the situations turn out well, leaders are left with the impostor syndrome and shaky confidence ("It went okay this time, but what about the next?"). Here are some of the ways in which leaders get caught in this vicious circle.

The Need to Be Liked

Perhaps this is you. You want everyone to like you. You don't want to offend others or be rude. You are frequently concerned about whether you have stepped on someone's toes or upset someone. Some call you a people-pleaser. Others call you a yes-man or yes-woman.

Your need to be liked comes from a wonderful place. You are socially oriented, and you value your relationships and other people's opinions of you. You're probably high on empathy, which means that you have a highly tuned radar for the feelings of others. Women, in particular, are naturally prone to honing in on other people's facial expressions. The problem is that your radar can misfire. It may give you misinformation (that you aren't pleasing others) because you misread people's expressions. Some common overcompensating responses include the following:

- Agreeing with others and being tentative in the language you use
- Avoiding controversial subjects of conversation and not expressing your opinions
- Being overly quiet when others are talking
- Asking for reassurance, such as, "Did I offend you?" or, "Is everything okay?" more than is needed
- Overanalyzing other people's facial expressions and assuming the negative when in fact it is not the case

The solution is to drop these reactions. Retain your need to be liked, but take the risk of showing more of yourself. You don't need to *try* to be likable, because trying is what makes you appear insincere. Show some of your faults. Take a risk and express your opinion or state something controversial. What people really like is others who are true to themselves and show a genuine dedication to sharing who they are.

The Need to Be Right

Many leaders have an excessive need to be right. It's often *not* out of their own grandiose belief that they're always right (although for some it is). Instead, it's a combination of a need to be seen as decisive and a fear of being wrong. They're concerned that others will see them as weak and ineffective if they don't say the right thing. One of my clients told me that she was overly self-promotional because she worried that if she didn't promote herself, no one else would, and she wouldn't get where she wanted to go in her career.

Remember that compensating behaviors are useful until they're used too much and become *over*compensating behaviors. As we'll discuss in the next chapter, you need to promote yourself. If, however, you're concerned that you don't promote yourself and as a result do it too much, you'll get a negative outcome. You'll look pushy, aggressive, and arrogant. When my client promoted herself more effectively, through the results she delivered and her work relationships, she was more successful than she was with her self-promotional comments where she tried to show that she was right.

Some of the most common overcompensating behaviors with the need to be right are these:

- You take credit for other people's work.
- You fail to acknowledge the contributions of other people.
- You speak over others or cut them off when you have something important to say.
- You correct people too often and focus on inconsequential errors.
- You tell people what to do rather than ask questions and gather feedback.

Of course, the rebound effect in all of these situations is that you don't look right. Or you might look right for a while, but in the end you really look like a jerk.

Confident Leader Action Steps for Ending the Impostor Syndrome

The goal is to be real and not always be right. Here's how:

- *Step 1: Get Your Vision and Intention*—*picture yourself as a Confident Leader* who capitalizes on being wrong by seeing it as an opportunity to show poise. You'll hold this image in your mind to help you navigate through the discomfort.
- *Step 2: Realize Your Commitment*—*figure out if you and your team are ready for a change now.* Any changes you make will upset the balance that you have in place and will throw you and your team off. Your stepping aside at times will require others to step up. Consider discussing this change with your team members to get their buy-in. If they agree, stepping aside can be a very effective strategy in developing your talent and improving your retention rates when people gain more visibility. They just need to be on board.
- *Step 3: Organize Your Support*—*allow your direct reports to shine.* The best way to get support is to give it. And the best way to support your team members' and direct reports' goals is to allow them to share the glory and the spotlight.
- *Step 4: Win with the Right Decisions*—*be strategic in your decisions to speak and what to say.* Before you say something, ask yourself the million-dollar question, "Is it worth it?" Is it really worth it to point out someone's mistake, get into a heated debate, or nitpick on unimportant details just so that you can be right?
- *Step 5: Turn Anxiety into Optimal Energy*—*when it is worth it, show how right you are.* Being right in the *right situations* will boost your confidence and energy. It's like the boy who cried

wolf. If you're always doing it, no one will listen, but if there really is a wolf and you let people know about it, you'll be a hero.

• *Step 6: Harness Your Strengths and Release Control—admit to your mistakes and apologize* when needed. As discussed earlier, you don't want to apologize excessively out of a need to be liked; however, if you have made a mistake, take responsibility. If you're overly concerned with being right, you're probably too careful or perfectionistic in your work. You're likely to be defensive when you are corrected. Instead, take more risks. When you do make mistakes, own them. Public opinion of leaders goes up when they take ownership of their screw-ups. They're seen as more genuine, transparent, and trustworthy. If you apologize, do so with no excuses. These are crutches that will make you look worse. Instead, simply say, "I'm sorry for the negative impact my actions had on you, and I will do better in the future." Then do better in the future.

Remember that these actions are not designed to make you invisible; they're designed to tone down overcompensating. Don't let the pendulum swing in the other direction so that you lose your voice. When you practice these strategies, you'll no longer look or feel like you're trying so hard, and you'll allow your natural insight to shine through.

What If You're Shy?

It's difficult to talk about yourself and meet strangers when you feel uncomfortable or worry that you'll embarrass yourself. Shy people can be socially skilled, but they take longer to warm up and get comfortable or they get overwhelmed when they are in groups or are the center of attention. Researcher Jennifer Beer recently conducted a study in which she filmed people who were meeting for the first time. She measured their shyness level and their mindsets, and their behaviors were coded by trained evaluators. A fascinating result emerged: those who had a fixed or stable mindset (seeing their success as the result only of their abilities) and were shy faired less well in meeting new people, appearing anxious and awkward even after five minutes of interacting. Those who had a growth mindset (seeing their success as a work in progress that improves with practice) were similarly uncomfortable during the first five minutes, but after that, they appeared more likable and sociable. Why did this happen? The growth-minded people were able to see the situation as a challenge, whereas the fixed-minded people were focused on not making mistakes.

What this means for you if you're shy is threefold. First, you absolutely can be shy and be a Confident Leader. Second, the growth mindset is important in becoming more confident. Look at the situation as an evolving challenge rather than as a judgment of your worth as a person. Remember that a fixed mindset drains confidence over time, whereas a growth mindset helps you build confidence. Third, if you are shy, you need to stay with a social situation long enough to get more comfortable—in the study, that took around five minutes. When you persevere, you will soon show your natural likability.

The Active Listening Challenge

Active listening is arguably the most important skill in business, and it is the most necessary skill for likability. It is also one of the most difficult skills. If you interrupt and don't pay attention to others' ideas, you aren't likable. If you aren't able to show genuine interest and curiosity, people will assume that you don't care about them. They'll feel unimportant. One of the keys to whether someone likes and respects you is *how you make that person feel about him- or herself.* If you make someone feel uninteresting and unimportant, that person will not like you or respect you as a leader. If you're trying to sell something and you're focused on your sales pitch and your script, you aren't listening to the needs of your customer. And you're unlikely to make the sale.

Listening is one of the most uncomfortable things to do until you get really good at it. When you listen, you're tempted to interject, react, correct, impress, and multitask. Just sitting there and listening is tough.

To truly listen, you'll have to inhibit many of your natural tendencies, but the payoff will definitely be worth it.

If you aren't investing energy and effort in listening, you aren't really listening. The goal is to use an optimal level of energy. If you're exhausted or distracted, you're probably trying too hard and focusing on yourself and what you'll say next. Or you're doing everything right, but the person you're speaking with has poor communication skills. If your direct report is disorganized and rambling, you'll need to try hard to follow him. This is an instance of your discomfort illuminating both a problem and a solution. Your discomfort in conversations with your direct report shows you that he needs coaching to improve his ability to express his ideas concisely. Likewise, if you sense that others are tuning out, getting frustrated, or getting distracted when you speak, it may be a sign that you need to work on your communication style.

Confident Leader Action Steps for Active Listening

- *Step 1: Get Your Vision and Intention—picture yourself listening attentively.* What do you see? Are you making eye contact? Nodding? Leaning forward? Making good facial expressions? What is the other person doing? If you ever have the opportunity to videotape yourself during a conversation, turn the volume down and compare what you see with your image of great active listening to look for areas to improve.
- *Step 2: Realize Your Commitment—what's the right amount of time to listen?* Active listening is not passive listening. It's doesn't mean sitting there mute so that the other person feels heard. If someone has a long-winded communication style, let it go a bit past your comfort zone so you can work on your patience, and then interject. Practice the "bottom-lining" technique, where you ask for the essential information: "I see that what you're saying is very important. I'm also aware of the time. Can you give me the bottom line?"

- *Step 3: Organize Your Support*—*create follow-up systems* so that information can be delivered in small chunks. Managers often make the mistake of throwing a ton of information at their staffs, only to have it be quickly forgotten. What works much better is to deliver information one piece or a couple of pieces at a time. This makes your communication concise and does not put a strain on your listeners or make them want to run away when they see you coming.
- *Step 4: Win with the Right Decisions*—*ask yourself if it's better to speak or to listen.* There's a good chance that you'll want to speak when it's better to listen. The components of active listening include reflecting ("It sounds like that's a tough situation"), which validates the other person's view; summarizing ("So what I hear you saying is … [summary]), which shows that you're putting it together; and questioning ("Can you describe how you handled that?"), which clarifies and furthers the dialogue.
- *Step 5: Turn Anxiety into Optimal Energy*—*create optimal energy while you listen.* Use your personality to guide you. If you are introverted, you can do well with sitting back, taking information in, and thinking about it. Extroverts, on the other hand, tend to get more energized by a back-and-forth volley of conversation. Also recognize the personality and communication style of the person you're speaking with, because mirroring someone's style helps that person explain her ideas and gain more from the conversation.
- *Step 6: Harness Your Strengths and Release Control*—*don't try to control the conversation* or feel that you're responsible for carrying the whole thing. A common cause of overcompensating in conversations is feeling that you need to do all the talking. Conversation needs to go back-and-forth like a tennis game. It's okay to have some pauses or to end a conversation when it appears to be done.

Visibility, Visibility, Visibility

In real estate, it's location, location, location, but in business, visibility is absolutely critical. Those people who network well and are most visible in their companies come up for promotion most often. Those who have a great keep-in-touch marketing strategy to stay in front of their customers and clients are the most successful business owners. And, interestingly, simple things like where you sit can play a major role. I host free teleseminars on topics related to positioning yourself as the expert (get invitations to attend by signing up in the green box at www.AchieveExpertStatus.com), and I recently had the privilege of interviewing Dr. Kevin Hogan. Dr. Hogan is a leading authority on body language and persuasion, and the author of bestselling books such as *The Science of Influence: How to Get Anyone to Say "Yes" in 8 Minutes or Less!* He shared an interesting piece of data that he had discovered: when you sit on people's right-hand side, they find you more attractive. This is because when people look to their right, they engage the left hemisphere of their brain, which is responsible for reason and logic. This is preferable to engaging the right hemisphere, which is where emotion (anxiety, irritation, and other things you don't want to bring up) resides. Whenever possible, take the seat to the right of the decision maker.

We know from decades of psychology research that familiarity breeds likability. Studies of students in dorms show that those who live near one another and whose walking paths cross like each other more than those for whom this is not the case. This means that in your workplace, you want to go out of your way to be around those whom you want to have notice you. In your business, you want to know your neighbors (those whom you naturally come across) and to get in front of those whom you may not naturally come across.

While this is intuitively obvious to people, there may be a limit to just how much familiarity breeds likability. A recent study found the opposite. Researchers Michael Norton, Jeana Frost, and Dan Ariely conducted a five-part study. In the first two studies, they found that people believe that the more they get to know others, the more they'll like them.

What was interesting was that they also found that the more traits (about an unknown person) participants were presented with, the less the participants liked a person. The reason was that the more traits presented, the more participants found reasons for dissimilarity. Those who perceived the first trait presented as being dissimilar perceived more traits as being dissimilar than those who perceived the first trait as being similar, and liked the individual less.

What this means for you is that there are times when ambiguity is a good thing, or when less is more, particularly with people to whom you are dissimilar. For business owners and marketers, the answer is finding the right prospects to be in front of. If you find people with key similarities, they will like you more over time. But if you find dissimilar prospects, they'll like you less and less the more they learn about you. Ben Franklin said that fish and visitors have something in common: both begin to stink after two days.

Visibility in front of the right people in the right amount and the right way is the key.

In *The Likeability Factor*, Tim Sanders points out that the success of business leaders rests in large part on how well they get along with others. Employees will go the extra mile for a likable leader.

Expert Interview

Tim Sanders

Tim Sanders is the *New York Times* bestselling author of *Love Is the Killer App*, *The Likeability Factor*, and his recent book, *Saving the World at Work*. Up until 2005, Tim served as a senior-level executive at Yahoo!, having been Yahoo!'s leadership coach and prior to that its chief solutions officer. He advocates for the uncomfortable actions of being a "lovecat" and showing compassion and values in the workplace. He teaches readers and seminar attendees how to achieve the likability factor by enhancing their natural friendliness, relevance, empathy, and realness. Learn more about his work at www.timsanders.com.

The title of your breakthrough bestseller, *Love Is the Killer App*, is creative and risky. Did it force anyone out of his comfort zone?

Yes, everyone at my publisher needed to go outside the comfort zone for this one. I spoke with my wife, and we decided that this title is "Tim." It's who I am and the battle cry for the book's message. With a great subtitle, we knew it would sell. So we advocated for it. I knew that if we wanted to be on the cover of *Fast Company*, the book needed an edgy title. The book was on the cover.

The idea of loving people as a business strategy sounds weird. What's actually weird is putting the compassion *back* into business. When you look at companies' founders, you see that they began with a great idea for improving the world, but as the companies grew, they needed to take on new responsibilities, such as pleasing shareholders. Love as a business strategy is actually getting back to its roots.

What is likability, and how can it be challenging to achieve?

After doing a lot of research, we discovered that likability reflects a person's capacity to consistently produce positive emotional experiences in other people. We learned that the norm for reciprocity is ingrained in us from birth. If someone says or does something nice, we can't help but respond. The secret for business is the law of reciprocity. The reason that we like people is that they make us feel good. If you make people smile when they think of you, you're likable.

Likable people create a positive psychological benefit for others. The greatest psychological need right now is reality. Because of information overload, global warming, and other such problems, we need to know the truth. Authenticity is comforting. Authenticity is about being yourself and being present. If I asked you whether your boss lies to you, and you said yes, you think he's dishonest. The main reason you feel this way is that he doesn't pay attention. He sits in meetings checking his BlackBerry. Presence is the secret to authenticity. The most likable people show you that there's no one else but you. This is very hard to do. I tell leaders to leave their gadgets in their cars and walk into meetings with nothing so that they will completely focus on others. Authenticity also includes promise keeping. The most successful people take the time to track not only the promises they make but also the promises they keep.

The second component of likability is consistency of friendliness. You want an outlook like a five-year-old or my pet dog (a tiny poodle), where you expect the best. Role-based gratitude also influences friendliness. A new guy in a job comes in happy and grateful to be there. When he loses this, he appears less friendly. People also use friendliness to determine whether you like them. If you do, they like you. If you're a leader and someone smiles at you, smile back regardless of who that person is and what position she's in.

The third component of likability is relevance, which is about building a bridge between yourself and others by showing your sincere interest. In business, we ask how someone's weekend was or how his kids are, but we never ask what he's enthusiastic about and then do some of that with him. When we do that, we add shock absorption, which helps us get through more together. It is impossible to be 100 percent consistent—something that I call "emotional gravity" sometimes takes over—so we need shock absorption to provide latitude through these times.

The fourth component of likability is showing empathy. I consider this to be the most difficult thing for modern business leaders. Treat other people's feelings as facts. A typical business exchange goes like this: A worker goes to the boss and says, "I'm really afraid, mad, hurt (any negative emotion) about the impact of the merger." The boss then goes on to try to change the worker's feelings. You might just as well tell him that you don't want to listen to him as do this, because both responses are equally invalidating. Empathy provides validation. Empathic souls are deep listeners who look into your eyes and focus on perceiving your emotions correctly. We tend to neutralize emotion, and it's important to first know what the emotion is so that we can best respond to it.

In addition to deep listening, powerless listening creates empathy. This means that you are not trying to fix something, you are just sitting with it. It also means *not* saying, "I know what you mean; I had that experience ..." because this comes across as sympathy, not empathy, and seems like you're turning the conversation back to you. If you've ever been sad and you had a pet come up and lie in your lap, you know that this is all you need; you don't need to try to change people's feelings.

How do values fit in with what you teach?
Any individual, regardless of his title, can transform just for profit into for good by bringing his values to work. The leaders of the future will be those who show responsibility. This is not a marketing issue; it is about changing the way you work. The only way to run a company like this is by bringing your values to work. You're successful because of your personal values, not in spite of them. Talk to entrepreneurs like Jeffrey Schwartz of Timberland or Ben Cohen of Ben & Jerry's—that's what they decided to do: build a company around their values.

The customers will no longer be casual about whom they buy things from. And workers will no longer work for a company that they're embarrassed by. They don't get embarrassed by profit margin and such; they do when a business treats the world wrong.

We've discussed how to be a likable Confident Leader by overcoming the impostor syndrome, developing exceptional listening skills, and capitalizing on familiarity and similarity. Now you're ready to use these skills to promote yourself. Many people think that the phrase "likable self-promoter" is an oxymoron, but it doesn't have to be. I'll show you how to market yourself in an authentic, likable way in the next chapter.

12

Promote Yourself to Propel Yourself

*"My Discomfort with Marketing Myself Is
Holding Me Back from Advancing in
My Career or Building My Business"*

To many people, *self* and *promotion* are dirty words when they are put together. We can promote the heck out of a product, our friend, or our employee, but when it comes to ourselves, it's another matter. We need to overcome this fear because research has shown that visibility and connections are the most powerful predictors of promotion. This means that you can be the best person in the world at what you do, but if your results are the world's best-kept secret, you will be too.

Think about *why* it's important for you to market yourself. If your answer is solely self-serving, you may remain uncomfortable with it. Of course, part of your answer should be to advance your career, grow your business, and such. If, however, you're clear about how what you do makes a difference to others (customers, clients, and so on), you will ignite your passion and want to share what you do. Consider also how your success has a positive impact on other people in your life: your spouse or partner, your kids, your parents, your community, your favorite charitable causes, and so on. These things will give you a burning desire to promote yourself, which

179

I think really means sharing your results. And when you think in terms of sharing results, some of the bad taste goes away.

Remember that our discomfort typically means one of three things: we should stop; we should continue, but modify our approach; or we should continue with the same approach despite our discomfort. Let's begin by exploring these three ideas to see which one best characterizes you and your current reluctance to promote yourself or your business.

You Don't Want to Be Promoted

I recently worked with a marketing executive, Leslie, who said to me, "I know that I need to get better at promoting myself within my company if I want to get promoted."

"Do you want to get promoted?" I asked her.

"Yes, of course," Leslie responded.

"How do you know that?" I pushed her.

"Well, that is the goal for everyone—to move up. Isn't it?" Leslie said.

"No," I said. Leslie looked at me like I was crazy.

I gave Leslie the task of completing a worksheet about her interests and her career ambitions. In doing so, she realized that she disliked her company and didn't want to be promoted. A couple of meetings later, it became clear to both of us that what she really wanted was to find a better match with the culture of another company. So my advice was to forget about self-promotion and find a new job.

A year later, I received a call from Leslie. She had found a new job in a company that was a great match for her. However, she was in a sales role, and she needed to put herself out there to network, meet prospects, and earn sales. She wasn't sure what to say and didn't want to turn prospective clients off by coming across as too much of a salesperson. This is one reason why discomfort is so helpful: it keeps us from making such mistakes. We all know people who self-promote obnoxiously or to excess, and we certainly don't want to be like them. On the other hand, if we go too far to the other extreme and are overly humble, no one will know the benefits of what we do or have to offer. I recommended that Leslie begin by using the feedback of others. She told the success stories of clients whom she had helped. The stories benefited her prospects because they showed them some solutions that they might try, and they highlighted the benefits of what Leslie was selling. It was a win-win solution, and she got comfortable with this approach after just a couple of experiences.

You Need More Practice

Another possible reason for avoiding calling attention to your achievements is that you lack experience. All you need is more practice in doing it in the right way. Remember that avoidance can be subtle, which is equally damaging.

For example, Jean told me that she was proud of herself for speaking up and expressing an off-the-wall idea in a meeting. She was frustrated, though, because no one heard her. Later in the meeting, her coworker Jennifer expressed a similar idea, and everyone was enthusiastic about it. It turned out that while Jean did take a step outside of her comfort zone to present her idea, she expressed it quietly, quickly, and in tentative language. This type of presentation is a form of subtle avoidance. As a result, Jean's idea got lost in the shuffle, and she did not get credit for it. When Jennifer presented the idea, she spoke loudly and slowly (showing that the idea was worthy of a few moments of thought), and her voice tone projected authority and commanded attention. Once you're sure that you aren't using any subtle avoidance or overcompensating strategies, then you're ready to practice. It will get easier over time.

Powerful Executive Presence

Confident Leaders have a strong executive presence. This means showing your most confident, commanding, and charismatic self. It in no way means that you are presenting something that you are not. One of my clients, a marketing specialist named Jules, came to me for coaching because, while he was an expert in marketing, he was not doing a great job of marketing himself. I'll share some steps that we took to help him create the presence he wanted and that you can use too. I gave Jules the task of observing people in his workplace who he thought had great presence. He listed the adjectives that he thought described them, including words such as *inspiring, powerful, charismatic, smart, networker, strategic,* and *great speaker.*

I then asked him to create a list of the positive adjectives that currently described him. We used a couple of assessments of his strengths to help inform this list, and we included words such as *connector, social, responsible, strategic, achiever, bright,* and *thoughtful.* We then went through both lists and looked for areas of overlap. This identified current attributes that were part of his desired presence. He added a couple of adjectives and came up with the list of the top three attributes for him — the three Ss: strategic, smart, and social. I think it's important that you create a specific vision for yourself to keep focused and not try to do it all.

Once Jules was clear on the executive presence that he wanted to convey, we set out to develop specific action steps to help him convey these key characteristics. For example, he took the time to articulate his strategic ideas in meetings. Previously he had cut to the bottom line, but I suggested that he tell the story and take the time he needed to express his high-level ideas. This was uncomfortable for him because he didn't want to hold up the meeting. Jules was smart and social in how he came across, people gave him the attention he commanded, and he was seen as strategic. It wasn't long before he was promoted to a vice president position, and he attributed his advancement to his polished executive presence.

BONUS ONLINE MATERIAL

For more information, read *How to Create Powerful Presence* at www.pascoaching.com/presence/.

How to Brag without Bragging

Catherine Kaputa, author of *U R a Brand*, recommends letting others brag for you. When you say how great you are, it's seen as bragging, but when others say how great you are, it's seen as a powerful endorsement.

She recommends asking important people (colleagues, clients, bosses) for endorsements to use on your résumé and Web site.

Most business owners know this, but not all of them routinely ask for endorsements because they don't want to be seen as self-serving or rude. People actually love to give endorsements of those who have provided a valuable service for them. If you don't think you provided outstanding benefit, don't ask (and work on improving!), but if you think you did, ask. I recommend planting the seed for an endorsement early on by putting it in your introductory materials.

For example, in your contract or on your Web site, you can include a statement such as, "Referring your friends or family is the greatest compliment," or "Our goal is to do such an outstanding job that you tell your friends and family." Include asking for testimonials as a standard part of your process—for example, at the end of all projects or, for ongoing clients, at the six-month mark. I also recommend asking for a referral in these words: "I'd appreciate a brief testimonial about the results that you've accomplished from our work together (or from the product)." The best endorsements don't say, "So and so is nice and wonderful"; instead, they focus on the specific results that were achieved. I also like to use the word *brief* (or say "one- to two-sentence") so that people know you are asking for something that requires minimal effort. If asked, I'd prefer to write a brief endorsement than a reference letter.

Kaputa recommends creating a brag book that can be presented at job interviews, meetings with prospective clients or customers, meetings with literary agents or editors if you're working on getting a book deal, and so on. This can include the following:

- Letters of recommendation
- Testimonials and endorsements of your work
- Key initiatives written up as case studies (challenges, action, results)
- Media clippings
- Articles that you wrote or were cited in

This is the easiest way to brag because it's all third-party endorsements rather than you saying how wonderful you are. Another great strategy is to align with a nonprofit organization, fundraiser, or corporate event—something that no one in your company would mind hearing about. You could, for example, promote the fundraiser (indirectly marketing yourself), and not risk company or team dissatisfaction with your marketing yourself directly.

Find a Need and Fill It

One of the most important keys to promoting anything is to position it around a market need. This means that you are constantly looking for the needs in the marketplace—either internal to your business or company or external. For example, in your job, you're looking for what your boss, coworkers, team members, or customers need. In your business, you're looking for what your employees, prospective customers, or clients need. When you find a need and fill it, you market yourself. What is a more powerful way to show others that you are valuable than providing value to them? I can't think of much. This goes back to the old adage, "actions speak louder than words." Well, this doesn't mean just any actions; it means those that are solutions to problems. When you solve other people's problems, you become invaluable to them, and they remember this.

Confident Leader Action Steps for Positioning and Promoting Yourself

- *Step 1: Get Your Vision and Intention—how do you want to be seen?* This is about your positioning: What words do you want to come into people's minds when they think of you and your business? Get uncomfortable here by not being humble. Think of your greatest strengths and how you really want others to see you.
- *Step 2: Realize Your Commitment—what steps can you begin with today?* While speaking in front of large groups to get exposure may be overwhelming, you could commit to sharing your riskier ideas with small groups that you already know.
- *Step 3: Organize Your Team—set up your team of endorsers.* We know that it's best to have others promote us. Figure out who's on your team—people such as clients, customers, colleagues,

your boss, your receptionist, your friends, members of the media, and so on. Then ask them. If you don't ask, the answer is always no. People may not promote you because they don't think of it, but when you ask, it will be on their minds. Ask them for something specific so that they know how they can help, such as, "Will you tell people you know who are starting a business about the business coaching I do?" or "In the meeting, how about if I share your important contributions and you share mine?"

- *Step 4: Win with the Right Decisions—select the key benefits to market.* If you share too much, people will remember nothing. In self-marketing or marketing your small business, promote only a few important value producers that reinforce your brand.
- *Step 5: Turn Anxiety into Optimal Energy—remember that you are sharing how you solve problems and help others.* Share the value in how you make other people's lives easier and more productive. If you aren't confident that you really produce value, then you need to get clear on that first.
- *Step 6: Harness Your Strengths and Release Control—never self-promote from a defensive position.* This is how you get caught in the vicious cycle of overcompensating. To use a sports metaphor, marketing yourself is an offensive move—you're scoring points. It's not a defensive move to keep others from scoring points. If you're uncomfortable and you realize that it's because you're on the defensive, take a step back and consider whether someone really needs what you offer. If so, explain it differently; if not, move on. Also, if you have an elevator speech way of describing yourself (which is helpful in getting yourself clear on the benefits of what you do), be careful not to overcompensate by reciting it verbatim and sounding like a robot. Instead, weave your points into conversations in such a way that they are relevant to others.

In the expert interview sidebar, marketing strategist and positioning expert Mark Levy provides guidance on how to promote yourself authentically and effectively.

> ### *Expert Interview*

Mark Levy--

Mark Levy is the founder of Levy Innovation (www.levyinnovation .com), a marketing strategy firm that helps consultants and entrepreneurial companies increase their fees by up to 2,000 percent. Joe Vitale, star of the film *The Secret*, calls Mark "a Superman of the Mind. He's a walking, talking, money-making brain on steroids. Computers want to grow up and be like him. And I'm probably underdescribing his abilities." Mark has written for the *New York Times* and has written or cocreated four books, including *How to Persuade People Who Don't Want to Be Persuaded* and *Accidental Genius: Revolutionize Your Thinking through Private Writing*.

Why is self-promotion so uncomfortable?
Four guesses:

Guess 1: In our society, people tend to tie their self-worth to their business. If their business is prospering, they consider themselves prosperous. If their business is failing, they consider themselves failures. It stands to reason that most people try to avoid situations, like self-promotion, where this success-or-failure dichotomy boils to a head.

Guess 2. When we're toddlers, or at least when I was a toddler in the mid–1960s, we were taught that "the nail that stands out gets pounded down." Self-promotion, which demands that we stand out, is more likely to expose us to a pounding.

Guess 3. When we "self-promote," we throw heavy attention on ourselves: "Here's what *I'm* promoting … here's why *I* think you should have this … here's why you should buy this from *me* …" Being family-oriented, friend-loving, community-minded creatures, all that self-focus goes against our natural way of being.

Guess 4. We don't know how to self-promote, so we hate doing it because we don't trust our ability to do it effectively. If we had interesting things to say, could get people's attention, and told them about things that could honestly help them, all the other reasons would largely recede. After all, we enjoy doing things we're good at.

Would you do anything differently to market yourself in a job and to market your own business?
Marketing your business and promoting yourself in an organization are leagues apart.

When you're marketing your business, you can be bold, dramatic, a maverick. You can experiment, trying one marketing tactic one week and doing something radically different the next. It's a big world.

When you're in a job, it's a closed environment. The landscape and players are fixed. You've got to be more cautious. If you promote yourself overtly and vigorously, you're liable to offend people that you work shoulder to shoulder with, day after day. Not good.

There is at least one piece of advice I can give you that you can use in either situation. My client and friend Dick Axelrod, of the Axelrod Group, is an advocate of it. The advice: Find out what's important to the people you're trying to influence, and do what you can to help them achieve it. As much as you can, take on their cause as your own. Show real interest. Offer counsel. If it's appropriate, pitch in. They'll love you for it, and they may very well help you get what you want.

What's the first step to exceptional self-promotion?
To promote, you first have to know what you're promoting.

When organizations hire an employee, a vendor, or a consultant, they're not really interested in that person's "deliverables," even if they say they are. What they're interested in is the results that those deliverables bring.

Promotional strategy 1, then, is not secretive and manipulative. It's open, honest, ethical persuasion. Promote the results of your work. That's the strategy. It'll help you win friends, influence people, and secure gigs.

What's an example of promoting the results?

If you head a research division and you want to move higher in the organization, understand and promote the results that your division helped the company achieve. Know the answer to questions like these: What did your division develop? How much did it help the company make? How much did stock prices rise? What new markets did it make inroads into? What awards did it win, and how did those awards increase the organization's valuation? What work methods did your department pioneer that reduced time and effort throughout the company? By how much did your methods reduce time and effort, and what things did the company gain from those savings?

If you're an organizational outsider—say, a consultant—the same rules apply. You acted as a coach to the CFO. Great. What happened?

What problems did she have? What advice did you give her? How did she translate that advice into action? How did it help make the company better? What were the results? If you don't know, find out.

To prove your worth, find internal and external measures.

An internal measure: "Due in part" to your help, the CFO came up with a new billing procedure that will help the company invoice its clients eight times faster. With the expected infusion of revenue, the organization is upgrading its manufacturing equipment, which will enable it to increase its yearly product output by half.

An external measure: Over the first three years, that productivity increase is expected to increase the organization's market share by 12 percent and make it $467 million in profits.

Notice, by the way, that I used the phrase "due in part" to your help. Memorize that phrase and use it when you promote yourself. It signifies that, while you were a significant contributor to the situation, and may even have been the catalyst, you were just a part of it. It honors the contributions of others and doesn't overstate your role.

You encourage people to use "the insight-based case study." What is this, and how can we use it?

I teach people to use such studies whenever they're trying to persuade someone: on a Web site; in a white paper; in a news release; when they're eye to eye with Mr. or Ms. Big, trying to close a deal.

To explain the insight-based case study, first I'll explain how a standard case study works.

The standard case study follows a problem-solution-results format. It first explains the problem that the client was experiencing. Then it segues into the solution you applied. Finally, it trumpets the results that the client enjoyed. Sounds good, right?

Where it usually falls apart, though, is in the solution section. Most case studies I've heard use the solution section to go on, ad nauseum, about the features of their solution. They talk about the studies they conducted, the meeting methodologies they used, the protocols they wrote, and so on.

Some talk about features is, of course, necessary. But stressing the features of your service is boring and makes you sound like a commodity. After all, all your competitors do pretty much what you do. They have their own studies, meeting methodologies, and protocols. Anything you can do, they can do (at least, that's the way it sounds to the casual listener). Where you can stand out is through insight.

Insight shows your mind at work, parades your abilities as a problem solver, and acts as a forceful differentiator because, while many people can conduct studies and the like, not everyone can come up with an insightful idea when the chips are down.

What does an insight-based case study sound like?

Here's an example for a sales consultant:

The Problem: "An IT firm called ACME Networking was having trouble. The salespeople it hired would start strong, but their sales and morale would predictably drop.

"The head of sales thought it was a hiring or training problem. He brought me in to study the company's hiring practices, training program, and sales methodology, and to make recommendations on how to fix them."

The Solution: "For a week, I studied ACME's processes and systems. I also conducted informal interviews with the salespeople themselves. It was during those interviews that I discovered something that no one was taking into account.

"The salespeople received a generous incentive. That incentive, however, was only in the form of money.

"Now don't get me wrong; the salespeople loved the money. But they had other needs—like getting time off or going after prospects in fields that interested them—that weren't being addressed.

"What I did, then, was to help the company restructure its incentive program. The salespeople would continue to receive monetary bonuses, but once they beat their sales goals, they'd also get additional rewards that were based on their personal needs and interests."

The Result: "Before the new incentive program, the company had experienced four down quarters, and revenues had slid from $52 million in 2005 to $45 million in 2006.

"Now, the new program has been up and running for a year. In that time, the company has had four consecutive up quarters, and the staff has generated $62 million in sales, which is $17 million over last year and $12 million over the goal. Not bad for a program that cost the company almost nothing to implement."

Do you see how the insight-based case study works? Rather than focusing on the details of the process, it focuses on the observation and shift in thinking that brought about the result. The insight is the pivot. It's the piece of information that drives the story. It's an x-ray of how you think, and it ties the results directly to your actions.

To create your own insight-based case studies, then, start with a result. In other words, think about some wonderful result that you helped generate for a client. Then, try recalling the insight you had that allowed you to generate that result.

If you have trouble remembering the dominant insight, try reliving the situation in your mind. Who was involved? Where were they stuck? Why were they stuck? What were they doing wrong? What surprised you? What was obvious to you, but escaped everyone else's radar?

Once you have the insight, write up the story in problem-solution-result format, putting your insight near the beginning of the solution step. Make the story turn there. You'll sound like a detective. You'll be talking about how you solved the case through observation and brains. It'll sound exciting and persuasive.

What makes it easier to promote yourself?
A strong elevator speech makes self-promotion a joy. It grabs attention, sets a context, and makes people all ears.

Most business people, though, freeze up when crafting an elevator speech. There are two reasons why. The first is that they don't realize that generalities bore, while specifics persuade. Here, for instance, is a boring generality: "We take our customers' businesses to the next level." Here is the same message in persuasive specifics: "Within five weeks of working with us, 98 percent of our customers double their productivity."

Second, they try to find their business's most distinctive point, instead of first finding *all* its distinctive points. Once they've found all its distinctions—in the firm's products, services, business model, people, infrastructure, and so forth—coming up with the most distinctive point becomes much easier.

By coming up with all the distinctions first, the business owner may, in fact, see a pattern that will allow him to come up with a new, powerful distinction that he had never thought about before.

When you focus on filling needs, providing value, creating a powerful presence, and branding yourself, you won't need to work at self-marketing— it will happen naturally. Something else that has a positive impact on your image and your brand is showing that you can stay calm and focused, even in high-pressure situations. We'll discuss this next.

13

Gain Composure and Keep Control over Your Emotions

"I Find It Difficult to Stay Composed and Focused When I'm Stressed or Frustrated"

CONFIDENT LEADERS HAVE high emotional intelligence (EI). Dozens of studies have linked EI with many areas of success. For example, in 2005, Dr. James Parker and his colleagues studied hundreds of college students and found that school grades are related to EI, and that EI scores predicted who would drop out of college. Another study by researchers from Yale, the University of Toronto, and the University of Surrey investigated EI in analysts and clerical staff in the finance departments of Fortune 500 insurance companies. The findings showed that EI (especially managing emotions) is significantly related to relationships, mood, attitude, and several performance indicators, more so than things like personality or verbal ability. Higher EI scores were related to higher pay.

There's much more support for this. David Rosete led a study in Australia that looked at 117 executives' IQ, EI, and personality. Supervisors provided ratings of the leaders' effectiveness. Rosete found that personality did not play a role in performance but that EI did, and it did in particular for getting things done. A recent study by Angelo Giardini and Michael Frese showed that the emotional competence levels of employees had a significant impact on the level of customer service provided. As you can see, EI is important for many areas of performance. Now I'll tell you what EI is and how you can boost yours.

What Is Emotional Intelligence, Anyway?

You may have heard of emotional intelligence, but you may not know exactly what it means, so let's begin there. In essence, emotional intelligence is your ability to recognize and manage your emotions and those of others. Emotional Intelligence has a solid research basis from the fields of psychology, neuroscience, and business leadership. There are four fundamental aspects of EI (as measured by the Emotional Competence Inventory, published by the Hay Group): self-awareness, self-management, social awareness, and relationship management.

Self-Awareness

This is how aware you are of your emotions and how accurately you can assess them. Most of us are so busy with the daily grind that we rarely take a step back and think about how we're responding to situations and how we come across. The other source of self-awareness is recognizing how others respond to us. This is often challenging because we tend to see what we want to see, and we tend to avoid the uncomfortable action of asking others for feedback. To grow in your self-awareness, consider building time for reflection into your day. Go over the ABCs: antecedents (situations that trigger emotion), behaviors (how you respond), and consequences (what is the result) so that you can see what caused you to respond as you did and how you can change. Also consider getting into the routine of collecting specific feedback from people who will be honest with you and whose ideas you value.

A large study that compiled thousands of data points found that leaders who sought out *negative* feedback were much more self-aware and effective than those who sought out positive feedback. Ask for and be open to hearing the good, but also the bad and the ugly.

Self-Management

Self-management is your ability to control your emotions. This component also includes your transparency, adaptability, achievement, and optimism. We discussed most of these concepts in other chapters, so we'll focus on the emotional self-control component. A key factor is whether you react or respond to situations. Answer these questions:

- When you get an irritating e-mail, do you reply right away?
- Do you sometimes find yourself regretting the way you handled yourself, wishing that you had been more calm and poised?
- Do you lose patience with or rush others?

If you answered yes to any of these questions, you may be in the habit of reacting rather than responding. When you react, you do what comes naturally, which is going with the emotional part of your brain. When you respond, you act against what is natural, which is why it is difficult. You engage the rational part of your brain and select the best response. To do this, you first need to use self-awareness, which you just learned how to do. Once you're aware of the antecedent, before you respond, ask yourself this question: "What is likely to result from this response?" This question engages the prefrontal cortex of your brain, the highly evolved part behind your forehead that is responsible for forethought and complex reasoning. It balances out any emotional reaction you had and will help you behave in an appropriate way to get the outcome you want.

Remember that accepting any emotions that arise is crucial to emotional control. If you aren't willing to have a feeling and try to fight it off, it will fight back, and you'll end up with more of it. Acceptance of emotions has been shown to be one of the most important determinants of work performance. Achieve acceptance by increasing your awareness of emotions and responses. Gather feedback from as many key players as possible, because you probably act differently around your boss, your business partner, your employees, your customers, and so on. The more views you have, the less likely you'll be to have a blind spot. Studies have shown that both peer and subordinate reviews have the most predictive power about a leader's true effectiveness and success, so be sure to get feedback from these sources.

Social Awareness

Your organizational awareness, focus on service, and level of empathy make up your social awareness. Remember from Chapter 11 that one of the most important keys to your likability is your empathy (seeing others' views, listening, and being open to diversity). Improve your organizational awareness by fine-tuning your radar for the emotional climate in groups and recognizing power dynamics. Improve your service orientation by fine-tuning your radar for your customers' or clients' needs. First and foremost do this by always taking personal responsibility, both when things are going well, as we discussed in the last chapter, and when things aren't going well. Other strategies to enhance your service orientation include being as available and responsive to your customers as possible and coming up with a system to regularly gather feedback.

Relationship Management

Developing others, serving as an inspiring leader and a catalyst for change, collaborating with a high-performing team, and managing conflict are part of relationship management. I discuss these concepts in detail in Chapters 8, 15, and 16.

The Downside of Achievement

A focus on achievement is an important part of emotional intelligence (part of self-management). Sometimes, however, the need to achieve can backfire. Here's how.

The Need to Be Smart

One of my clients, Vince, an engineer turned marketing executive in a pharmaceutical company, often sounded like he was showing off how smart he was. He'd use jargon and big words, make reference to all kinds of current and historical events, and throw useless trivia into the conversation. After my first conversation with him, I had two hypotheses: the first was that he didn't feel that he was smart enough, and the second was that he was trying to distract people from other things. Both turned out to be true.

"Vince," I said on our second call when he started in with the overly intelligent language, "I have no idea what you're talking about. I'm a reasonably bright person, so if I can't follow you, I'm sure that others feel the same way."

"Huh?" I had clearly caught him by surprise, and his overcompensating guard was down (if it was up, he would have said "pardon me?").

"I don't understand why you *try* to sound smart when you clearly *are* smart. You really don't need to try," I added.

"I'm not nearly as smart as the others here who are from Harvard Business School and Wharton, and I don't even have an MBA." Ah, the first hypothesis confirmed.

"Do you feel that if you act smart, people won't notice your lack of an MBA or extensive experience in marketing?" I inquired.

"I never really thought of it like that, but yes," Vince replied. The second hypothesis confirmed. It turned out that he tried to sound intelligent so that people wouldn't notice his lack of education and experience in marketing. He figured that if he used jargon, people would see him as an engineer and look at what he has rather than what he doesn't have. It is an interesting theory, but when executed in an overcompensating way, it backfired.

The Need to Win

Your need to win is a very helpful strength. I bet it's why you're as successful as you are. However, you must be willing to lose if you want to be sure to win. The more you try *not* to lose, the worse off you'll be. One of my clients was a poker player, and he told me about something called "tilting"—when you're distressed because the game isn't going well, you try harder to win. You end up playing based on emotion rather than on strategy, and you continue to lose.

Your focus on the end zone may also entail neglecting to focus on how you'll get there. Your mind is thinking, "win, win, win ..." and therefore is not thinking about the systems and processes. Others may not be with you, and they will feel dismissed and rushed while you're trying to win. Your need to win can also signify an impostor syndrome because you're afraid that you'll be fired or lose business when you stop winning.

Confident Leader Action Steps to Excel

- *Step 1: Get Your Vision and Intention—picture yourself appearing naturally and effortlessly intelligent.* Ironically, when you stop trying to look smart, you appear more confident and intelligent. Envision how you'd handle a loss or a setback. Many inventors say that their moment of greatest discovery occurred after their biggest failure.
- *Step 2: Realize Your Commitment—be prepared for all reactions.* When you drop your overcompensating behavior, you must be ready for all kinds of reactions, both from yourself and from others. You'll feel more vulnerable initially but stronger over time.
- *Step 3: Organize Your Support—ask questions.* The best way for you to be helped by others is by learning from them. When you're always the one talking and trying to look good, you miss out on valuable opportunities to hear other people's points of view. As a manager, the best way you can help your direct reports grow is to ask them questions to encourage critical thinking.

- *Step 4: Win with the Right Decisions—make better decisions by focusing on the situation.* When you try to sound intelligent and focus on winning, you're unlikely to make great decisions because you're focused on yourself, not on the situation. Instead of weighing what you're going to say, weigh the variables at hand and make better decisions. Focus on the journey, not just the destination.
- *Step 5: Turn Anxiety into Optimal Energy—become less self-conscious and more confident.* Allow your discomfort to energize you to thrust yourself out of your head and into the situation. You'll be less self-conscious, and you'll get better results.
- *Step 6: Harness Your Strengths and Release Control—speak in layperson's language.* Don't go in a totally opposite direction and speak in overly casual language; just focus on speaking as straightforwardly as possible. I was going over a 360-degree feedback evaluation with a client, and one of his peers wrote, "If I hear one more analogy, metaphor, riddle, proverb, quote, simile, or SAT word, I'm going to lose it. Just talk to me like a normal person, man." I think that sums it up.

Your Mood Determines Other People's Moods—And Results

In *Primal Leadership,* renowned emotional intelligence researchers Daniel Goleman, Richard E. Boyatzis, and Annie McKee explain, "This emotional task of leaders is *primal*—that is, first—in two senses: It is both the original and the most important act of leadership." The emotions of leaders are contagious. You can have a positive impact on the mood and performance of others. Whether you want to influence your team members, boss, customers, clients, or others, you can use mood contagion to your and their advantage. In the sidebar, one of the authors of this book, Dr. Annie McKee, talks about how to be a resonant business leader.

```
Expert Interview
```

Dr. Annie McKee

Dr. Annie McKee is a thought leader in emotional intelligence theory and practice. She is the coauthor of several influential books published by Harvard Business School Press, including *Primal Leadership: Realizing the Power of Emotional Intelligence*, with Daniel Goleman and Richard Boyatzis, and *Becoming a Resonant Leader* with Richard Boyatzis and Fran Johnston. Dr. McKee cofounded the Teleos Leadership Institute, where she advises senior level executives in Fortune 100 organizations on the intersection of leadership, culture, and strategy. Dr. McKee serves as adjunct faculty of the Graduate School of Education at the University of Pennsylvania and teaches at the Wharton School's Aresty Institute of Executive Education. Learn more at www.teleosleaders.com.

In your experience, is there any aspect of emotional intelligence that leaders find particularly challenging?
The first thing that comes to mind is self-awareness. The higher you go in an organization, the less accurate the information you receive about yourself is. People often don't tell a leader the truth, especially if it's negative, because they don't want to harm the relationship. Oddly, I've noticed that people are also afraid to tell a leader positive things, perhaps because they don't want to look like a brownnoser. The higher you go, the less likely it is that people will give you accurate feedback, and the less able you will be to make an accurate self-assessment. Even with leaders who have a natural capacity for accurate self-assessment, when they get mixed messages for a long period of time, they lose their accurate self-awareness.

The best leaders I know have some type of reflective practice to help them keep in touch with themselves and how they're feeling. This practice could be meditation, prayer, spending time in nature, independent exercise, building empty space into their calendars, doing activities that have nothing to do with business, or working in a very different context. For example, one powerful business leader we work with spends time working in South Africa with people dealing with HIV and AIDS. In reality, and unfortunately, it is all too easy to let such practices slip. Frankly, when you get very busy, the first things that you drop from your schedule are the things that replenish you.

While self-awareness can be compromised as you move up in an organization, leaders often remain highly aware of the superficial aspects of themselves, such as how they dress. While of course it's important to be aware of how you present yourself, the real challenge is to develop your capacity to recognize what's going on inside yourself and how this affects your teams and your organizational culture.

Can you describe the open-loop limbic system and how it affects emotions and performance?

Research in the last few years has taken us light-years forward in our understanding of how emotions affect groups, communities, and large organizations. We're at a special place in time in this field. There's hard science behind emotional contagion; in fact, there are new studies on "mirror neurons." These appear to be structures whose function is to reflect another person's electromagnetic pattern that is associated with emotions.

In organizations, human emotions dramatically affect group emotions. This is especially true for the leader. To be blunt, because we're mammals, we seek hierarchy and naturally follow the leader. We want to see what the leader can and will do, so we pay special attention to the nuances of expression that the leader shows.

The emotions of others, especially leaders, can affect performance because people don't perform well when they're too stressed, angry, or afraid. The brain goes into survival mode, and we respond to perceived anger from the leader in the same way we'd respond to a saber-toothed tiger in our village.

I like to focus on the other side, too—when people are enthusiastic, cheerful, and optimistic, these feelings are also contagious. The open limbic system enables us to share positive emotion, which effectively leads to others feeling inspired. We open up and think more creatively, solve problems, and innovate. The key, then, is to embrace all emotions—positive and negative—and to push ourselves past discomfort and then transform these emotions into new areas of comfort, which will have a positive impact on ourselves and others.

Let's talk about self-regulation. What are some signs that it would be helpful for someone to increase emotional self-control?

If, after the fact, you find yourself asking, "Why did I do that?" or "That was not like me; what was I thinking?" chances are that you were actually not thinking rationally and that it was your amygdala (the emotional part of the brain) that was responding. If your responses are disproportionate to the situation, that is another clue.

It's also helpful to look in more depth. Over time, you may find yourself feeling that you aren't expressing yourself as well as you have in the past (this is that stuck, paralyzed feeling). Have you noticed that you're giving in to impulses or that you aren't finding much meaning in things? If you're feeling bored and restless, chances are that you're out of balance and need to manage your emotions. We need to manage ourselves to a place of openness and learning, not shut down.

Is there a risk in having too much emotional self-control?

Absolutely. This is dysfunctional self-monitoring. Behaviorally, too much self-control results in your putting a cocoon around yourself and being closed down, which can lead you to appear inauthentic. Even if people can't articulate why, they pick up on this excessive self-control. There is also a somatic component to it—it can affect your immune functioning. Basically, you turn in on yourself. While it's good not to express *everything*, when you express too little, either you appear out of touch or you get sick.

How do you increase self-regulation?

Extensive personal change is hard to bring about because we're set in our habits. If you recognize that you're not living or showing up the way you want to, then first, think about what life would be like if it were the way you want it to be. Unless you get in touch with what's really important to you, you're likely to struggle with change and slip back into your old patterns. The only thing that truly energizes us is to tune into the vision of what we really want. If, for example, you're trying to change solely to help your team, you may be motivated intellectually, but this is not a powerful driver of change until you engage what's most important to you. Intentional change starts with a vision for oneself.

Once you have this vision, you can then consider who you are now. What's really going on? How can you discover your real self? You may want to collect data to help you see where you currently are. Then ask, "What are the gaps between my real and my ideal self?" and "What can I do to remove these gaps?"

What are the benefits you've observed when leaders have improved emotional self-control?
A couple of examples come to mind.

One person is the CEO of a Fortune 100 company. He's always been engaging, optimistic, and charismatic, but over the years, and because of the constant pressure of his role, he lost the capacity to see the impact of his behavior on his team and his organization. He had tight relationships with some people, and the others felt left out. His sense of humor was taken as flippant.

This CEO began to deliberately and consciously attend to the way people responded to him. This helped him to boost his self-awareness. He also focused on building empathy, and he was able to truly adjust the way he reacted to people. His company went through a difficult merger, but he was able to turn the extreme tension in the organization into optimism during this challenging time.

Another example is a senior executive who had lost touch with what was most important to her. As with many women at high levels, her emotions and behaviors particularly stood out because she was different (there are still few women at the top levels in organizations). Through the process of discovering her vision and the meaning in her organization and in her life, she left her teams healthier, got results, and, most importantly, built a resonant environment.

We've discussed how to accurately assess your emotions, maintain poise no matter what, and achieve more by not trying so hard. Let's move on to another challenge that helps you become a Confident Leader—how to put yourself out there and shine.

14

Stand Out! Be Different and Get Better Results

"I Know I Need to Really Put Myself Out There, but Part of Me Would Rather Blend In"

HAVE YOU EVER been house hunting? If so, you probably got sick of seeing beige walls, neutral-colored bathrooms, and the same kitchen in every new or updated house. In real estate, developers and house flippers use neutral color schemes to appeal to the most buyers. There is, however, an exception to this rule: the high-end homes. In the very high end homes, buyers expect to see unique finishes. These buyers don't want their house to look like every other house, and they're willing to pay a premium for creativity, top-of-the-line amenities, and an exquisite style. Do you want to be seen as ordinary or high end?

Don't Be Beige, but You Don't Have to Be Neon Green

While the high-end homes have unique finishes, you rarely find ones that have wild color schemes. This is because high-end sellers are smart and know that while they don't want to be bland, they also don't want to be so outrageous that they appeal to no one. What does all this mean for you? It means that while you don't want to play it safe and blend in, you also don't want to be totally out there in situations and cultures that don't call for it. You've heard the idea of "be yourself" preached time and again, and I certainly agree with this idea, but there are additional considerations.

If a house had neon green walls, visitors might be distracted and miss everything else that the house has to offer. This is why it's always important to be authentic, as we discussed in Chapter 11, *and* to tailor your approach to the situation. One of the fundamental rules of change is that you need to meet people where they are and then walk them along with you to where they want and need to go. Any other approach will be taken as a push, and a push is typically met with resistance.

Similarly, one of the fundamental laws of communication is to mirror the individual you're speaking with. This doesn't mean being less of yourself; instead, it means slightly toning down or amping up your natural style so that the other person is able to hear your ideas. If I'm being interviewed by a high-energy, fast-talking radio show host and I answer calmly and thoughtfully, I'm not appropriately mirroring the individual, and she's likely to cut my interview short. Whenever possible, get a sense of the culture and context of a new business situation that you're entering so that you can be in the right mindset.

To follow through with the color metaphor, if someone's natural personality is sage green (cool, calm, serene, and soft-spoken) and you come at him with a fire-engine-red approach (loud, urgent, and very high energy), he may be overwhelmed and not hear what you are trying to say. If you have a red personality, it can be to your advantage to tone it down when you are dealing with a sage-green type of individual. Interestingly, if you are mixing paint, the way to tone down red is by mixing in some of the complementary color, which is green. Mirroring modifies your style so that other people can best benefit from your ideas.

Here are a few examples to illustrate this concept:

1. Mark is the manager of a team of engineers. He does not love being the center of attention and prefers to let his

results and those of his team members speak for themselves. While he prefers a beige approach, it is likely to keep him stuck in a middle management position. Mark needs to take the challenge of standing out if he really wants to move ahead.

2. Shantelle is a sales manager, and one of her representatives wasn't making her numbers. Shantelle discovered that her rep was afraid of offending customers and was playing it safe. She encouraged this rep to be bolder and less careful. She gave her rep a pep talk, but nothing happened. It turned out that Shantelle had approached her sage-green rep with a fire-engine-red approach and did not get the message across. She tried again, and this time she toned down the emotions in her voice, approached her rep calmly, and asked the rep questions to help cocreate an action plan. Questions are a great way to draw out a quieter or more reserved individual. This approach was very effective.

3. Jessica is a customer service representative who had to deal with an irate customer. The customer was beyond fire-engine red. He was acting like there was a five-alarm fire, and you could almost see the smoke coming out of his ears. Jessica was uncomfortable, but she knew that she had to deal with his concerns. She figured that the best way to help him calm down was for her to be very calm because that was what she saw all the other customer service representatives doing. "Sir," she said in a slow and soothing voice, "this is no problem at all; it happens all the time. I know that we can satisfy your needs." "Satisfy my needs?!" he bellowed back as if fuel had been added to the fire. Jessica was correct in her need to remain calm, but she took it too far and didn't mirror back any of his energy. He felt patronized and thought that she wasn't taking his problem seriously, and as a result he escalated his approach. If Jessica had added a bit of red to her approach, she'd have shown some energy and said, "Yes, this is very important, and we must get it taken care of right away." This would have responded to his five-alarm fire, not in a five-alarm way, but

in a strong enough manner to let him see that he would get immediate attention.

4. Vijay is the owner of a small technology business. He took the huge risk of leaving his corner office executive suite in favor of self-employment. When he was just getting going, he didn't want to lose any potential customers. As a result, he had a very large target market—essentially anyone who owns a computer, which is everyone. What he needed to do was to become, as Seth Godin says, a Purple Cow. He was lost in a sea of technology consultants and didn't stand out. Vijay needed to challenge himself to own a niche. A niche is composed of expertise plus credibility. Vijay needed to be clear about his expertise and build credibility (via testimonials, quotes in the media, and work samples).

Naked in the Boardroom

While it's tempting to be beige, doing so is hiding. When you stand out, on the other hand, you feel naked in front of all your peers, your colleagues, your bosses, your customers, and the world. Is this a risk you are willing to take? And are you ready to take it right now?

It's scary to put yourself out there. The more you believe in something, the harder it is to offer your ideas publicly because they truly are a part of you. The more you stand out, the more you will be opened up to critics. If you don't acknowledge this to yourself and plan how you will handle it, you may hold yourself back and avoid maximum exposure.

The only way to manage the risk that comes with exposure is to know that there will be critics and to be willing to accept their differing opinions. Instead of seeing criticism as negative (although it certainly feels negative), see it as evidence that you have done what you are meant to do. You've raised the benchmark for yourself, and your ideas are now highly visible. They can have a positive impact on dozens, hundreds, thousands, perhaps millions of people. As long as you've presented your ideas with integrity and the intent to benefit others, then you can feel great that you've put yourself out there.

Exceed or at Least Defy Expectations

One way to make yourself remarkable is by shocking people with how much value you deliver beyond their expectations. Being unexpected makes you memorable. Research on advertising has illustrated this point. For example, in one study, researchers analyzed top advertisements (as measured by winning or being finalists in ad competitions) and found that almost all (89 percent) of the ads fit into one of six templates and that most of the templates were about something unexpected. If it works for advertising, it can work for you, too. And that leads us to the idea of branding.

The best way to take control of how you are seen by others is to create a brand for yourself. Whether you own your own business or work for someone else, a brand helps you stand out, win a promotion, get more business, and achieve the reputation you want. A brand makes you more memorable and marketable. Catherine Kaputa, author of *U R a Brand*, says,

> *Self branding is about making the most of what you've got. It's about daring to put forth a different idea. It's about responding to changes in the marketplace.*
>
> *Many of us keep doing the same things long after they're not working anymore. Self-branding is about playing an active role in your career and life and learning how to position and market yourself to maximum advantage.*
>
> *After all, it's a myth to think that you'll be rewarded solely on the basis of your hard work. And if you don't brand yourself, someone else will. Chances are that their brand description won't be quite what you have in mind.*

Self-branding is all about differentiating yourself, being visible, and showing the specific value that you offer. You cannot be humble when creating your brand because if you are, you won't stand out enough, but you do need to remember the idea of niche that I mentioned earlier—you want your brand to be based on your true expertise, credibility, and relevance for a particular group of people. Also realize that you may have several different brands, just as you wear different hats in your work and your personal life, but that they work best when they are all connected.

I recently served as a communications coach for a hit show on MTV called *MADE*, where I coached a 17-year-old to change the way she came across. While my typical style is highly encouraging, energetic, and friendly, I had to modify it for this show. To make her take me and the work she needed to do seriously, I had to be more stern, calm, and direct with her.

In statistics, there's something called a confidence interval, which is an estimate of how reliably something falls within certain parameters. If you have a huge confidence interval around your estimate, the estimate will probably be less reliable. Let's say you have an estimate of 5, but your confidence interval begins at 1 and goes to 10. This means that 5 is not a very accurate estimate. If your interval were smaller, you could feel more confident that your estimate was accurate. You don't need to get this statistically, but I like to apply the concept of confidence intervals to your self-branding and standing-out strategy. Within a certain range, you are seen as genuine, and you promote your brand. If you stray too far from this range, you lose the power of your brand, and you can be seen as a jack of all trades or as indecisive or, at worst, inauthentic. If you keep your brand somewhat narrow, it will be more reliable and memorable, and you will be more confident.

Your SWOT Analysis

You may be familiar with the SWOT analysis used in marketing—strengths, weaknesses, opportunities, and threats—but have you conducted a SWOT analysis on yourself? Have you assessed your internal strengths and weaknesses and determined the marketplace opportunities and threats? You want to stand out in your areas of strength as they relate to business opportunities. You can't successfully be a star in everything, but when you conduct a SWOT analysis, you see where you should shine.

Branding and Color

We've been using the metaphor of color, and color is one component of a brand. When you think of a brand, you think of things like Coca-Cola (red), ING (orange), and Best Buy (blue and yellow). For example, I put a good deal of thought into the colors for my company, Performance & Success Coaching. Our tagline is "When the Change You Need to Make Is Too

Important to Leave to Chance," and our unique selling proposition is that we help people do the tough things that lead to the best results, using a cutting-edge, research-based approach. I help people be courageous and face their fears, but I wanted to show them that we do so in a smart, strategic, and fun way, so I chose the professional colors of blue (trust and professionalism) and green (growth), but I made them contemporary and warm. Instead of a cool blue and a bluish green, I chose a brighter blue and a light celadon green that has a lot of yellow for warmth. How can you use color to brand yourself or your business? Here are a few ideas:

- Your clothing. Consider not just the colors you select, but also the pairings. Using complementary colors (blues with oranges, greens with reds, and yellows with purples) makes everything brighter and pop more. This can be great if you own a graphic design business but too much if you're in financial services, unless perhaps the warm color is used in small amounts as an accent color.
- Your accessories. Again, as with clothes, consider the way your accessories go together, not just their colors. A overly matching look can indicate that you play it safe, while having nothing matching can say that you're disorganized.
- Your car exterior and interior.
- Your hair. Consider its style as well as its color.
- Your logo and business cards.
- Your Web site.
- Your office decorations.
- Your keep-in-touch stationery, cards, and other such documents.

BONUS
ONLINE MATERIAL

As you probably know, every color evokes a different mood. You can get an article on color theory written by Angela Nielsen, creative director of the award-winning Web design company One Lily Web Solutions, here: www.pascoaching.com/colors.htm.

Be an Antileader

Kaputa points out that as humans, we have a soft spot for underdogs. Sometimes taking an antileader approach reveals you to be a rebel, an innovator, and an antiestablishment symbol. In companies, this is a risky approach, but you can apply some elements of it and pass on others. For entrepreneurs, an antileader model can be enormously successful. Think of rebel entrepreneurs such as Richard Branson.

Kaputa states that while the characteristics of leaders include being big, inflexible, and unresponsive, the characteristics of antileaders include being small and nimble, flexible, and responsive. Many small business owners fear being seen as "the little guy," so they go to great lengths to appear larger. Remember that the sixth step in the GROWTH model is harnessing your natural strengths rather than over-compensating for your weaknesses. You could, therefore, use your small size, new and cutting-edge status, and responsiveness to customers as your unique selling proposition rather than trying to be something you're not.

Profile of an Antileader

Sir Richard Branson, founder and chairman of Virgin Group Companies, exemplifies living and working on the edge of your comfort zone and being an antileader. By following his instincts, he built a net worth of nearly $300 million by the time he was 35, owns two tropical islands, and, by his account, loves the challenge and joy that comes from doing business. No doubt Sir Richard had his share of fears along the way, but he converted them into inspiring energy to accomplish everything he wanted. He is a master of creating an emotionally based brand. The products in his brand don't go together, but this doesn't matter at all because the strong brand image stands out.

Despite having dyslexia and being challenged with reading and writing, he began a magazine called *Student* when he was 15 and left school at 16 to pursue work at the magazine full time. As a teenager, he interviewed people like John Lennon and Mick Jagger. Sir Richard founded

Virgin when he was just 20. Virgin began as a mail-order company, but right after he established it, there was a six-month postal strike in Britain. He had to think fast, and he opened the first Virgin Records store to take care of the distribution problems that the strike presented. He continued to grow Virgin, and 20 years later he sold his music company for close to $1 billion.

In *Screw It, Let's Do It,* Sir Richard Branson tells stories of death-defying feats in which he set new records for time spent in a boat and a hot-air balloon, but he points out that you don't need to do such dramatic things to live by the lesson that if you want to do something, you should prepare well, help others, never give up, and just do it. He says, "Whatever your goal is, you will never succeed unless you let go of your fears and fly" (p. 11). Sir Richard also lives by the goal of challenging himself. He seeks to do the best he can at work and to find adventure. His first challenge came at the age of four. His family was on vacation at the shore, and he longed to swim in the sea but didn't know how. His Auntie Joyce bet him 10 shillings that he couldn't learn to swim. He took the challenge, and he tried and tried despite the cold water and rough waves. He didn't learn to swim. On their way home from the vacation, he was disappointed that he hadn't learned to swim. He gazed out the window, and suddenly he noticed a stream. "Stop the car!" he hollered, and he ran into the river. His family cheered him on from the bank. After going under and choking on water, he found himself swimming around in a circle. He collected his 10 shillings and a powerful lesson about believing in yourself and not giving up.

In the foreword to *The Rebel Rules* by Chip Conley, Sir Richard Branson says,

> *For the longest time I felt like an oxymoron, a rebel business-man. I was a black sheep among sacred white cows. But during the past decade I haven't felt so lonely … companies are actively recruiting rebels into their ranks to initiate innovation and change…. My vision has never been rigid. It's constantly changing, just like the company. Visionless companies are dead organisms. Yet, companies like Virgin are constantly mutating,*

organically synthesizing new ideas that help build the brand in the heart and mind of our customers. Virgin enjoys being the underdog. Our goal is to be the consumer's champion, finding stodgy industries like air and train transport, financial services, and cola, and shaking them up. As someone once said, vision is about seeing the invisible. I think it's also about imagining the unimaginable.

You may not be quite as rebellious and adventure seeking as Sir Richard Branson, but there are some great lessons to be learned from his mindset and his approach to business.

Confident Leader Action Steps for Showing Your Brilliance by Standing Out

- *Step 1: Get Your Vision and Intention—how do you want to stand out?* Ask yourself, "What one thing, if I stood out in it, would dramatically boost my career or my business results?" Get a clear image of how it would look when you stand out in this area.
- *Step 2: Realize Your Commitment—are you willing to risk feeling naked for the world to see right now?* If you really were going to be naked for the world to see, you might want some time to cut sugar out of your diet or jump on a treadmill. Likewise, consider the optimal timing for putting yourself out there. You want to find the right balance between presenting your best work and being perfectionistic and obsessive.
- *Step 3: Organize Your Team—who can help you stand out in the best way?* Compile a team of mentors, advisors, and coaches (who will give you accurate feedback and ongoing guidance), supporters (who are fans of what you do and will share it with

others), and administrators (who will do the behind-the-scenes work to make you shine). Also, realize that there will be people who resist your standing out, so be prepared to deal with them with empathy and patience.

- *Step 4: Win with the Right Decisions—when you want to hide, put yourself out there even more.* The critical decision will be what to do when you first put yourself out there and have that moment of terror. If you've followed Steps 1 through 3, you are ready, so you need to decide to persevere. My rule of thumb is to hold on at least until you are feeling calmer, because you don't want your decision to be based on fear.
- *Step 5: Turn Anxiety into Optimal Energy—interpret discomfort as growth.* Remember that the only difference between energy and anxiety is your interpretation. If you tell yourself, "This is fabulous; I'm really pushing myself beyond my limits," you will feel in control and energized. Also use the feedback that you get when you stand out as a powerful indicator of further growth opportunities.
- *Step 6: Harness Your Strengths and Release Control—use your differences to your advantage.* Remember how Richard Branson and others have used the underdog principle to their benefit. Consider how your differences are actually your greatest strengths and promote them rather than hide them.

Purple Cows

Imagine that you are driving in the country, looking at field after field of black-and-white cows. Sometimes there's a brown cow. Sometimes there's a baby cow. But overall, the cows all look the same. Then you see a purple cow. Talk about standing out! In the expert interview that follows, you'll read a few thoughts on standing out by Seth Godin, the author of *Purple Cow.*

Seth Godin

Seth Godin is a bestselling author, an entrepreneur, and an agent of change. His most recent titles include *The Dip* and *Meatball Sundae*. *Permission Marketing* was a *Fortune* Best Business Book, *BusinessWeek* bestseller, and *New York Times* business book bestseller. *Purple Cow*, a *New York Times* and *Wall Street Journal* bestseller, is about how companies can transform themselves by becoming remarkable. Seth was chosen as one of 21 Speakers for the Next Century by Successful Meetings. The founder and CEO of the direct-marketing company Yoyodyne, which Yahoo! acquired in 1998, he holds an MBA from Stanford and was called "the Ultimate Entrepreneur for the Information Age" by *BusinessWeek*. Learn more at www.sethgodin.com.

You are a perfect example of being a Purple Cow because you boldly put your ideas out there. Does this put you outside your comfort zone, and why do you do it?

I try to get outside of my comfort zone at least once a day! It turns out that it's not fatal, as previously reported.

Why is it uncomfortable but important to give up interruption advertising?

Interruption marketing keeps getting more expensive at the same time it gets less effective. That's because consumers have more choices, and the few who are left watching unanticipated, impersonal, irrelevant commercials are the people who are least likely to buy what you have to sell.

In your book *The Dip*, you discuss the importance of strategic quitting. Why do you think that people resist quitting even when they should?

Quitting is scary, because it requires you to acknowledge the end of one road and the beginning of another. Quitting means committing to something new. You know it's time to quit when you're on a dead end ... when the future promises more of the same, not a chance for a breakthrough.

To be a Purple Cow, you've really got to put yourself out there. To succeed in today's business climate, why is it essential to be remarkable?
Because safe is riskier. Safe guarantees mediocrity and ultimately failure. It's better to embrace the discomfort now and enjoy the benefits tomorrow.

You've learned not only that you need to put yourself out there if you want to be exceptional but also how to do so by self-branding, by exceeding expectations, and perhaps even by being an antileader. You've almost completed the journey toward becoming a Confident Leader, but first I'd like to provide you with tools for something that puts most people far outside their comfort zones: dealing with conflict and difficult people.

15

Handle Conflict and Difficult Situations with Ease

"I Want to Improve My Skills in Managing Conflict and Dealing with Difficult People"

As CONFIDENT LEADERS, we need to manage conflict, hold high-stakes conversations with decision makers, present our ideas to people who may shoot them down, and deal with difficult people. While challenging, these skills are crucial to our growth.

Navigating Conflict and Tension

For many people, conflict is extremely uncomfortable. Simply being around conflict can be upsetting and disruptive, and needing to manage conflict is even more difficult. The way most people handle their dissatisfaction, frustration, or fears about others is the opposite of what works. Remember how upset Joe's wife was about how much Joe worked? He and his wife handled the tension in the best way that they knew. She criticized him for giving priority to his work and told him how stressful it was for her to have to do everything alone. He got defensive and said that he needed to work that much to support the lifestyle that they had created. As they went back and forth like this, they both became more attached to their original views. As one pushed for change, the other resisted and dug his or her feet in. Little did they know that they were acting out a classic relationship pattern.

The Push-Pull Relationship Dynamic

This pattern has been studied by family and couples researchers, and they have found that it's at the heart of many interpersonal conflicts. While it's been studied primarily in couples, the same pattern holds true in business relationships: peer to peer, manager to direct report, salesperson to customer, or any other business interaction. The idea is congruent with Newton's third law, "For every action, there is an equal and opposite reaction." The following figure shows how the cycle works, with an example of a boss and a direct report.

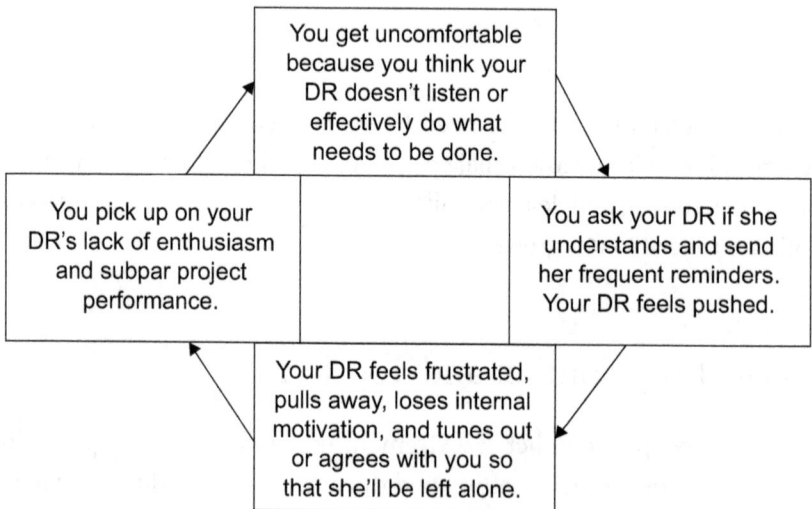

	You get uncomfortable because you think your DR doesn't listen or effectively do what needs to be done.
You pick up on your DR's lack of enthusiasm and subpar project performance.	You ask your DR if she understands and send her frequent reminders. Your DR feels pushed.
	Your DR feels frustrated, pulls away, loses internal motivation, and tunes out or agrees with you so that she'll be left alone.

DR = Direct Report or Supervisee

The real problem occurs not when you start to feel uncomfortable, because discomfort is fine and informative, but rather when you attempt to act on your discomfort. Remember, *it isn't the discomfort that's the problem; it's how you respond to it.*

Picture these scenarios:

- You interview a job applicant who really wants the position and has a wonderful interview. Although you're impressed with her, you need to interview other applicants. When this applicant doesn't hear back from you right away, she leaves messages for you and e-mails everyone she met during the interview. You and your team find her too pushy and back away from her as a top choice.
- You're concerned that one of your direct reports is not staying on top of all of his projects. You monitor his progress and try to hold him accountable, but he feels infantilized and loses his internal motivation for the project.
- You're a sales manager, and one of your representatives generally makes his numbers but never goes much over plan. Together you go to a meeting with a prospect, and you observe your rep's communication. He does more talking than listening and subtly gives the impression that the prospect would be stupid not to buy the product. The prospect feels pushed and says that she'll follow up. She does not, and when your sales representative contacts her, she avoids his calls.

There is an optimal level of tension that is needed. If the job applicant did not express interest or follow up, she would not be perceived as being enthusiastic about the job. If, as a manager, you did not hold your direct report accountable, you would not be an effective manager. And if the salesperson did not provide key information, the prospect would not be able to decide whether she wanted to purchase the product.

A little push is helpful, but once you go beyond the right level, you will get resistance and avoidance. It's like lifting weights at the gym — with too little tension on the machine, you won't improve in your lifting abilities. With too much, however, the weights won't move, and you'll be stuck. Or you'll try to lift weights that are too heavy and end up hurting yourself. As a Confident Leader, you strike the right balance in the tension you create for your employees. They have the optimal levels of anxiety, energy, and drive to perform, but they do not feel pushed.

Confident Leader Action Steps for Reducing Tension

- *Step 1: Get Your Vision and Intention—what do you want?* Do you want effortless communication? More motivation or follow-through from your staff? More purchases from your customers? Less resistance from others?
- *Step 2: Realize Your Commitment—figure out where you're pushing.* Take a week and observe how people behave when they interact with you. Do you sense resistance? Do you feel frustration? Do you have to constantly stay on top of people and follow up? Are you taking up all the slack in your team and working harder than the others? If you notice any of these types of things, then ask yourself how ready you are to address them.
- *Step 3: Organize Your Support—put everyone on the same team working toward the same thing.* Research has shown that one of the best things for resolving conflict is a common goal. When you notice yourself or others squabbling about details and specifics, get people aligned with a vision to help them reach the common goal.
- *Step 4: Win with the Right Decisions—decide to change your approach.* If you're the one doing the pushing, commit to one month in which you are less demanding and less haranguing. See what happens at the end of that time. If you're the one being pushed, decide if it's worth it to change, and recognize that people may not like your changes because they're used to taking advantage of your work ethic. If you do all the work, others don't have to. But if you stop doing all the work, others will need to step up.
- *Step 5: Turn Anxiety into Optimal Energy—observe the different energy levels when you stop pushing.* When you push and someone else resists (or vice versa), the energy goes to maintaining equilibrium. This is Newton's third law. This is why people like Joe feel that they are pushing a boulder up a mountain (with gravity pushing it in the opposite direction).

When you stop pushing, you and others are heading in the same direction, and everyone will notice significant increases in energy.

- *Step 6: Harness Your Strengths and Release Control—you will feel out of control at first, and that is great!* The approach-avoidance or push-pull relationship dynamic develops to help you feel more in control. When you commit to ending the cycle, you will initially feel off guard and out of control. If you feel like this, congratulate yourself, because you're making progress. Be careful not to revert to your old ways, because if you do, you'll continue to feel the discomfort, but it will no longer be helpful to you.

Your Business Relationships as Mirrors

It's easy to point the finger at someone else and say that it's that person's problem, and it's hard to accept responsibility and force yourself to change. If you find yourself constantly doubting what someone else is saying, being irritated by that person's behaviors, or being frustrated, take your reaction as a sign that there is probably something that *you* need to work on. I call this the "mirror technique." When you have a negative reaction to someone, ask: how does your reaction reflect you more than it does him?

For example, if you find yourself getting frustrated when a team member doesn't get right back to you on a project, try saying, "What does my response show me about myself?" It shows that one of your areas for growth is impatience and urgency addiction. In these cases, the default thought process is to think that everything is important and should be done right away. Instead, step back and ask:

- "Is this really so important that it needs to be done right away?"
- "Did I communicate the sense of urgency?" and if so, "Do I always communicate a sense of urgency and have therefore created a boy-who-cried-wolf situation?"

- "What's most important in this situation—that this gets done right this second, or that I preserve the relationship with my assistant, who is overall phenomenal?"
- "How can I improve my patience and flexibility?"

Remember the push-pull relationship pattern. For example, in my case, my natural impatience can make my assistant less efficient. If I communicate a sense of urgency about nonurgent things, she is likely to think to herself, "Jeez, relax, it isn't that serious," and therefore not get right to it. If she responded to my sense of urgency by always getting right to it, her response would probably be out of fear. And if my goal was a positive long-term relationship, I would not reach this goal if she was always fearful.

The High-Stakes Situations

Kerry Patterson, Joseph Grenny, Ron McMillan, and Al Switzler, the authors of *Crucial Conversations*, define a crucial conversation as one in which opinions vary, the stakes are high, and emotions run strong. One of my clients was in charge of creating a marketing campaign for a new product. When the time came for him to discuss his strategy with his boss and their vice president, he was nervous. It was a crucial conversation because the vice president had an entirely different agenda. He was looking for ways to cut costs, whereas my client was about to present him with a fantastic marketing opportunity that would be very expensive. My client felt that if he didn't get the organizational support he needed, he would be forced to look at other job opportunities—the stakes were high. And, of course, my client's emotions were elevated because he was presenting something that had he worked extremely hard on, and he wanted a specific result.

My advice was to be prepared and to not attempt to control the situation. If his vice president had concerns, my client's role was *not* to overcome the objections. If he approached the conversation this way, he would get the push-pull dynamic. His vice president would feel pushed, and therefore would pull back. Instead, my client's goal was to meet the vice president where he was and collaboratively discuss the pros and cons. Remember that working through pros and cons moves you or someone else through the readiness for change stages that we discussed in Chapter 2.

In *Crucial Conversations*, the authors caution you not to get stuck in what they call the Sucker's Choice. This is a feeling that you need to choose between two unattractive options. My client's vice president could have gotten stuck in the Sucker's Choice of thinking, "Either I save money and we have no innovation, or I have to spend a great deal of money on this project at a time when I'm supposed to be cutting costs." When the stakes are high and adrenaline is pumping, you're prone to looking at things as black or white. The alternative is to look for the "and." "Is there a way to innovate and stay within budget?" "Is there a way to test out the new marketing plan on a small scale before investing the big bucks?"

When I see my clients get stuck in black-and-white thinking, I recommend that they make a list of all the gray areas. I'm not talking one or two possibilities, but every possibility—perhaps it's 5, 10, 20, or 50. When they do this, something remarkable happens—they begin to think differently.

Let's say that you're a business owner and you have a high-stakes conversation with an investor. You'll be tempted to think in black and white: either he'll love my idea and provide capital, or he won't. See how much pressure this puts on you and your presentation? If you write a list of every other alternative, you'll see that this initial meeting is just that— an opening. It may also help you to reformulate your goals. If your initial goal is to get the investor to fund your business, you may be nervous for a reason: it's too large a goal for a first meeting. If you reframe your goal as securing a follow-up meeting to present your analysis in greater depth, you'll feel differently.

I help my business owner clients to set up joint venture partnerships. One thing that they routinely dread is making the initial calls to people. After working with many clients on this issue, it became clear to me that they dreaded this for a reason: they had the wrong goals. They were putting so much pressure on themselves to sell their businesses that of course the calls were intimidating and unsuccessful. Marketing is a cycle, not a one-time thing, so I helped my clients reframe their calls to action to be much smaller, such as agreements to receive white papers by e-mail, follow-up phone calls, or lunch meetings. When my clients took this pressure off themselves, they took the pressure off the calls and their prospective business partners, and they achieved much better results.

Performance Situations

One of the greatest challenges many people face is performance situations, such as public speaking. We fear negative evaluation, public mortification, and career devastation. The fear of public speaking ranks higher than the fear of death. This is why the comic Jerry Seinfeld is quoted as saying, "If you were at a funeral, you'd rather be the one in the coffin than the one giving the eulogy." This topic is covered in detail in *The Confident Speaker*, which I coauthored with Harrison Monarth, so I won't go into great detail here except to say that the GROWTH model works very well for the fear of public speaking.

You first get your vision of what you want. Why is it important to you to be a confident speaker? (Step 1: Get Your Vision and Intention.) Then you determine how ready you are to begin working on this goal today. If you have a speaking engagement booked, but it isn't for eight months, you may not be motivated to work on this yet. If you rarely need to present in your job, your motivation may be low. (Step 2: Realize Your Commitment.) Then ask yourself whom you know and what resources you need if you are to make the change. You may look up Toastmasters groups, sign up for a course, ask friends to listen to your speech and give you feedback, and so on. (Step 3: Organize Your Support.) Then make the right decisions. If you're uncomfortable about making a presentation, is it because you aren't prepared? Do you know the needs of your audience and the true objective of your talk? Find out if there's a reason for your discomfort. (Step 4: Win with the Right Decisions.) Next, use your anxiety to achieve optimal energy by using your focus of attention. When you focus on your audience rather than on yourself, you feel less self-conscious, and your anxiety turns into optimal energy. (Step 5: Turn Anxiety into Optimal Energy.) Finally, be sure that you aren't using crutches and overcompensating behaviors that can mask your talent as a speaker and make you look like you're trying too hard. (Step 6: Harness Your Strengths and Release Control.)

What about Those People You Can't Stand?

What's more difficult than dealing with people you can't stand? I can't think of much. Not only is it difficult, but it's not much fun. The first step is to figure out what type of people you can't stand. We all do things that are annoying at times and that irritate others, but certain people are irritated by certain things. When you know yourself and know what kinds of behaviors are like nails on a chalkboard to you, you can handle them proactively.

The first and most important step is to understand the person you can't stand. The best way to do this is to figure out what that person's intention is. Rick Brinkman and Rick Kirschner, the authors of *Dealing with People You Can't Stand,* say that people's motives fall into four categories: getting it done, getting it done right, getting along, and getting appreciation. They provide their insight on dealing with people you can't stand in the expert interview sidebar.

Brinkman and Kirschner recommend listening to the person's communication style to discover his or her primary motivator. For example, someone who is motivated by getting it done is likely to be direct, concise, and quick in her speech pattern. Such people may come across as controlling. The person who wants to get it done right will back up his idea with examples and facts and may be more tentative or perfectionistic. An indirect and considerate communication style would be a getting along focus and appears to look for approval. And a flamboyant or elaborate communication style indicates the intent of getting appreciation and can be attention-seeking. Once you understand the other person's intent and communication style, you can mirror it and align yourself with that person rather than battle her. Once the two of you are aligned, you can redirect the conversation to reduce conflict and disagreements and improve results.

Dr. Rick Brinkman

Dr. Rick Brinkman is the coauthor of the book *Dealing with People You Can't Stand: How to Bring Out the Best in People at Their Worst*, which is an international bestseller that has been translated into 17 languages. Through his company, Rick Brinkman Productions, Inc. (www.rickbrinkman.com), he provides keynote speeches and training for corporations and associations on Conscious Communication for leadership, teamwork, and service. He is frequently in the media as a communication expert and has been featured on CNN and in the *Wall Street Journal*, the *New York Times*, and *O, the Oprah Magazine*.

In your book, you and Dr. Kirschner describe the top 10 most unwanted types of people. Are there any that stand out as provoking discomfort or anxiety in others?
Difficulty is in the eye of the beholder. If you don't know how to handle the behavior, it will be challenging for you. For others, the same behavior that gives you problems wouldn't even show up as a blip on their radar. I remember doing a seminar for a company, and out of 75 people, 74 people were there to learn how to deal with one "tank" vice president. However, the 75th one stood up and said, "I don't see what the problem is that you people have with him. He's a no-brainer to deal with." She was wired differently; she had the right attitude, and she knew the right things to do to deal with this person's behavior, so she didn't perceive him as difficult.

All of us already have the attitudes and skills to handle some behaviors, and therefore we don't find them difficult to deal with. But with other behaviors, we're missing the correct attitude and skills, so those behaviors will make us crazy. That's where I come in—to train people on what to do to successfully transform difficult behaviors.

Are there any behaviors that are more difficult to deal with than others?
In general, I find that people who are aggressive, get-it-done types are driven crazy by whining and wishy-washy behaviors. That's because

neither of those behaviors is getting things done. Whiners sit and wallow, and wishy-washy people are likely to make commitments but not keep them. On the other hand, people who are friendly and want to play nice are intimidated by an aggressive type of behavior. And people who are more expressive or emotional are driven crazy by nothing people who are quiet and withdrawn, and vice versa.

It's tempting to avoid those whom we can't stand. When do you need to deal with them?
Avoidance can be a valid strategy. You have to ask yourself if the job or the relationship is worth the energy needed to deal with this person. If it's not, then leave or get him to leave. But sometimes you may not have the choice of leaving. Maybe you don't want to leave your job. Perhaps this person is a relative and you are stuck with her. In that case, you have to change your attitude toward this person, and the first step is to consider what's in it for you if you learn how to successfully deal with him. When you learn how to handle a difficult behavior, you're doing yourself a favor not only in the current situation, but also in all the future times that you will face this behavior. For someone in a leadership position, knowing how to deal with challenging people is a must-have skill. That's because leaders will have all kinds of people on their teams over the course of their careers. The leader's job is to bring out the best in others and orchestrate a successful working environment. You can't have a difficult behavior destroying the morale or productivity the team.

What are some of the skills that turn conflict into cooperation?
One is listening. Many times we think that we're listening, but we're not really. Just because sound is coming into your ears doesn't mean that you really hear it. You could be thinking about what you are going to say. Or even if you are listening, the assumption that you know what the other person really means by her words can lead you astray. I would suggest that you assume you don't know and ask questions to find out more. Sometimes people don't communicate clearly, and you need to help them get out what they really are trying to say. We've all had the experience of someone telling us something

and we wonder, "Why is he saying that?" When that happens, what you are missing is the person's *intent*. What is the purpose behind his communication? A good listener is paying attention like a detective, trying to figure out what the other person is really trying to say. And before we leave the subject of listening, here's an important sign to watch for: people repeating themselves. That's a sign that the speaker doesn't feel heard. When you hear a repetition, treat it as a signal to give the person feedback on what you heard and understand.

Another critical skill is really an attitude. I suggest that you think of the difficult person as a workout machine at the gym. This will help you build your communication muscles. This person is an opportunity to figure out what works with that type of behavior. If you don't do this, you'll continually be plagued by that behavior in the future. I find a great question to ask oneself is, "What is the last thing I want to do right now?" Then whatever occurs to you, just do it. It's amazing how often this can transform the situation. For example, if someone's being a know-it-all, the last thing you want to do is validate her point of view, but if you do, she will shut up and listen to you. Think about it. Because it's the last thing you want to do, of course it's the thing you have not done, and that's why you have a problem with this person or this type of behavior.

Also keep in mind that not everyone responds the way you do. For example, when being upset, one person may need to talk about the problem immediately, while another person really needs time to think. Very naturally, each of these people will do unto the other as he would like the other to do unto him. The problem is that if the person who needs time to think is upset, he will withdraw, but his friend who needs to talk about upsets will try to support him by talking to bring him out. Although the friend will have the best of intentions, she will actually annoy her friend and disrupt his process for dealing with being upset. By learning the style and needs of those around you and being flexible, you can supply what they really need and fulfill your positive intentions. This type of mismatch is a common cause of conflict that really doesn't need to be there.

What are some of the ways in which technology creates interpersonal challenges?

There are basically three forms of communication: face to face, phone, and written. Each one brings something and loses something. For example, on the phone, you lose the visual cues, but you have more control over how you sound. If you're getting stressed while you're on the phone, put yourself into a relaxed position. Put your legs up, use the mute button, and take a deep breath.

In written communication, you have time on your side. I've been teaching communication since the 1980s, and as e-mail took hold in the 1990s, all of a sudden written conflicts were happening, even though people had been writing to each other for hundreds of years. Time used to be built into the system. With a typewriter, you had to take the time to write a response. What makes things even more tricky with e-mail is that we hallucinate a tone of voice with e-mail that is based on *our* stress level, blood sugar, and so on. In the past, when we had more time, we'd arrive at other points in our blood sugar curve, and we'd reread and edit.

In the electronic age, it's too easy to throw away the time advantage. People are dealing with high volumes of e-mail, so we get into get-it-done mode. We've all had the experience of rereading an e-mail 24 hours later and seeing a sentence that we hadn't seen before. That's because the e-mail elves come in at night. So we need to recognize when to bail on e-mail and what it's good for.

There are three things that suggest that it would be a good idea to go interactive (talk in person or by phone rather than through e-mail). The first is if you suspect emotional content. The second is if you write something, and as you reread it, you are concerned about how the person will take it. The third is if you have to gather information; if you have to ask more than one yes or no question, then go interactive to make sure you're on the same page. On the other hand, there are times when it's better to go with e-mail, such as when you need something documented, or you're intimidated and wouldn't say your true feelings face to face, or you need to make the same communication to multiple people and logistics prevent you from getting together face to face or on the phone—with teams scattered across the globe, face-to-face interaction can be impossible.

One of the most difficult things to do is to recognize when you are the person that people can't stand. What are some signs that would show you that this is the case?
If you're having a problem with someone, there's a good chance that that person is having a problem with you—two sides of the same coin. Put yourself in the other person's shoes and consider what he may be feeling. Then give voice to it. For example, with a teenager, you can say, "It must be hard to have a parent nagging you." You'll get his attention real fast. Another obvious clue that you may be difficult is if someone says that you're being difficult! Keep in mind that a behavior that is perfectly comfortable for you may be a behavior that drives the other person crazy. If you're comfortable being quiet and thinking about things, whereas the person you are with is more expressive and needs communication, your quiet may be driving her crazy. Difficulty is in the eye of the beholder. If someone tells you that you're difficult, don't waste time being defensive. Just utilize this as feedback and as an opportunity to grow. Ultimately, the more flexible you can be in your behavior, the greater your success at handling the difficult behaviors of others. In this way, you become an agent of communication change and bring out the best in those around you.

Increase your awareness of the push-pull relationship dynamic and practice the tension-reduction techniques, and you'll master the challenge of dealing with difficult situations and people. In the final chapter, we'll discuss one of the most important roles of a Confident Leader: creating meaningful innovation and change.

16

Master the Challenge of Championing Change

"I Want to Innovate, Create Powerful Change, and Make a Real Difference"

ALEKSANDR SOLZHENITSYN SAID, "If you want to change the world, who do you begin with, yourself or others?" You've been focused on creating change by changing yourself. And in this final chapter, we'll look at one of the most uncomfortable and powerful things you can do: innovate and lead widespread change. Nothing creates resistance more than change. Of course, change is both inevitable and necessary, so as a Confident Leader, you must know how to not only manage change but champion it. When you help others to navigate their own fears about change and take steps outside their own comfort zones, you'll see monumental improvements occur in your organization.

Building Momentum for Change

As you now know, the best way to start doing something that is difficult is to find the right pace. Sometimes you want to encourage small steps because they feel manageable, although you don't want to go so slowly that you lose momentum and get stuck. Other times, the first step is in an entirely new direction, and it requires a giant leap. Whether the movement is in small steps or giant leaps, explain the process to the people who are making the changes or the ones who are indirectly affected by the changes you're making. Anxiety increases in the face of uncertainty, so explain as much as you can about the road ahead. At times you won't know what lies ahead, so you can simply discuss the first guidepost as the goal. Turn the uncertainty and anxiety into energy by focusing on the excitement of the journey and the potential results.

When you present an innovative concept to others, help them to move out of their comfort zones, but not so far out that they resist the change initiative. The first thought that will come to most people's minds is, "Will this create more work for me?" Build motivation and address this concern with two steps.

1. *Paint an inspiring picture.* If you're going to ask people (or yourself) to do something difficult (make a change), it's important that they first answer the question, "Why the heck would I want to do that?" when it's hard for them to imagine what "that" would even look like. A picture speaks a thousand words, so answer this question by explaining what the end result will be. Use concrete descriptions, stories, emotions, and the five senses to bring your image to life. Keep this concise so that you don't overwhelm yourself or others.

2. *Start at square one.* Imagine that you were learning how to play Monopoly and your instructor said, "You get to be one of the characters like a shoe, and you roll the die and move around the board, and you earn money and build hotels, and you might have to go to jail, but you can get out …" You'd probably think, "I don't have the time or energy for all this." And this is just a board game — not a nerve-wracking change! If, however, your instructor gave you one sentence about how the game works and then said, "Starting is simple; just roll the die and the box you land on will determine the next step," you'd be intrigued and think, "I can do that!"

Recall the principle of habituation, or getting used to our discomfort if we remain in it. Walk people from step to step, giving them some time to habituate to each step. The challenge comes when we want to jump ahead or when we're being pressured by others to rush the process. I frequently come across this challenge as a business coach—I'll hear my client's vision for change, and I'll want to serve as a catalyst and help her. My natural inclination is to tell her all the great things that she can do, but if I launched into everything, she would think, "I don't have time (or money or energy) for all of this." We need to share our enthusiasm but rein it in so that people can experience it for themselves rather than feeling that it is being thrust upon them. Likewise, if we're being pressured by others to make a change all at once, we need to hold our ground and educate them about why one thing must happen before the other and why the pace we've chosen makes sense.

Exploiting Change Rather Than Starting It

In *Innovation and Entrepreneurship,* management guru Peter Drucker explains that entrepreneurs search for change. They see change as a great thing, but they usually are not the ones to start it. Instead, they find evidence of change and then exploit it as an opportunity. For example, an innovator notices a movement toward a new technology and then exploits the trend by taking the technology application to a new level. Whether you're an entrepreneur or you're entrepreneurially minded, this concept is helpful because it takes the pressure off of catalyzing change. To use a metaphor, in research on memory, there are two ways in which you can remember information; one is to freely recall it, and the other is to recognize it. Which do you think would be easier: to fill in the blank, or to spot the answer among choices? Recognition is typically easier. So as a change leader, you can fine-tune your radar for evidence of change to capitalize on, rather than think that you must come up with something from scratch.

Drucker points out that to innovate, you must create a resource. There is no such thing as a resource until it is made. Penicillin mold, for example, was seen as a pest because it killed bacteriologists' cultures until Dr. Alexander Fleming realized that it could kill unwanted bacteria and offer a cure for bacterial infections. So how do you recognize change and create resources? Here are several opportunities that Drucker recommends:

1. *A surprise or unexpected success, failure, or outside event.* Discover what you can learn from unexpected (or expected) failures. The question to ask yourself is, "Was the failure merely a mistake and I'll improve with practice, or is there something else causing it that can be capitalized on?"

2. *Incongruity between reality and what people assume it is.* For example, Frank Rumbauskas Jr., author of the *New York Times* bestselling book *Never Cold Call Again,* realized that cold calling was the number one sales tool but was not as effective as other approaches, such as giving away valuable information and educating prospects so that they come to you rather than you cold-calling them.

3. *A process need.* This is the idea that "necessity is the mother of invention." The question to ask yourself, your clients or customers, your employees, or other stakeholders is, "What isn't working or is missing from how it is currently done?"

4. *Changes in the industry or marketplace.* Look for changes in the structure of your industry and those of your customers and business partners.

5. *Changes in demographics, perception, and knowledge (both scientific and nonscientific).* When you observe or anticipate these changes, you can consider what opportunities and needs will emerge that you can fill.

Is Innovation Idealistic?

You must think beyond "realism" to lead a change initiative. Pessimists like to say that they are "realists," which can be helpful at times, but can also be limiting. Social reformers, on the other hand, focus on mobilizing the masses for change and must have some level of optimism and idealism to believe that they can make change happen. Earlier in the book, we discussed self-efficacy, or believing that you can bring about change and being resilient in the face of failure. That is a key to being an innovator or a social reformer. Innovations often entail a good deal of trial and error, failure, skepticism and criticism, and effort. The leading authority on self-efficacy, Albert Bandura, says, "It is, therefore, not surprising that one rarely finds realists in the ranks of innovators and great achievers." Be careful that your realism isn't holding you back from your true potential. In the expert interview that follows, you'll hear how innovator Jen Groover used her belief in her idea to persevere in the face of skepticism and failure.

Expert Interview

Jen Groover

Jen Groover is the CEO and founder of Jen Groover Productions and the innovator behind the internationally bestselling and award-winning Butler Bag handbag company. A Momentum Award winner and an entrepreneur expert for PBS's *Real Savvy Moms*, Jen was recently named a one-woman brand by *Success* magazine. Jen has appeared on CNBC, ABC, CBS, PBS, and in *Success* magazine, and her products can be found everywhere, from *O, the Oprah Magazine* to the *Washington Post*. Jen's motto is, "What if and why not?" Learn more at www.jengroover.com.

When you got the idea for your innovative Butler Bag, what fears went through your mind?
There were many—the cost to launch, how to create a higher-grade leather handbag, how to penetrate a market that is so brand-demanded (many people buy handbags based on the brand name), how to show that fashion and function can go together (which many people had already attempted and had failed to do), and time to launch because the longer the delay, the greater chance that someone could create a knockoff.

How did you handle these concerns?
Basically, I listened a lot. My philosophy has always been that if everyone is doing one thing, I'll do the other thing. If you go the same

way as everyone else, you'll get the same results as everyone else. You won't get anything new. So I listened to hear what people were doing and analyzed the results they got, and I found ways to do something different. I also analyzed other industries and read success stories to give me more ideas.

In the accessories industry, you usually launch by going to a trade show. I was concerned that if I went to the trade show, I'd be sitting there next to Coach or Marc Jacobs, and they'd have big, beautiful booths. My booth would pale in comparison. And I'd be opening up my product to exposure and knockoffs.

So I took a totally different approach and didn't go to a trade show. Instead, I invested in a PR firm that specializes in strategy. We discovered that telling my story was the best way to get people interested. We even include a tag with the story on the bags. Basically what happened is that I looked at how my dishwasher organizes silverware and thought, "Hey, the way the silverware is organized is how I want my handbag to be!" People relate to a story, and people remember a story. Telling the story has been incredible in creating viral marketing and empowering the consumer to spread the message.

How has staying true to yourself helped you navigate business challenges?
I believe that it's so important to be true to who you are, your values, and your integrity because your credibility is everything—to your consumers, your employees, the media, and others in the industry who can open doors for you. It's funny; I've always done things that I think have depth and purpose, so I never really saw myself as being in the accessories industry, which can be shallow and cutthroat. I chose to do it differently and not get engaged with the superficial things, which can mean avoiding industry events.

Staying true to your vision and not getting off course is the key—that's when innovation happens. If someone says, "That doesn't work; we've tried it before," question it. Maybe that person hasn't tried it in the same way, or maybe it was a while ago and things have changed. Possibly, the world is different now from the way it was when your idea was tried before.

When people try to get you off course, that's your greatest challenge to prove yourself as a true pioneer and innovator. Engage your competitive spirit and focus on catalyzing change. I wake up every day knowing that I focus on change and innovation, and this makes me not fearful of being deterred. I invite the challenges, and I invite constructive criticism, which I listen to but don't get lost in. When things become difficult, there's a thrill for me because I know that I'll grow from it.

What limits innovative thinking?
A problem in the world of innovation is that people talk about it in terms of math and science. People think that they cannot innovate and lead change if they aren't strong in these areas. I'm not strong in math or science! And many girls are brought up to believe that they aren't either. Math and science are only a small part of innovation. Innovation is about integrative thinking and creativity (which most girls and women are excellent at). Innovators identify problems and have a unique ability to connect the dots to solve those problems. As a change catalyst, you must be a visionary, which takes conviction and courage. You can always hire the engineers, designers, and quantitative people to execute your ideas.

What are some of the top challenges to being a change leader and innovator?
There are internal and external struggles, but I believe the internal is more important. Once you're okay with being different and having people think that your ideas are strange, you develop the confidence and conviction to share these ideas anyway. I spent most of my life suppressing my ideas. People thought I was ADD, and I kept quiet. Once we get comfortable with who we are and how we're different, everything else gets easier. But remember that creating a change or movement isn't supposed to be easy. And sometimes you're gone by the time what you put out into the world is celebrated. I welcome the challenges, and use comments such as, "That's a bad idea" to make it a better idea.

What do you recommend as first steps for people who recognize the ability to innovate, either in their jobs or in their own businesses?

First, analyze why a change is needed. Is there an economic or an efficiency gain? Will you create a new industry?

Second, get clear on what the benefit is. People need to realize and understand the benefit of your idea. We're trained to qualify and quantify, so, when possible, focus on numbers and the bottom line. This isn't always possible, and if it isn't, stick to your guns and explain that there aren't data because this has never been done before.

Third, prepare yourself for a challenge. Recognize that people don't like change. If your idea doesn't work out, realize that your failures are your opportunities to learn. People are afraid of signing on for change because they think that if they do and it doesn't work out, they'll lose their jobs. At my company, there is no failure because change is our goal. Be sure that your environment encourages creativity and innovation. If you're in a corporate culture that's full of red tape and roadblocks, and the culture is to stay the same (rather than change), then I suggest a different environment. There's always another way.

What are some everyday ways for us all to innovate?

I believe the most important thing that we can do each day as businesspeople, parents, and community members is to teach kids and others that failure is an opportunity to grow. Anytime you attempt something, you will learn something. People are so afraid to fail that they don't try anything. Sharing an attitude of, "Let's try it and see what happens, and if it doesn't work, we'll keep going," is the best thing you can do. When schools and parents eliminate the failure-versus-success type of thinking and replace it with the mentality of growth, they bring about great change and make the world a better place.

How necessary is discomfort for innovation?

Completely necessary. You must be awkward, be uncomfortable, and have growing pains if you are to innovate. I invite all of these things, because I know that if I'm comfortable and content, I'll never improve. My mom used to say something to me that at the time I didn't get, but that is now the most important rule I live by and share: "If you are not uncomfortable today, you did not grow and change today."

Joe's Revelation and Authenticity Revolution

Throughout the book, we've been focusing on Joe's transformation to a Confident Leader. When Joe realized how much time and energy he was wasting by playing things safe, he was astounded. He was trying so hard to look like the leader that he thought he should be that he wasn't doing much else. He wasn't using his true strengths and talents. He wasn't approaching the tough things he needed to do if he was to grow in his role, grow the company, and grow as a person. He figured that if he had this problem, others did too.

"I've decided to do something crazy!" Joe told me.

"I love it. What is it?" I responded.

"I've decided to institute a quarterly Confront Your Fears day."

"Whoa—what will that look like?" I was curious.

"Well, in our team meeting, each person will go around and say one thing that he is struggling with. He'll indicate whether it's something that he wants to address on his own and tell the team about next quarter or whether he wants to get someone to help him. Let's say that my marketing director says, 'I'm struggling with the technology necessary to do this new project.' If she wants help, someone else on the team will volunteer. Of course I'll participate, too. People will be recognized for their openness, for their eagerness to grow and build a more innovative company, and for helping each other out," Joe explained.

"Wow, people will be encouraged to be and improve upon who they really are. This will help them to feel more authentic and connected to your company, which can help you develop and retain your talent. They'll feel more at ease around you and may start to give you more accurate feedback, which will improve your self-awareness and development. This will be an intimidating proposition, so you'll need to model it and explain the purpose well, but you might just see some pretty remarkable results," I said.

It turns out that the best result was in Joe's being more of who he was, taking more risks, and putting himself out there. The more he did this, the more his team followed suit. Joe's work and home relationships were revolutionized, and he became the leader we knew he could be.

Action Is Everything

Many great inventors and change leaders say that good ideas are a dime a dozen. What really matters is how you act on the idea. Most people get stuck because their doubts and insecurities keep them from taking exceptional action.

Confident Leader Action Steps for Innovative Change

- *Step 1: Get Your Vision and Intention—what powerful change do you want?* Paint your picture of this change, and share it with others.
- *Step 2: Realize Your Commitment—what are the first steps?* Big changes sometimes begin small. What is the first thing you can do?
- *Step 3: Organize Your Team—assign roles.* Because change is scary and uncertain, make sure that people are crystal clear about what their roles are and how they can help.
- *Step 4: Win with the Right Decisions—pick your battles.* Begin with the battles that you're likely to win. Get into the winning mindset with these victories. At the same time, embrace any losses as victories by asking the question, "How can we use this new information?"
- *Step 5: Turn Anxiety into Optimal Energy—bring the fears to light.* Take the time to acknowledge your concerns and apprehensions as well as those of others. Often simply exposing them will be enough to keep them from getting in the way.

Recognize and reward all the efforts (regardless of result) and accomplishments along the way, and the results you want will multiply exponentially.

- *Step 6: Harness Your Strengths and Release Control—use your strengths in new ways each day.* And drop all crutches. Remember that you aren't really putting yourself out there as a change leader if you're holding on to all your old crutches.

Uncomfortable Action, Unbelievable Results

Take uncomfortable action in small ways and big ways each day, and you'll be on the road to accomplishing more than you ever thought possible. You're a Confident Leader. The people you bring along for the ride will also be surprised and delighted by the changes and the incredible rewards that this journey holds. It's bumpy and it's tough. It shakes you to the core at times, and it makes you question everything. You'll see: it's definitely worth it.

Endnotes

Chapter 1

9   *In fact, biological studies show that business leaders with a drive for power ...*
—D. C. McClelland, R. J. Davidson, C. Saron, and E. Floor, "The Need for Power, Brain Norepinephrine Turnover and Learning," *Biological Psychology* 10 (1980), 93–102.

10   *It's called the Yerkes-Dodson Law ...*
—R. M. Yerkes and J. D. Dodson, "The Relation of Strength of Stimulus to Rapidity of Habit-Formation," *Journal of Comparative Neurology and Psychology* 18 (1908), 459–482.

12   *In* Business Psychology in Practice, *Charles Mead and Rachel Robinson, consultants and authors of one of the chapters, say ...*
—Charles Mead and Rachel Robinson, "What Clients Want," in P. Grant (ed.), *Business Psychology in Practice* (Philadelphia: Whurr Publications, 2005), p. 11.

13   *In a seminal study, sixth graders solved word puzzles that were ranked either very easy ...*
—S. Harter, "Pleasure Derived from Challenge and the Effects of Receiving Grades on Children's Difficulty Level Choices," *Child Development* 49 (1978), 788–799.

14   *Research suggests that three categories of philosophy influence your values ...*
—R. E. Boyatzis, A. J. Murphy, and J. V. Wheeler, "Philosophy as a Missing Link between Values and Behavior," *Psychological Reports* 86 (2000), 47–64.

16   *A personal goal is more likely to be achieved ...*
—H. J. Klein, M. J. Wesson, J. R. Hollenback, and B. J. Alge,
"Goal Commitment and the Goal-Setting Process: Conceptual
Clarification and Empirical Synthesis," *Journal of Applied
Psychology* 84(6), 885–896.

17   *Harvard psychology professor Daniel Gilbert, in his intriguing
book* Stumbling on Happiness ...
—Daniel Gilbert, *Stumbling on Happiness* (New York:
Knopf, 2006).

Chapter 2

21   *Two influential researchers, James O. Prochaska and Carlos C.
DiClimente ...*
—James O. Prochaska and Carlos C. DiClimente, "Toward a
Comprehensive Model of Change," in W. R. Miller and N.
Heather (eds.), *Treating Addictive Behaviours: Process of
Change* (New York: Plenum Press, 1986).

26   *Recent evidence shows that when people are asked what they
regret the most ...*
—T. Gilovich and V. H. Medvec, "The Experience of Regret:
What, When, and Why," *Psychological Review* 102 (1995), 379–395.

33   *In 2002, researchers Daniel Gilbert and Jane Ebert assigned ...*
—Daniel T. Gilbert and Jane E. J. Ebert, "Decisions and
Revisions: The Affective Forecasting of Changeable Outcomes,"
Journal of Personality and Social Psychology 82 (2002), 503–514.

34   *This finding can be explained in part by cognitive dissonance ...*
—Leon Festinger, *A Theory of Cognitive Dissonance*
(Palo Alto, CA: Stanford University Press, 1957).

34   *Research by Peter Gollwitzer on intentions and what actually
gets implemented ...*
—Peter Gollwitzer, "Implementation Intentions: Strong Effects
of Simple Plans," *American Psychologist* 54 (1999), 493–503.

Chapter 3

37   *Transformational leadership* ...
      —B. M. Bass, *Leadership and Performance beyond Expectations*
      (New York: Free Press, 1985).

37   *In 2006, Australian researchers Simon A. Moss and Simon Ngu* ...
      —Simon A. Moss and Simon Ngu, "The Relationship between
      Personality and Leadership Preferences," *Current Research in
      Social Psychology* 11(6) (2006), 70–91.

39   *In Good to Great, Jim Collins highlights the importance of
      having the right team* ...
      —Jim Collins, *Good to Great* (New York: Collins, 2001).

40   *In 2000, researchers Paul R. Nail, Geoff MacDonald, and David
      A. Levy* ...
      —Paul R. Nail, Geoff MacDonald, and David A. Levy,
      "Proposal of a Four-Dimensional Model of Social Response,"
      Psychological Bulletin 126(3) (2000), 454–470.

41   *We tend to ask questions in ways that get the answers we want.* ...
      —L. Hunt, "Against Presentism," *Perspectives* 40 (5) (2002), 1–2.

43   *Marilee Adams, author of* Change Your Questions, ...
      —Marilee Adams, *Change Your Questions, Change Your Life: 7
      Powerful Tools for Life and Work* (San Francisco: Berrett-
      Koehler Publishers, 2004).

46   *Gallup studies of over 80,000 managers presented in the book* First,
      Break All the Rules *by Marcus Buckingham and Curt Coffman* ...
      —Marcus Buckingham and Curt Coffman, *First, Break All the
      Rules* (New York: Simon & Schuster, 1999). (Questions cited are
      presented on pages 33–34.)

48   *In one study, Dr. Martin Seligman of the University of
      Pennsylvania* ...
      —M. E. P. Seligman, T. A. Steen, N. Par, and C. Peterson,
      "Positive Psychology Progress: Empirical Validation of
      Interventions," *American Psychologist* 60(5) (2005), 410–421.

Chapter 4

52   *We'd even pay our hard-earned money, as shown in one study ...*
—Amos Tversky and Eldar Shafir, "The Disjunction Effect in Choice under Uncertainty," *Psychological Science* 3 (1992), 205–209.

59   *Participants in a study conducted by Timothy D. Wilson and his colleagues ...*
—Timothy D. Wilson et al., "Introspecting about Reasons Can Reduce Post-Choice Satisfaction," *Personality and Social Psychology Bulletin* 19 (1993), 331–339.

60   *In a study of 60 successful entrepreneurs ...*
—A. G. Ettinger, *Make Up Your Mind* (Santa Monica, CA: Merritt Publishing, 1995).

60   *As we learn, often by trial and error, a deep part of the brain ...*
—M. D. Lieberman, "Intuition: A Social Cognitive Neuroscience Approach," *Psychological Bulletin* 126 (2000), 109–137.

60   *Our thoughts can lead us astray in decision making because they're affected ...*
—Amos Tversky and D. Khaneman, "Judgment under Uncertainty: Heuristics and Biases," *Science* 185 (1974), 112–131.

63   *In one study, researchers asked participants if they'd rather go on an average island ...*
—Eldar Shafir, "Choosing versus Rejecting: Why Some Options Are Both Better and Worse than Others," *Memory & Cognition* 21 (1993), 546–556.

63   *In 2000, Sheena Iyengar of Columbia Business School and Mark Lepper ...*
—Sheena Iyengar and Mark Lepper, "When Choice Is Demotivating: Can One Desire Too Much of a Good Thing?" *Journal of Personality and Social Psychology* 79 (2000), 995–1106.

64   *An interesting psychological process happens when we think ahead:* …
—T. Eyal et al., "The Pros and Cons of Temporally Near and Distant Action," *Journal of Personality and Social Psychology* 86 (2004), 781–795.

Chapter 5

67   *When you turn over rocks and look at all the squiggly things underneath* …
—Jim Collins, *Good to Great* (New York: Collins, 2001), p. 72.

72   *A classic study conducted by Donald G. Dutton and Arthur P. Aron showed that* …
—Donald G. Dutton and Arthur P. Aron, "Some Evidence for Heightened Sexual Attraction under Conditions of High Anxiety," *Journal of Personality and Social Psychology* 30 (1974), 510–517.

76   *Researcher Dan Wegner and his colleagues set out to investigate this issue* …
—D. M. Wegner, D. J. Schneider, S. Carter, and T. White, "Paradoxical Effects of Thought Suppression," *Journal of Personality and Social Psychology* 53 (1987), 5–13.
—D. M. Wegner, "Ironic Processes of Mental Control," *Psychological Review* 101 (1994), 34–52.

77   *Research by Stanley Rachman and Padmal de Silva shows that 80 percent of people* …
—Stanley Rachman and Padmal de Silva, "Abnormal and Normal Obsessions," *Behaviour Research and Therapy* 16 (1978), 233–248.

77   *The reason that people with OCD experience more of these obsessive thoughts* …
—B. A. Marks and D. W. Wood, "A Comparison of Thought-Suppression to an Acceptance-Based Technique in the Management of Personal Intrusive Thoughts: A Controlled Evaluation," *Behaviour Research and Therapy* 43 (2005), 433–445.

77   *This may be why people who are prone to having panic attacks …*
       —M. S. Schwartz and N. M. Schwartz, "Problems with
       Relaxation and Biofeedback: Assisted Relaxation and Guidelines
       for Management," in M. S. Schwartz (ed.), *Biofeedback: A
       Practitioner's Guide*, 2nd ed. (New York: Guilford Press, 1995).

78   *In London in 2003, investigators measured the job performance
       of 412 customer service workers …*
       —F. W. Bond and D. Bunce, "The Role of Acceptance and Job
       Control in Mental Health, Job Satisfaction, and Work
       Performance," *Journal of Applied Psychology* 88 (2003), 1057–1067.

78   *In 1995, psychology and economics researchers Daniel Read and
       George Loewenstein conducted an experiment …*
       —Daniel Read and George F. Loewenstein, "Diversification
       Bias: Explaining the Discrepancy in Variety Seeking between
       Combined and Separated Choices," *Journal of Experimental
       Psychology* 1(1) (1995), 34–39.

Chapter 6

82   *In 1971, David Glass conducted a seminal study …*
       —D. C. Glass and J. Singer, *Urban Stressors: Experiments on
       Noise and Social Stressors* (New York: Academic Press, 1972).

83   *Harvard professor Ellen Langer conducted several classic studies …*
       —Ellen J. Langer, "The Illusion of Control," *Journal of
       Personality and Social Psychology* (1975), 36: 311–328.

83   *She teamed up with Yale professor Judy Rodin …*
       —Judy Rodin and Ellen J. Langer, "Long-Term Effects of a
       Control-Relevant Intervention with the Institutional Aged,"
       Journal of Personality and Social Psychology 36 (1977), 897–902.

83   *Dr. Steven C. Hayes, the founder of Acceptance & Commitment
       Therapy …*
       —Steven C. Hayes, *Get Out of Your Mind and Into Your Life:
       The New Acceptance and Commitment Therapy* (Oakland, CA:
       New Harbinger Press, 2005).

86   *In one study, participants listened to a classical music song; ...*
—J. W. Schooler, D. Ariely, and G. Loewenstein, "The Pursuit
and Assessment of Happiness Can Be Self-Defeating," in I. Brocas
and J. Carillo (eds.), *The Psychology of Economic Decisions:
Rationality and Well-Being*, vol. 1 (Oxford: Oxford University
Press, 2003).

Chapter 7

100   *Daniel Kahneman, a psychologist who won a Nobel Prize ...*
—Daniel Kahneman, "Objective Happiness," in Daniel
Kahneman, E. Diener, and N. Schwarz (eds.), *Well Being:
The Foundations of Hedonic Psychology* (New York: Russell
Sage, 1999).

100   *My colleague Dr. Max Vogt, who coauthored a book with me ...*
—Personal conversation, Max Vogt and Larina Kase, 2007.
Learn more at ImproviseLife.com.

101   *Instead, I like to use the definition [of success] put forth in the
book* Just Enough ...
—Laura Nash and Howard Stevenson, *Just Enough: Tools
for Creating Success in Your Work and Life* (Hoboken, NJ:
Wiley, 2005).

103   *We become prone to making thought errors, such as
overestimating risk ...*
—A. T. Beck, *Cognitive Therapy and the Emotional Disorders*
(New York: Penguin Books, 1991).

105   *Phillip G. Clampitt, Robert J. Dekoch, and M. Lee Williams, the
authors of a 2002 article ...*
—Phillip G. Clampitt, Robert J. Dekoch, and M. Lee Williams,
"Embracing Uncertainty: Hidden Dimensions of Growth," *Ivey
Business Journal*, January/February 2002, 57–61.

108   *In Richard Branson's autobiography ...*
—Richard Branson, *Screw It, Let's Do It* (London: Virgin
Books, 2006).

Chapter 8

115   *In* Accidental Genius, *author Mark Levy shows readers …*
—Mark Levy, *Accidental Genius: Revolutionize Your Thinking through Private Writing* (San Francisco: Berrett-Koehler Publishers, 2000).

118   *Dr. Martin E. Seligman's research on optimism shows that our explanatory style …*
—Martin E. Seligman, *Learned Optimism: How to Change Your Mind and Your Life* (New York: Vintage, 2006).

119   *Research has shown that mild forms of positive distortions of reality …*
—S. E. Taylor, *Positive Illusions: Creating Self-Deception and the Healthy Mind* (New York: Basic Books, 1989).

120   *Charles Garfield is a computer scientist who led the team of the Apollo 11 project …*
—Charles Garfield, *Peak Performers* (New York: Harper Paperbacks, 1987).

122   *Flow is a concept that has been researched for decades, spearheaded by a former …*
—Mihaly Csikszentmihalyi, *Flow: The Psychology of Optimal Experience* (New York: Harper Perennial, 1991).

126   *Research by psychologists such as Robert Emmons shows that gratitude is a strength …*
—R. A. Emmons and C. A. Crumpler, "Gratitude as a Human Strength: Appraising the Evidence," *Journal of Social and Clinical Psychology* 19 (2000), 56–69.

126   *The positive psychology research of Dr. Seligman and his colleagues …*
—M. E. P. Seligman, T. A. Steen, N. Park, and C. Peterson, "Positive Psychology Progress: Empirical Validation of Interventions," *American Psychologist* 60(5) (2005), 410–421.

126 *In his bestselling books such as* The Attractor Factor, *Joe Vitale ...*
—Joe Vitale, *The Attractor Factor* (New York: John Wiley &
Sons, 2005).

Chapter 9

129 *In 2002, motivation researchers from Rochester, New York, and
from France learned ...*
—F. Cury, A. Elliot, P. Sarrazin, D. Da Fonseca, and
M. Rufo, "The Trichotomous Achievement Goal Model
and Intrinsic Motivation: A Sequential Mediational Analysis,"
Journal of Experimental Social Psychology 38 (2002),
473–481.

130 *A recent study conducted by Johannes Michalak and colleagues
at Ruhr University ...*
—J. Michalak, O. Puschel, J. Joormann, and D. Schulte,
"Implicit Motives and Explicit Goals: Two Distinctive
Modes of Motivational Functioning and Their Relations to
Psychopathology," *Clinical Psychology and Psychotherapy* 13
(2006), 81–96.

131 *Power motivation is linked with leadership, and those who are
high in the power motive ...*
—K. Sokolowski, H. D. Schmalt, T. A. Langens, and R. M.
Puca, "Assessing Achievement, Affiliation, and Power Motives
All at Once—The Multi-Motive Grid," *Journal of Personality
Assessment* 74 (2000), 126–145.

131 *A 2000 study by Sigal G. Barsade, Andrew J. Ward, and
colleagues showed ...*
—Sigal G. Barsade, Andrew J. Ward, et al., "To Your
Heart's Content: A Mode of Affective Diversity in Top
Management Teams," *Administrative Science Quarterly*,
45 (2000), 802–836.

In Mindset, *researcher Carol Dweck describes two types of mindsets ...*
        —Carol S. Dweck, *Mindset: The New Psychology of Success* (New York: Random House, 2007).

132   *When employees taking a computer training course were put into a fixed mindset ...*
        —J. J. Martocchio, "Effects of Conceptions of Ability on Anxiety, Self-Efficacy, and Learning in Training," *Journal of Applied Psychology* 79 (1994), 819–825.

133   *Marilee Adams, author of* Change Your Questions, Change Your Life, *...*
        —Marilee Adams, *Change Your Questions, Change Your Life* (San Francisco: Berrett-Koehler Publishers, 2004).

133   *The way in which you attribute success or failure is your locus of control...*
        —J. B. Rotter, "Generalized Expectancies for Internal versus External Control of Reinforcement," *Psychological Monographs* 80 (1966), no. 609.

133   *Studies have shown that an external locus of control is associated with ...*
        —P. E. Spector, "Development of the Work Locus of Control Scale," *Journal of Occupational Psychology* 61 (1988), 335–340.

133   *A related concept is that of self-efficacy, developed by Albert Bandura, ...*
        —Albert Bandura, "Self-Efficacy," in V. S. Ramachaudran (ed.), *Encyclopedia of Human Behavior*, vol. 4 (New York: Academic Press, 1994), pp. 71–81. Reprinted in H. Friedman (ed.), *Encyclopedia of Mental Health* (San Diego: Academic Press, 1998).

136   *Another interesting point: we think that ...*
        —C. Heath, "On the Social Psychology of Agency Relationships: Lay Theories of Motivation Overemphasize Extrinsic Rewards," *Organizational Behavior and Human Decision Processes*, 78 (1999), 25–62.

136 *In another study, Susan Harter explored intrinsic and extrinsic motivation ...*
—Susan Harter, "Pleasure Derived from Challenge and the Effects of Receiving Grades on Children's Difficulty Level Choices," *Child Development* 49 (1978), 788–799.

137 *In 1989, graduate students in business participated in a study ...*
—Robert Wood and Albert Bandura, "Impact of Conceptions of Ability on Self-Regulatory Mechanisms and Complex Decision-Making," *Journal of Personality and Social Psychology* 56 (1989), 407–415.

137 *Gary Chapman wrote the bestselling book* The Five Love Languages *about how to express feelings ...*
—Cary Chapman, *The Five Love Languages: How to Express Your Heartfelt Commitment to Your Mate* (Chicago: Northfield Publishing, 1995).

139 *In their book* Encouraging the Heart, *Kouzes and Posner point out ...*
—James M. Kouzes and Barry Z. Posner, *Encouraging the Heart* (San Francisco: Jossey-Bass, 2003).

Chapter 10

154 *In* Refuse to Choose, *Barbara Sher creates a profile of what she calls "Scanners."*
—Barbara Sher, *Refuse to Choose! A Revolutionary Program for Doing Everything That You Love* (New York: Rodale, 2006).

156 *The five steps in the STING model by Rita Emmett, the author of* The Procrastinator's Handbook, *...*
—Rita Emmett, personal telephone interview conducted by Larina Kase.

157 *According to David Allen, author of the bestseller* Getting Things Done *...*
—David Allen, *Getting Things Done: The Art of Stress-Free Productivity* (New York: Penguin, 2001).

Chapter 11

169 *Researcher Jennifer Beer recently conducted a study in which she filmed people …*
—Jennifer S. Beer, "Implicit Self-Theories of Shyness," *Journal of Personality and Social Psychology* 83 (2002), 1009–1024.

173 *Dr. Hogan is a leading authority on body language and persuasion …*
—Kevin Hogan, personal conversation, 2008.

173 *Researchers Michael Norton, Jeana Frost, and Dan Ariely conducted a five-part study.*
—M. I. Norton, J. H. Frost, and D. Ariely, "Less Is More: The Lure of Ambiguity or Why Familiarity Breeds Contempt," *Journal of Personality and Social Psychology* 92(1) (2007), 97–105.

174 *In* The Likeability Factor, *Tim Sanders points out that the success of business leaders …*
—Tim Sanders, *The Likeability Factor* (New York: Three Rivers Press, 2005).

Chapter 12

182 *Catherine Kaputa, author of* U R a Brand, *recommends letting others brag for you.*
—Catherine Kaputa, *U R a Brand* (Mountain View, CA: Davies-Black Publishing, 2005).

Chapter 13

193 *For example, in 2005, Dr. James Parker and his colleagues studied …*
—J. D. A. Parker, J. Duffy, L. M. Wood, B. J. Bond, and M. J. Hogan, "Academic Achievement and Emotional Intelligence: Predicting the Successful Transition from High School to University," *Journal of First-Year Experience and Students in Transition* 17 (2005), 67–78.

193   *Another study by researchers from Yale, the University of Toronto, ...*
—P. N. Lopes, S. Cote, D. Grewal, J. Kadis, M. Gall, and P. Salovey, "Evidence that Emotional Intelligence Is Related to Job Performance, Interpersonal Facilitation, Affect and Attitudes at Work, and Leadership Potential" (submitted for publication).

193   *David Rosete led a study in Australia that looked at 117 executives' IQ, EI, ...*
—D. Rosete, and J. Ciarrochi, "Emotional Intelligence and Its Relationship to Workplace Performance Outcomes of Leadership Effectiveness," *Leadership and Organizational Development Journal* 26 (2005), 388–399.

194   *A recent study by Angelo Giardini and Michael Frese showed that the emotional competence ...*
—Angelo Giardini and Michael Frese, "Linking Service Employees' Emotional Competence to Customer Satisfaction: A Multilevel Approach," *Journal of Organizational Behavior* 29(2) (2007), 155–170.

194   *A large study that compiled thousands of data points found that leaders ...*
—P. A. Mabe III and S. G. West, "Validity of Self-evaluation of Ability: A Review and Meta-analysis," *Journal of Applied Psychology* 67 (1982), 280–296.

195   *Acceptance of emotions has been shown to be one of the most important ...*
—E. J. Donaldson and F. W. Bond, "Psychological Acceptance and Emotional Intelligence in Relation to Workplace Well Being," *British Journal of Guidance and Counseling* 34 (2004), 293–312.

196   *Studies have shown that both peer and subordinate reviews ...*
—T. H. Shore, L. M. Shore, and G. C. Thornton III, "Construct Validity of Self- and Peer Evaluations of Performance Dimensions in an Assessment Center," *Journal of Applied Psychology* 77(1) (1992), 42–54.

—G. M. McEvoy and R. W. Beatty, "Assessment Centers and Subordinate Appraisals of Managers: A Seven Year Examination of Predictive Validity," *Personnel Psychology* 42 (1989), 37–52.

199   *In* Primal Leadership, *renowned emotional intelligence researchers Daniel Goleman* ...
—Daniel Goleman, Richard E. Boyatzis, and Annie McKee, *Primal Leadership* (Boston: Harvard Business School Press, 2004).

Chapter 14

209   *For example, in one study, researchers analyzed top advertisements* ...
—J. Goldenberg, D. Mazursky, and S. Solomon, "The Fundamental Qualities of Top Ads," *Marketing Science* 18 (1999), 333–351.

209   *Catherine Kaputa, author of* U R a Brand, *says* ...
—Catherine Kaputa, *U R a Brand* (Mountain View, CA: Davies-Black Publishing, 2005), p. 8.

212   *Despite having dyslexia and being challenged with reading and writing* ...
—Richard Branson, *Screw it, Let's Do It* (London: Virgin Books, 2006), pp. 15–16.

213   *In the foreword to* The Rebel Rules *by Chip Conley, Sir Richard Branson says* ...
—Chip Conley, *The Rebel Rules* (New York: Simon & Schuster, 2001), pp. 15–18.

215   *Imagine that you are driving in the country, looking at field after field* ...
—Seth Godin, *Purple Cow: Transform Your Business by Being Remarkable* (New York: Portfolio, 2003).

Chapter 15

222   *Research has shown that one of the best things for resolving conflict is a common goal.*
—F. Dukes, "Public Conflict Resolution: A Transformative Approach," *Negotiation Journal* 9(1) (1993): 45–57.

224   *Kerry Patterson, Joseph Grenny, Ron McMillan, and Al Switzler, the authors of* Crucial Conversations, *define a crucial conversation as ...*
—Kerry Patterson, Joseph Grenny, Ron McMillan, and Al Switzler, *Crucial Conversations: Tools for Talking When Stakes Are High* (New York: McGraw-Hill, 2002).

227   *Rick Brinkman and Rick Kirschner, the authors of* Dealing with People You Can't Stand, *...*
—Rick Brinkman and Rick Kirschner, *Dealing with People You Can't Stand* (New York: McGraw-Hill, 2002).

Chapter 16

235   *In* Innovation and Entrepreneurship, *management guru Peter Drucker explains that entrepreneurs ...*
—Peter Drucker, *Innovation and Entrepreneurship* (New York: Collins, 2006).

236   *For example, Frank Rumbauskas Jr. ...*
—Frank R. Rumbauskas Jr., *Never Cold Call Again: Achieve Sales Greatness without Cold Calling* (New York: Wiley, 2007).

237   *The leading authority on self-efficacy, Albert Bandura ...*
—Albert Bandura, "Self-Efficacy," in V. S. Ramachaudran (ed.), *Encyclopedia of Human Behavior*, vol. 4 (New York: Academic Press, 1994), pp. 71–81. Reprinted in H. Friedman (ed.), *Encyclopedia of Mental Health* (San Diego: Academic Press, 1998).

Index

Ariely, Dan, 173
Aron, Arthur P., 72
Assessment
    motivation, 137
    readiness for change and team
        building, 39–40
    StrengthsFinder assessment (Gallup
        Organization), 93–94
Attitude, dealing with people you can't
    stand, 230
The Attractor Factor (Vitale), 91, 126
Authenticity
    innovative change, 241–242
    and likability, 175–176
Avoidance
    anxiety responses, 73–78
    apprehension as, 53

B

Bad worry action step, 71
Balance
    and anxiety, 68–69
    push-pull relationship dynamic,
        220–221
Bandura, Albert, 133–134, 137, 237
Barsade, Sigal G., 131–132
Basal ganglia, and intuition, 60
Beer, Jennifer, 169–170
Behaviors
    activation control, 123–124
    likability and projecting confidence,
        166–168
    strengths, focus on, 87–89
Bias and intuition, 60–61
Big 5 personality traits, 38
"Big It," focus on, 99–113
    action steps, 108–109
    big picture solution, 104–105
    courage, 109
    expert interview: Michael Port, 110–112
    finding, 99–102
    shoulds, 101–102

tunnel vision, 102–103
urgency and importance, 106–109
vision, as limiting, 105–106
Book Yourself Solid (Port), 110
Boyatzis, Richard E., 199
Brag book, 183
Brag without bragging, promotion,
    182–185
Branson, Richard, 108–109, 212–213
Breaking rules, team building, 46–48
Brinkman, Rick, 227-228
Buckingham, Marcus, 46, 93
Building momentum for innovative
    change, 233–234
Business Psychology in Practice (Mead
    and Robinson), 12–13
Buy-in, creating, 43–44

C

Center for the Treatment and Study of
    Anxiety, University of Pennsylvania, 8
Challenging work projects, and
    procrastination, 148
Change principles
    focus on "Big It," 99–113
    focus on conflict and difficult
        situations, 219–232
    focus on emotional competence,
        193–204
    focus on energy, 115–128
    focus on innovative change, 233–243
    focus on likability and projecting
        confidence, 165–177
    focus on motivation, 129–145
    focus on overcoming procrastination,
        147–163
    focus on promotion, 179–191
    focus on standing out, 205–217
*Change Your Questions, Change Your
    Life* (Adams), 43–44, 133
Chapman, Gary, 137–138
Cholesterol analogy for anxiety, 69

T

U

U R a Brand (Kaputa), 182–183, 209
Uncertainty
  decision-making, 52
  fear of, 152
Undesirable work projects, and
    procrastination, 148
Urgency and "Big It," 106–109

V

Value, providing excellent, 209–211
Values
  clarification, and anxiety, 70
  discomfort and growth, 13–14
Visibility and projecting confidence,
    173–174
Vision and intention
  action steps, 17
  "Big It," focus on, 105–106
  comfort zone, moving past, 10–13
  common mistakes, 11
  goal setting, 7–8, 14–15
  in GROWTH step formula, 3–18
  knowledge into action, 8–9, 55
  as limiting, 105–106
  mental rehearsal, 120–121
  motivation, 134, 139
  optimal anxiety as key to change, 9–10
  preparation stage, 25–26
  treasure map creation questions, 15–16
  vignette, 3–7
Vitale, Joe, 91, 126–127
Vogt, Max, 100
Voice, neutral tone of, team building,
    41–44

W

Ward, Andrew J., 131–132
Weakness, focus on, 81–82
  (*See also* Strengths, focus on)
Web sites
  David Allen, 159
  Rick Brinkman, 228
  color theory, 211
  creating a presence, 182
  Rita Emmett, 157
  Seth Godin, 216
  Jen Groover, 237
  James M. Kouzes, 141
  Mark Levy, 186
  Annie McKee, 200
  motivation assessment, 137
  Michael Port, 110
  positioning yourself as an expert, 173
  readiness assessment, 20
  Tim Sanders, 174
  strength assessment, 93
  Joe Vitale, 127
Wegner, Dan, 76
Why *vs.* how in future decisions, 64
Williams, M. Lee, 105
Wilson, Timothy D., 59
Winter Notes on Summer Impressions
    (Dostoyevsky), 76–77
Wood, Robert, 137
Work projects, and procrastination,
    148
Worry (*See* Anxiety)

Y

Yerkes-Dodson Law, 10

About the Author

Larina Kase, Psy.D., MBA, is a business psychologist, a professional speaker, and the founder of Performance & Success Coaching LLC, an international consultancy based in Philadelphia. She helps executives, entrepreneurs, and professionals guide themselves and others to success and become leaders in their fields. Using solidly researched change principles, Larina helps people achieve more than they ever thought possible.

Before founding her business, she served on the clinical faculty at the world-renowned Center for the Treatment and Study of Anxiety of the University of Pennsylvania, where she contributed to cutting-edge research on anxiety and confidence. Larina is sought out by the press for her expertise in the psychology of business success. She is often featured in print media such as *Entrepreneur*, *SELF*, and *Inc.*; is interviewed on TV and radio; and was a communications coach on the MTV hit show *MADE*. She is a regular on the speaking circuit, and audiences call her inspiring. Larina is the author or coauthor of seven books, including the *New York Times* bestseller *The Confident Speaker* (McGraw-Hill, 2007) and *Anxious 9 to 5* (New Harbinger, 2006). She lives in Philadelphia with her husband and two dogs. You can find additional resources at www.pascoaching.com and learn more about Larina's ideas at her blog, www.TheMindsetofSuccess.com.

www.ingramcontent.com/pod-product-compliance
Lightning Source LLC
Chambersburg PA
CBHW060329100426
42812CB00003B/927